TRACES
OF THE
PAST

TRACES
OF THE
PAST

A FIELD GUIDE TO
INDUSTRIAL
ARCHAEOLOGY

DAVID WEITZMAN

Charles Scribner's Sons · New York

Grateful acknowledgment is made to use the following illustrations: pages 114 and 115, from *Structural Design* by Hale Sutherland and Harry Lake Bowman, copyright © 1938, and from *Structural Design in Steel* by Thomas Clark Shedd, copyright © 1934, both reprinted by permission of John Wiley & Sons, Inc.; pages 116 and 117, from *Movable and Long Span Steel Bridges* by George A. Hool and W. S. Kinne, copyright © 1943, used with the permission of McGraw-Hill, Inc.; pages 123, 124, 130, from *Steel and Timber Structures* by George A. Hool and W. S. Kinne, copyright © 1942, used with the permission of McGraw-Hill, Inc.; page 19, reproduced from *The Steam Locomotive in America* by Alfred W. Bruce, by permission of W. W. Norton & Company, Inc. Copyright 1952 by W. W. Norton & Company, Inc. Copyright renewed 1980.

Library of Congress Cataloging in Publication Data

Weitzman, David L
  Traces of the past.

  Bibliography
  1. Industrial archaeology.   2. Railroads—
History. 3. Bridges—History.   4. Iron industry
and trade—History.   I. Title.
T37.W44   609'.73   79-65975
ISBN O-684-16107-9

1 3 5 7 9 11 13 15 17 19 F/C 20 18 16 14 12 10 8 6 4 2

Printed in the United States of America

For Peter

CONTENTS

TRACES
OF THE
PAST

1. MIRRORS OF RUST

Railroad rights-of-way are historical places, roads upon which to travel the past, having the power to envelop the curious trackwalker and would-be historian in a very different, very distant era. Entering upon the roadbed from a busy street and taking the first hesitant steps onto a silent abandoned or seldom-used track, we are drawn into the scene farther and farther as though entering an old photograph, down the track, just around the next curve, out toward the horizon, where the rails converge on another place and time.

I discovered the joy of such journeys as a child, when, finding a railroad track, I would follow it until I had lost all sense of time or how far I had come, and I'm still discovering these doorways quite by accident. I stopped recently near my home in northern California, to discover that not 10 yards away from the edge of a busy highway stands just such a doorway. And only slightly hidden by the trees and brush that separate the single-track roadbed from a shopping-center parking area stand two section houses, with dull, flaking red-painted boards and battens, and hand-car tracks leading directly to the side of the rail—there, much as they were fifty, perhaps seventy-five years ago.

Scattered around the sheds are some artifacts of railroad archaeology. A stack of "fishplates," or track connectors, for example, contains a telling clue. One of them is smaller than the others, a leftover from some

earlier day, when lighter rail was in use here. Nearby are piles of tie plates, metal bearing plates placed under the rail at each tie to keep the rail base from cutting into the wood; and, of course, spikes are everywhere. Partly hidden under the brush is a blackened old tie with narrower impressions than the tie plates at the section house would have made. Here is another clue to the changeover to heavier rail. Farther along, some of the lighter rail is still on the old ties. Only one short section remains, and all but a couple of ties are gone. But you can still follow the roadbed to where it ends amid some piles of gravel and the rubble of a foundation. Beyond, a timber trestle crosses a little creek, which, sadly, emerges into the daylight from a steel culvert just long enough to give purpose to the old trestle before disappearing into another culvert and under the parking lot.

"Only a little ways more," I told myself that day, just around that turn, but I stayed until darkness sent me back to the car. Around that turn, about a quarter of a mile from and just out of sight of the highway, stood the giant redwood-staved barrel of a water tank atop a frame of sturdy timbers. In its accustomed place hung the sheet-metal spout and rope awaiting the gloved hand of the fireman, who stopped by each day to pull it down toward the open manhole or filler opening and send a torrent of water into the nearly empty locomotive tender.

Iron grade-crossing marker on the Virginia Blue Ridge Railway, Piney River, Virginia.

The peace of an old roadbed covered over with grasses and wild flowers, long empty of its rails and ties, or even one whose life is still reflected in its shining rails and well-kept right-of-way has a magic of its own. But if we are old enough to have known steam locomotives, our imagination fills in the movements, the sounds, the smells that once animated this empty place. It is quiet here. No train has passed this way for many, many years. But it isn't empty. Let's continue our railroad hike down a track somewhere, anywhere, using our historical imagination, our past experiences and sense of history. We'll weave a life around things we find along the way, even seemingly insignificant things like signposts, for instance. . . .

We would probably walk no more than a mile or two in either direction before coming upon a bit of railroad history like a weathered whistle post, its $\frac{W}{X}$ warning the engineer of a grade crossing coming up in a quarter of a mile; $\frac{W}{S}$ is his warning of a station coming up. The post is painted white, and under the black letters are painted two long and two short bars that would have brought forth two long and two short calls of the whistle. A few more minutes of walking and, sure enough, there it is—a dusty country road leading up over the edge of the roadbed, rattling across the tracks on old wooden planks that kept cows, pigs, sheep, and goats off the track, and down the other side on its way to a crossroads somewhere in the distance.

The experienced railroad walker looks forward to meeting old friends like mile-

Abandoned water tank at Crested Butte, Colorado.

Whistling post.

posts. The one up ahead is a piece of careful stonework, nicely hewn from granite, about 4½ feet high, 12 inches on a side. The lower half is uncut; the upper half has been bush-hammered, and on its smooth whitened face, pointing in the direction from which we've come, are two figures, B and 6, painted in black, one above the other. Walking around to the opposite side, we find the figures P and 109. At this point on the line we're six miles out of Boston and 109 miles from Portland, the initial showing the city from which the mileage was reckoned. This is how it was done on the Boston & Maine. On the Grand Trunk Railway in Canada, mileposts of triangular section were used, with an edge pointed toward the track so that both mileages could

be read at once. This was intended as a convenience not only for train crews but for passengers who might be following their progress over the hours. On the old Michigan Central, minor posts were set at half-mile and even quarter-mile points, and on the Lehigh Valley Railroad the milestones were cut from slabs of flagstone to about 20 inches wide and 3 or 4 inches thick. The Chicago & Eastern Illinois Railroad was one of the first to put up milestones cast in concrete, the numbers and letters molded into the post and painted white against a lampblack background mixed into the concrete. The Southern Pacific marked mileage along its right-of-way on boards that were nailed to the telegraph poles running along the tracks. On the Atchison,

Topeka & Santa Fe, the mile was painted on a steel plate attached to the nearest telegraph pole, but the exact mile points were marked by an old piece of boiler flue driven into the roadbed at the end of a tie, the upper 12 inches of the flue having been flattened and the number, about ¾ inch high, stamped into the metal.

There will be other signposts along the way, too. Diamond-, pentagonal-, and hexagonal-shaped yellow signs with black numbers warned of speed limits through busy areas or over switches, as did the "Yard Limit" (often just a yellow **V** with no lettering), "Junction," and "Water Tank — (however many) Miles Ahead" signs. On the Buffalo, Rochester &

Pittsburgh, a triangular sign was placed on a telegraph pole at each curve, giving the number of the curve and the degree of curvature. On other railroads this information was put on stakes or stone monuments at the side of the track, on the back of which might be found the superelevation, or curve elevation. Along the Nashville, Chattanooga & St. Louis and the Pittsburgh, Ft. Wayne & Chicago, every fifth telegraph pole was numbered for easy location of bridges and other structures. You might even come across a "Close Sand Valve" post, warning the engineer that just ahead were switches or other devices possibly fouled by sand poured onto rails where better traction was needed.

Around the next bend or over that grade, we might find an old trestle, a semaphore signal bridge (color-light signals replaced them in the late 1940s), a hand car, a turntable, or a switch stand still guarding a turnout onto a weed-covered siding. The stand might be crowned with a bright red disk and a lamp of red and green lenses— "pot signals," the oldtimers called them, which once brought visits every day at dusk from the lamplighter, who carefully trimmed the wick, refilled the oil pot with kerosene or lard oil, and, finally, lit the burner and set it inside the lamp for another night's vigil, before moving on to the next one down the track.

Such trackwalking experiences can be found anywhere, and they make us realize the historical richness of even long-abandoned railways. Some rights-of-way have been in continuous use from the 1800s to the present day, their historical locus remaining fixed. Others are nothing more than a gravel path cut through a hillside, traces of activity long ago. Still, even where tracks have been moved to avoid a steep grade, or because the line is no longer needed, or for any number of reasons, much remains of archaeological interest.

From iron strap rails on stones and then ties on which ran little steam locomotives weighing 8 or 9 tons, to wide gauge, to standard gauge, from 30-pound rail to 80-pound and 100-pound and then to 152-pound rail for locomotives of over 300 tons, from hand-operated mechanical interlocking to electric signals, from wood to coal to diesel oil, we move on and on through the salient developments in railroad technology. All occurred on narrow rights-of-way, protected from modern intrusions but always public—permanently established, in most cases, by state and federal charters and land grants. Some run right down the middle of Main Street.

The value of any museum lies not in the artifacts collected there but in the feelings, the ideas, the images they evoke. Just as the work of the historian and archaeologist does not end with the collection of artifacts but is really only the beginning, the "collecting" of railroad artifacts—seeing and becoming aware, sketching, photographing—is but a first step toward broader and deeper understandings of life in this place before our time, in other generations. Through track walking and the collecting of images, we become sensitive to another aspect of history and acquire a new set of symbols, a new vocabulary, which helps us to see even further back into the past. We'll learn to read these newly acquired symbols as though they were words in a new language, as indeed they are, and then use this new language to help us toward new perspectives on the commonplace.

We've all learned well that lesson describing the impact of the railroads on American history. The locomotive is, I suppose, one of the first images (after brick factories humming with belt-driven machinery) evoked by the familiar term "industrial revolution." The importance of the railroads in the growth of the American economy is, to be sure, an essential and interesting fact. But even more interesting and, for the amateur historian, more enlightening is the fact that in their every aspect—company names, locomotives, freight and passenger cars, gauges, design innovations—the railroads have been affected, their philosophy and operations

A Trackwalker's Guide to Wayside Structures

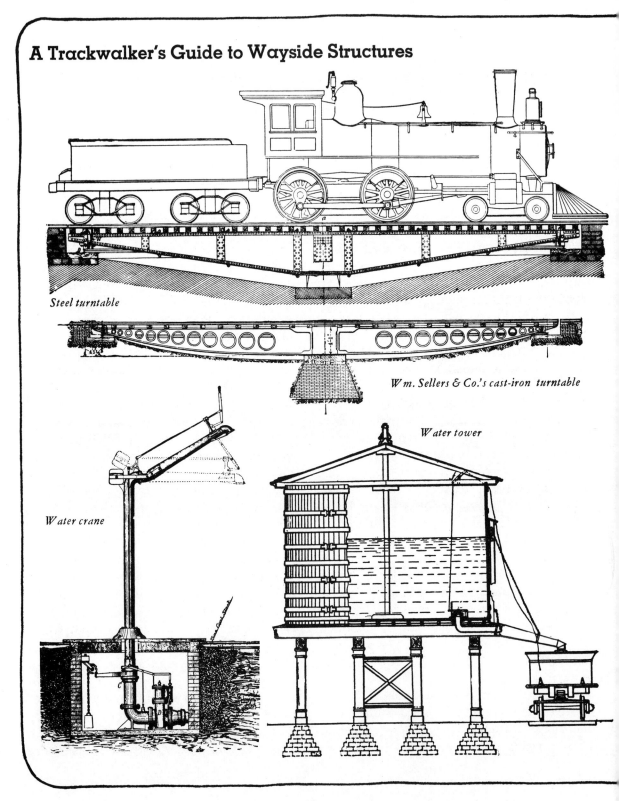

Steel turntable

Wm. Sellers & Co.'s cast-iron turntable

Water crane

Water tower

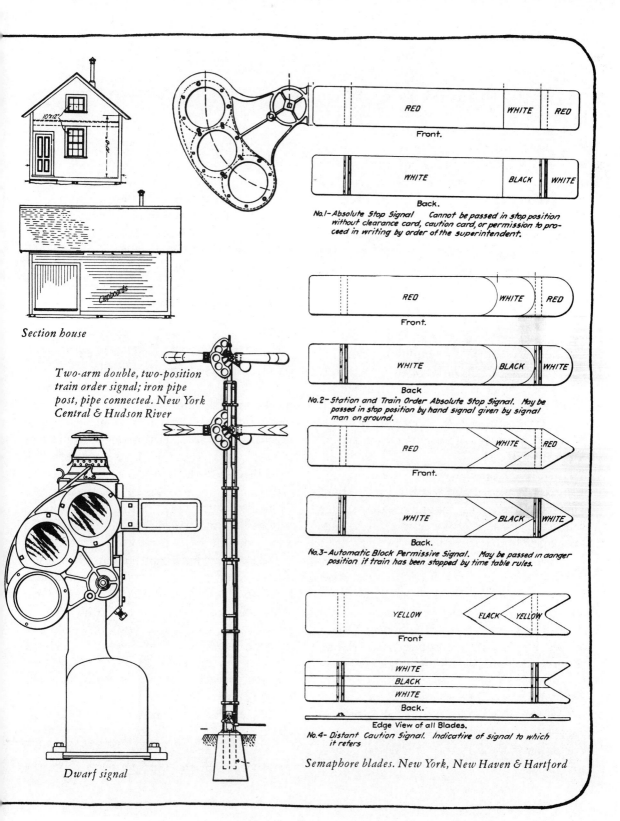

Section house

Two-arm double, two-position train order signal; iron pipe post, pipe connected. New York Central & Hudson River

Dwarf signal

Front.

RED | WHITE | RED

Back.

WHITE | BLACK | WHITE

No.1–Absolute Stop Signal   Cannot be passed in stop position without clearance card, caution card, or permission to proceed in writing by order of the superintendent.

Front.

RED | WHITE | RED

Back

WHITE | BLACK | WHITE

No.2– Station and Train Order Absolute Stop Signal. May be passed in stop position by hand signal given by signal man on ground.

Front.

RED | WHITE | RED

Back.

WHITE | BLACK | WHITE

No.3–Automatic Block Permissive Signal. May be passed in danger position if train has been stopped by time table rules.

Front

YELLOW | FLACK | YELLOW

Back.

WHITE
BLACK
WHITE

Edge View of all Blades.

No.4– Distant Caution Signal. Indicative of signal to which it refers

Semaphore blades. New York, New Haven & Hartford

9

fundamentally shaped and altered, by the people and institutions among whom they grew. The railroads have mirrored every step in America's history to a greater extent and with a greater degree of accuracy than any other industry of the period. All of this lends considerable significance to the artifacts of railroading scattered so profusely about our national landscape. For the working historian and archaeologist, then, where the emphasis is placed—the effect of railroads on history, or the railroads as mirrors of national culture—is a subtle but crucial distinction.

In the first instance, the railroads stimulated the growth of heavy industry, the iron and steel and locomotive-building industries being certainly the heaviest of the nineteenth century. Each need created by the railroads—larger rails, stronger iron (and then steel) bridge girders, heavier locomotives, more capacious freight cars—was met, in turn, by American industry.

But our concern here is "reading" the artifacts of railroading for information about what was happening in nineteenth-century America. Let's look, for example, at the railroad maps in a historical atlas of the 1830s and 1840s. There we'll discover something that to our way of thinking seems very strange indeed: numerous little railroads all over the map, east of the Mississippi, but most of them with less than a hundred miles of track and few of them connecting with one another! By 1860, according to another map, the problem seems to be solved. The railroads are much longer now and *seem* to be connecting, but now they're all different gauges! What's happening? Let's go back into American railroad history and try to answer this question.

Railroads, as we'll soon see, have a historical direction and probably several "beginnings" and "endings." Where tracks begin and end, what kinds of places they pass along the way (a ghost town, mining settlement, or the site of an early American village), and where the sidings lead you from the main line (to a cattle pen, grain elevator, lumber mill, quarry, or little factory) will provide much of what we need to complete the picture.

Suppose you are visiting friends in Lowell, North Billerica, Wilmington, or one of the other original stops along the old Boston & Maine right-of-way, and you're doing some track walking, and you've begun to wonder: Where does it go? Where did it begin? In fact, why is there a railroad here at all?

The Boston & Maine never was one of the giants of the industry (which makes it just that much more attractive to me as a local historian). For as long as anyone around there can remember, the B & M has been their link with Boston to the south. True, the line was extended north to Nashua, Manchester, and Concord, New Hampshire, and on to Woodsville, and then across to Wells River in Vermont; but the *historical direction,* the view of the longtime inhabitants of these towns and others along the way—and of their ancestors—is *toward* Boston. In fact, there are two more principal lines of the road, one reaching westward to Rotterdam, New York, and one north to Portland, Maine. Standing at any one of these points, looking down the line, one can see that the rails run straight and true to Boston (a map of the entire system forms a perfect arrow pointed at the city).

But let's return to our trackside vantage point at Lowell and our questions about the

Dating a Railway

Establishing the age of an abandoned railway becomes a simple matter if, during the years of its operation, track crews used one of the usual methods of dating ties: dating nails, stamping, or notching. The dating of ties—a practice which apparently began sometime in the 1880s —provided engineers with information on the length of the tie's service as well as on the durability of various woods and the effectiveness of preservatives on them, and helped track crews determine when the ties would need to be replaced.

Dated nails were used the most extensively— galvanized-iron or copper nails with, stamped on their heads, the last two figures of the year the tie was laid. The nails were sometimes driven into the top of the tie about midway between the rails, and sometimes on the end— depending on the railroad. The nails were usually about 2½ inches long with a ⅝-inch-diameter head.

Some roads, among them the Southern Pacific and the Lake Shore & Michigan Southern, stamped ties as they were put into the track. A cast-iron hammer with raised figures indicating the year on its striking face was used. The figures were much larger than those on dating nails and they were stamped on both the top and the end of each tie. At the end of each year the hammers were called in, scrapped, and new ones cast for the coming year—to be issued to the section foremen.

A third method, which, luckily, was not so widely used, consisted of cutting notches on the edge of the tie face in a certain position fixed for each year of the decade. In the event that you come upon such notches, it may be possible to decipher them by this explanation from a turn-of-the-century manual: "Say the road runs north and south: then let the odd numbered years be marked on the north edge of the face and even numbered years on the south edge. Starting at the east end of the tie, let successive notches toward the west end thereof indicate years increasing upwards to ten. As distinct positions for the notches, points can be taken outside the rail, just inside the rail, and at the middle of the tie, making positions for five notches on each side of the tie face." There seems to have been no provision in this system for numbering the decade, even though ties were often in service longer than ten years; however, it may be possible to learn this from other clues.

origins of this railroad. If we were to look again through the railroad maps arranged chronologically in a historical atlas of the United States (an essential tool for the amateur historian), we would discover that the maps for the 1600s, 1700s, and early 1800s show only one city in Massachusetts, consistently: Boston. Other cities come and go on the maps. Salem shows up on the early maps but is gone by the time of the American Revolution, when, of course, Lexington, Concord, and Bunker Hill appear. On the maps for the first two or three decades of the 1800s, these too have disappeared; only Springfield (scene of Shays' Rebellion and the Springfield Armory founded by Washington in 1794) and Boston are shown. Then, suddenly, in the maps from the 1840s a new name appears to the north of Boston: Lowell. We know that Boston was, from its founding, a commercial center and port, but what about Lowell? What was happening there? This time, taking a close look at the map, we see that there is a fine black line between the two cities, with evenly spaced crossbars. A railroad has been built.

A visit to Lowell answers remaining questions about the origins of the Boston & Lowell, the B & M's predecessor. Through the city run five miles of power canals, seven canals in all. The canals are essential factors in the growth of the city. Along them may be found today a number of textile mills, the Hamilton-Appleton Mills, Massachusetts Mills, and New Market Mills among others. On Amory Street still stand the six original buildings of the Boot Mills, built between 1835 and 1843, the machinery driven by waterwheels and turbines on the Eastern Canal. On Perkins Street stand two other mill buildings, the site of the Lawrence Manufacturing Company, which in 1848 had 105,000 spindles powered by steam engines and wheels on another of Lowell's waterways, the Lawrence Canal. A visit to the local history shelf of the library would reveal the extent of the freight traffic between Lowell and Boston. By 1848 these two mills alone were producing 24,000,000 yards of cloth annually. Lowell became America's first great industrial city. So the run—once described in romantic terms by Charles Dickens—was, in fact, of signal importance in American industrial history. The Middlesex Canal and a stagecoach had earlier been the freight and passenger carriers between Boston and Lowell. Then, in 1829, a group of textile manufacturers in Lowell petitioned the state for a charter to build a railroad between the two cities. The twenty-six-mile trip by canal boat took eighteen hours; the train made the trip in an hour and seventeen minutes! The canal system was doomed and, in the years to follow, American visions and energies were used for the building of railroads.

The historical purpose of the Boston & Lowell, then, was to provide first one city and eventually others along the line access to the markets and port of Boston. In this way it was no different from hundreds of other railroads that emerged in the early decades of the last century. Because of this "local" nature of the road, the Boston & Lowell and, later, the Boston & Maine were to have a profound effect on the villages, towns, and cities along the route—and, indeed, they've become institutions. In the reminiscences of generations of trainmen, passengers, and grownups—who remember with fondness the childhood hours spent walking along or sitting by the tracks to catch a glimpse of the locomotive, to hear its puffing and chuffing, and to exchange waves with the engineers—is the feeling that there is in the Boston & Maine something decidedly "New England." The B & M, like so many other little railroads in America that grew up with the settlements they served, made a distinctive, albeit intangible, statement in regional mood and style, and the scene in which it grew up is reflected in every railroad artifact of the period.

Throughout the 1700s, business in colonial America was conducted and dominated by merchants who had established their businesses in the large cities and ports of the

Tie Woods

Track walking does have its uneventful moments—as when you've been stepping from tie to tie to tie for hours, and the next railroad artifact is still a mile or two away. But such moments might just be used for thinking about those ties underfoot: how they came to be the size and shape they are and how they speak of that part of the American lumbering industry that grew up, literally, alongside the railroads over the past century and a half. So . . . these simple timbers *do* have a story to tell.

Throughout the 1800s, railroad engineers preferred ties hewed from small trees to sawed ties from larger trees. The former shed water better and lasted a year or two longer (the average life of a tie then being about seven years), though they did not offer as smooth a bearing as sawed ties did. Railroad builders looked for compromises between softwoods—which weathered better but were more easily cut and abraded by the rail and didn't hold spikes as well—and hardwoods—which resisted cutting but which checked, or cracked, badly in the hot sun. Also, heartwood checked worse than did sapwood, but it held a spike better and lasted longer in the ground.

In 1900 and for several years before, the standard tie dimensions were 8 feet long, 6 to 7 inches thick, and 6 to 8 inches wide. As heavier rail came into use in the early decades of this century, ties became longer—anywhere from 8'6" to 9', depending on the wood and the surface on which they would be used. An inch here or there, by the way, was no small matter; engineers had calculated that beam strength varied by the square of its depth, or thickness, so that a 7-inch-thick tie had a strength of 343 and a 6-inch tie 216—a difference of 59 percent.

The variety of woods used for ties offers a sampling of what is to be found in North American forests. In 1890, about 60 percent of all ties in use were hewed from the many varieties of oak. That percentage lessened as the years went by, but the ties are probably still of oak if you are walking tracks in the Allegheny Mountains, the Middle Atlantic States, the Lake States (including Ohio), or the states of the

Trackwalkers may come upon some early experiments, such as concrete ties. These were laid in 1914 at the Southern Pacific yards in Oakland, California.

Mississippi Valley. Yellow pine has been used extensively in southern Atlantic Coast and Gulf states, and some yellow pine has found its way into New England. A mountain pine has been the favorite of railroads in western Texas and in New Mexico and Arizona. The soft black and the red cypress have been much used in the Gulf States. Among the longest-lasting ties are those of cedar, found in Canada, Maine, Michigan, Wisconsin, and Washington; these ties have averaged fifteen to twenty years' service. One red cedar tie in the track of the Boston & Providence was in use from 1834 to 1876—a total of forty-two years. Chestnut was much used throughout the Middle Atlantic and New England states, hemlock in the northern states east of the Mississippi. The ties you'll walk along in Montana may be of tamarack (but, most likely, of cedar); tamarack was also used in Canada, along with hemlock, spruce, and fir. Few states could compete with those of the Ohio Valley for color—there wild cherry, honey locust, and black walnut were once used. And, while redwood would not appear to be suited for use under heavy steel rails, it has in fact been used extensively throughout California, where, in 1900, Southern Pacific records showed redwood ties on sidings that were still perfectly sound after forty years of service—without tie plates!

Atlantic coast. When railroads appeared on the scene, the American economy was undergoing a transition from this merchant-dominated capitalism to industrial and finance capitalism, from an economy in which local and regional interests prevailed to a truly national economy. (Actually, historians see the beginnings of this trend in the later part of the eighteenth century and the earliest decades of the nineteenth century.) Nevertheless, the attitudes that shaped business and the new railroads up to about the time of the Civil War were still those of the merchant capitalist, whose principal concern was winning the competition with rival merchants in other cities for the markets of an America expanding toward and across the Mississippi. The bickering and maneuvering were endless. Railroads were built to "capture" markets the way the Boston & Worcester Railroad was built to capture the Worcester trade for Boston and keep it from going to Providence via the Blackstone Canal. Laws were passed in state legislatures and city governments prohibiting the building of railroads or changes in gauge that might give another city in the same state—or just over the line in another state—some economic advantage.

The locations of railroad terminals reflect this struggle for dominance of local markets. In many American cities there are two, three, four, or perhaps more terminals several blocks apart, if not clear across the city from one another (central terminals were built later), each serving separate railroads. Railroads were prohibited from going straight through cities, ostensibly for reasons of clean air and peace and quiet; but the real reason was that it would be too easy for freight to pass through to another market. Some of it would go through anyway, but at least local carriers and teamsters would have the business of moving the freight from one depot to another. In Civil War Augusta, Georgia, thousands of soldiers marched through the streets of the city between railroad stations, changing trains. In Richmond, Virginia, in 1861, four railroads entered the city, each terminating at a depot a mile or so away from the others. Terminals in Chicago are so far apart one wonders if many of those who came to the city and stayed had originally intended to pass through to St. Louis or Kansas City, but just couldn't make it across town to the other terminal. Although there were some exceptions, passenger and freight railroad cars did not continue on to another railroad's track, but traveled only on their own line.

There were more reasons, but the pattern is there on the maps of the period and along the rights-of-way and track we walk. Railroads—some not five miles long—fan out from the principal river and ocean ports in each state to small towns and industries in the backcountry: New Orleans, Louisiana, to Kenner (ten miles); Detroit, Michigan, to Ann Arbor (twenty-five miles); Sandusky, Ohio, to Tiffin (thirty miles); Toledo, Ohio, to Adrian Junction, Michigan (twenty-five miles); Annapolis, Maryland, to Harpers Ferry, West Virginia (sixty-five miles); Bridgeport, Connecticut, to Danbury (twenty miles); Chicago, Illinois, to Elgin (thirty miles); Sacramento, California, to Folsom City (twenty miles, and the only railroad in California in 1860).

In a very real sense the railroads belonged to the communities they served, beginning with the two they were meant to connect and growing to include others that became stops in between. The completion of a line was an occasion for a grand celebration. Nowhere were the pride and the local interests of the original little railroads proclaimed more clearly than in their names—lovingly hand-lettered in gold and other bright colors on locomotive cabs, tenders, cars and cabooses, stations, overpasses and bridges: Louisville & Nashville, Camden & Amboy, Natchez & Hamburg, Petaluma & Santa Rosa, Memphis & Little Rock, Pensacola & Georgia, Bullfrog & Goldfield, Chicago & Milwaukee, Stockton & Copperopolis, Painesville & Youngstown, Wasatch & Jordan Valley. . . . Well, you'll be making your own list soon enough.

In this day of thoroughly standardized industry, it is difficult for us to credit that each of the railroads of the last century had a uniqueness about it, the magnificent locomotives seeming less like technology than a local craft. Looking at pictures of early railroads in operation—from the very beginning they were attractive to artists and photographers—reading the reminiscences of those growing up around them and the trainmen that made them go, just being in the presence of antique locomotives and cars restored to their original delivery-date brightness, the overwhelming impression is one of style and craftsmanship. Everything about the little railroads spoke of regional custom and pride: the railroad's name, the names given a locomotive and train, the decoration and color scheme, terminal- and wayside-building architecture, special colors each road used for semaphores and switch-stand targets (art forms in themselves), even distinctive modifications of stan-

dard locomotives and cars. A shortline or narrow-gauge railway in upstate New York, or Mississippi, or California, or Michigan was no less a reflection of the times and the locale than were dialects, architectural styles, kitchen recipes, and dress of those areas. You may not be persuaded to take the study of early railroads from the realm of industrial history and archaeology and place it, instead, under the heading of American arts and crafts, but the little railroads were a form of individual and regional expression and as such can be "collected"—that is recorded, photographed, sketched, restored, and preserved—not only as artifacts from a particular historical period of industrialization but also as a folk art!

The local character of small railroads owes much to geography, but that doesn't explain why railroads operating in similar terrain under similar conditions still developed individual styles. Their attention to details of construction and operation of equipment, and the personal involvement of small-railroad management as well as crews seems a better answer, and makes each railroad just a little bit different from the next. All of this might have disappeared with the standardization and consolidation of the post–Civil War years, but it was so much a part of railroading by then that much of it survived until the early years of our century. This is important, by the way, not just for the railroad buff or collector of lore, but for the historian and archaeologist, who, becoming aware of these differences and small points of style can use them to date locomotives and cars and, most important, return abandoned equipment to its proper historical context.

One of the niceties of early railroading

Moguls, Decapods, Mastodons...

Locomotives are classified by their number of wheels. In this system—devised by Frederic M. Whyte in 1900—the first figure represents the number of wheels in the leading truck, the second figure the number of drivers, and the third figure the number of wheels in the trailing truck. A 4-6-2, then, has four leading wheels, six drivers, and two trailing wheels. Mallets have two sets of drivers and are recognized by series such as 2-6-6-2 or 0-8-8-0. Locomotives are also referred to informally by names such as Mogul, Atlantic, American, etc.—acquired in a number of ways. For example, the first 2-8-2s were built by Baldwin in 1897, on order from the Nippon Railway in Japan; these turned out to be successful freight locomotives and were subsequently introduced into the United States, appropriately named Mikado.

Many of the wheel arrangements shown in the chart are for locomotives which were in service throughout the 1800s and early 1900s; several, such as the Forney 4-Coupled (four wheels coupled by side rods) and the 8-Wheel Mallet, have not been manufactured in a modern form. Names in parentheses are those of modern types based on the preceding early wheel arrangement.

Arrangement	Diagram	Name
0-4-0		4-Wheel Switcher
0-4-2		4-Coupled and Trailing
0-4-4		Forney 4-Coupled
0-4-6		Forney 4-Coupled
0-6-0		6-Wheel Switcher
0-6-2		6-Coupled and Trailing
0-6-4		Forney 6-Coupled
0-6-6		Forney 6-Coupled
0-8-0		8-Wheel Switcher
0-8-2		8-Coupled and Trailing
0-10-0		10-Wheel Switcher
0-4-4-0		8-Wheel Mallet
0-6-6-0		12-Wheel Mallet
2-4-0		4-Coupled
2-4-2		Columbia
2-4-4		4-Coupled Double Ender
2-4-6		4-Coupled Double Ender
2-6-0		Mogul
2-6-2		Prairie
2-6-4		6-Coupled Double Ender
2-6-6		6-Coupled Double Ender
2-8-0		Consolidation
2-8-2		Mikado

was the naming of locomotives. The custom, probably borrowed from the English tradition, continued up through the 1870s and 1880s. Only a few modern locomotives received names: the Baltimore & Ohio's *Philip E. Thomas* and the Delaware & Hudson's *John B. Jervis* were built in 1926 and 1927. But by 1900 it had become the standard practice just to assign road numbers.

Before road numbers were assigned to locomotives on the Atlanta & West Point Railroad in 1872, the road's 4-4-0 (see the

2-8-4	8-Coupled Double Ender (Berkshire)
2-10-0	Decapod
2-10-2	10-Coupled Double Ender (Santa Fe)
2-10-4	Texas
2-12-0	Centipede
4-4-0	8-Wheel American
4-4-2	Atlantic
4-4-4	4-Coupled Double Ender
4-4-6	4-Coupled Double Ender
4-6-0	10-Wheel
4-6-2	Pacific
4-6-4	6-Coupled Double Ender (Hudson)
4-6-6	6-Coupled Double Ender
4-8-0	12-Wheel
4-8-2	Mountain
4-10-0	Mastodon
4-10-2	Southern Pacific
4-12-2	Union Pacific
0-8-8-0	16-Wheel Mallet
2-6-6-2	16-Wheel Double Truck Mallet
2-8-8-2	20-Wheel Double Truck Mallet
2-4-6-2	14-Wheel Passenger Mallet

"Moguls, Decapods, Mastodons . . ." box above for an explanation of these numbers), "Americans" carried names like *Native, Dr. Thompson, Post Boy, L. B. Lovelace, Patriot,* and *Telegraph.* Among the names of locomotives on the Montgomery & West Point Railroad were *Abner McGehee* (the road's first financial backer), *Colonel J. P. Taylor, West Point, Charles T. Pollard* (M & WP's first president), *Columbus, Selma,* and *Savannah,* leaving little doubt of the road's geography and heritage. The roster of the last wood-burning railroad, the Boston, Concord & Montreal, records 4-4-0s named *Old Man of the Mountains, Winnipiseogee, Lady of the Lake, Ahquedauken, Pony, Tip Top, Mt. Washington,* and *Granite State.* And most people could guess the state within whose boundaries ran locomotives with such irreverent names as *Skaggs, Coffee-Grinder, Gypsy, Advance,* and *Bully Boy.* In case you can't guess, the roster also includes engines named *Eureka, Santa Rosa, General Vallejo, Eel River, San Rafael,* and *Sonoma.* It should be mentioned that these names were more than custom or decoration; they were actually used to refer to a specific locomotive. While railroad men of later years had to content themselves with referring to their locomotives by class or road number, the engineers and firemen who rode these earlier locomotives recalled them lovingly by name in their memoirs, recorded reminiscences, and railroad histories.

All along, cars and equipment had been as colorful as the road names, but the most lavish expression of a little railroad's style was in the distinctive detailing of its locomotives. The years from 1850 to 1870 stand out as a decorative period of locomotive design. The veneration with which Americans regarded the locomotive engine made it unthinkable to paint such a wondrous machine in somber black tones or to leave the gray metal unfinished. There was color, lots of color, in those early years. The bright, glossy paint, gilt lettering, elegant scrollwork and striping, and the painted vignettes of landscapes, factories, portraits, eagles, and other animals on the sides of the tender reflected the artistic exuberance of the period.

Contemporary descriptions of locomotives of this period are remarkable. The *Semi-*

nole, built by Thomas Rogers for the Union Pacific in 1867, had a wine-colored tender with gilt lettering. Matthias Baldwin's *Tiger,* built for the Pennsylvania Railroad in 1856, had an ornately gilded tender painted bright pink. Red wheels and green cabs, or "engineer's houses," as they were known then, were the favorites of many railroads. So were silver or white smokeboxes. A lithograph issued about 1856 shows the locomotive *Thomas Rogers* with driving and truck wheels done in white, rimmed with red stripes and the counterweights painted robin's-egg blue. Baldwin specifications for a Cleveland & Pittsburgh Mogul (2-6-0) called for the finish to be "Plain and smooth, wheels and cow catcher to be painted Indian red."

Though builder's painting specifications are rare, there remains this one for what must have been a most beautiful locomotive, the *Kittatinny,* built for the Delaware, Lackawanna & Western in 1855:

Wheels and cow catcher	Dark brown with vermilion stripes
Frames, belly band, braces, wheel covers and reversing shaft	Green with black stripes
Pumps	Vermilion with black stripes
Suction pipe	Green
Smoke-box front	Dark brown with scrolls
Smoke-box door	Green with vermilion stripes around it

A Closer Look at Cylinders

Cylinders enable us to guess the vintage of a found locomotive, and, more interesting, place it in a period in the historical development of the steam engine in America. Fortunately, the differences in cylinder design are reflected in the outward appearance of the cylinder block, and are easily recognized.

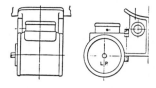

The two-cylinder simple engine with one cylinder on each side was basic throughout the nineteenth century. Locomotives imported from England and built in America in the 1830s had inclined cylinders, a design that continued up through the 1840s. Horizontal cylinders first appeared later in the decade, became standard in the 1850s.

CROSS COMPOUND

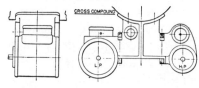

The 1880s and 1890s were a time of experimentation with various arrangements of "compound" cylinders, which used the steam twice —first in a high-pressure and then in a low-pressure cylinder. One of the earliest of these was the "cross compound," with a low-pressure cylinder on one side and a high-pressure cylinder on the other.

VAUCLAIN COMPOUND

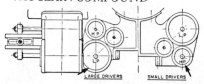

The first locomotive with compound cylinders based on the design of Samuel Vauclain was built by Baldwin in 1889. Differences in frame design for locomotives with large or small drivers resulted in two variants of the Vauclain cylinders—shown in the drawing.

TANDEM COMPOUND

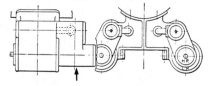

Three- and four-cylinder compounds with cylinders inside the frame (visible between the front drivers) and the "tandem compound" all appeared between c. 1900 and 1910. In this design the low-pressure cylinder is behind the high-pressure cylinder instead of above it, as in the others. Since both cylinders are on the same center line, two pistons are mounted on the same piston rod.

Three-cylinder compound

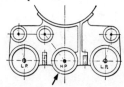

Four-cylinder compound

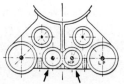

Some lines continued their distinctive color schemes well into the twentieth century, but for the most part the gaiety had ended by the 1880s. Still, locomotives that remained in service provide the historian with decorative touches more durable than paint, and which reveal regional tastes as well: ornamental metalwork. Polished brasswork is probably what comes to mind first—the brightly polished whistles, boiler bands, bells, headlamp brackets, steam domes, cylinder and steam-chest covers. But there were other metals too, polished-copper piping, silvery steel side rods and valve gear, planished or highly polished cast iron. The motifs were often classical Greek or Roman, or Gothic, and even Egyptian. In the early 1850s an acorn-shaped sandbox graced the boilers of engines built by the Taunton Locomotive Manufacturing Company, and whistles and bells would sit atop stands of fluted columns.

Railroads of the day could choose from a profusion of locomotive designs offered by numerous manufacturers, some of whom survived into the early 1900s; but few still make locomotives today. The manufacturer's name appears on the builder's plates of the locomotives we'll discover on our walks: Baldwin Locomotive Works (Philadelphia and Eddystone, Pennsylvania); Richmond Locomotive Works (Richmond, Virginia); Schenectady Locomotive Works (New York); Porter, Bell & Co. (Pittsburgh); National Locomotive Works (Connellsville, Pennsylvania); Rogers Locomotive & Machine Works (Paterson, New Jersey); Manchester Locomotive Works (New Hampshire); Brooks Locomotive Works (Dunkirk, New York); Heisler, Dickson Locomotive Works (Scranton, Pennsylvania); Hinkley (Boston); Canadian Locomotive Company Ltd. (Kingston, Ontario); Norris (Philadelphia); Davenport Locomotive Works (Davenport, Iowa); Vulcan Iron Works (Wilkes-Barre, Pennsylvania); Montreal Locomotive Works (Montreal); and Rhode Island Locomotive Works (Providence). The Baldwin Locomotive Works' *Record of Recent Construction 1898* called the prospective buyer's attention to the array of locomotives and styles available, noting that on file in their drafting department were "upward of two thousand designs for locomotives. . . . These designs are being added to at the rate of about one hundred and twenty-five complete designs each year."

In addition, there were locomotives built from scratch or modified considerably in the railroads' own shops. To the manufacturer's design were added little touches by the railroad's own engineering department, either when ordering the locomotive or after it arrived in the road's shops. Stacks, particularly, were a distinguishing feature of old locomotives, and they provide the archaeologist with the single most important clue to the fuel burned in the locomotive's firebox (see pages 22 and 23). Some stacks were the trademark of the manufacturer. The Baldwin "straight stack" was fitted to thousands of locomotives and became associated with Baldwin design. So did the "Rushton stack," named for the Baldwin draftsman who invented it. Others were designed by the railroad's own draftsmen and engineers. The "McConnell stack" was one of these. Used on the Union Pacific, it was designed by and named for the road's superintendent of motive power at Omaha. The "Congdon stack," too, was named for its designer, another Union Pacific superintendent, and was used

A Look at Drivers

The diameter of a found locomotive's drivers is the principal clue to its use. The dimensions are for standard-gauge locomotives built from about 1890 to 1910. Cast iron was the preferred material for driving wheels from about 1835 to the 1890s, when cast-steel wheels were introduced. Although one locomotive was built with 88-inch drivers, larger drivers were less common, most engines being built with 54-inch to 60-inch drivers and classified as general service. Drivers smaller than 40 inches were used on industrial, logging, and some narrow-gauge locomotives.

Design rule: Maximum safe speed of a locomotive in miles per hour was roughly the same as the diameter of the driving wheels in inches.

"Boxpok" (from box-spoke) drivers are modern, first appearing on locomotives throughout the 1940s.

Early Baldwin drive wheels with separately cast counter-weights bolted between wheel spokes

These counterbalances are characteristic of the first one-piece wrought-iron driver centers introduced by Baldwin in 1889. Counterbalance pockets were filled with lead poured through holes cored in wheel rims.

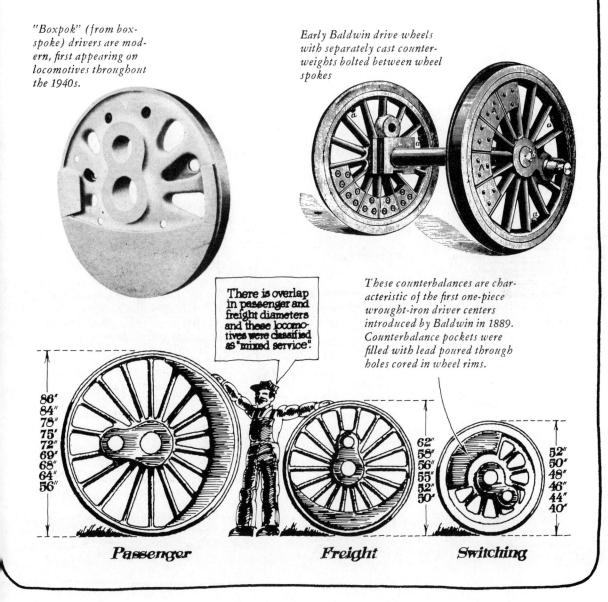

There is overlap in passenger and freight diameters and these locomotives were classified as "mixed service".

86"
84"
78"
75"
72"
69"
68"
64"
56"

62"
58"
56"
55"
52"
50"

52"
50"
48"
46"
44"
40"

Passenger   **Freight**   **Switching**

A Closer Look at Smokestacks

Stacks help us to determine the age of a locomotive, the name of its builder, and whether wood or coal fueled its firebox. Some of the accompanying stacks, such as the McConnell and the Congdon, were identified with a particular railroad, whereas the Baldwin straight stack became the builder's trademark. A few stacks do allow us to date locomotives within a decade or so, but most were used over too long a time to provide us with much more than an approximate date.

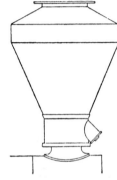

The Rushton stack, or "cabbage," is considered an improvement on the Radley and Hunter design. Kenneth Rushton was a Baldwin draftsman, and his design was introduced on their locomotives about 1910.

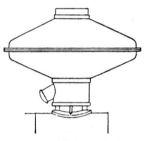

Another Baldwin variation on the Radley and Hunter design. Some appeared on Baldwin export locomotives, particularly ten-wheeled wood burners for Brazil.

Western "bonnet" stacks were very common from about 1840 to 1890.

This Radley and Hunter design was introduced by Baldwin in the 1840s. Its successful spark arrester made it popular with cotton-carrying railroads in the South. It is an improvement of an earlier design by French (master mechanic of the Germantown Railroad) and Baird (a Baldwin foreman).

Large diamond-shaped stacks such as this one designed by A. J. Stevens for the Central Pacific Railroad were used extensively on all types of engines from the early 1860s to the 1890s—though locomotives with such stacks remained in use even into the present century.

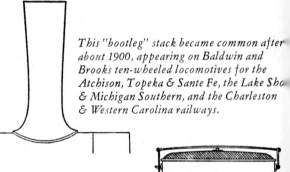

This "bootleg" stack became common after about 1900, appearing on Baldwin and Brooks ten-wheeled locomotives for the Atchison, Topeka & Sante Fe, the Lake Shore & Michigan Southern, and the Charleston & Western Carolina railways.

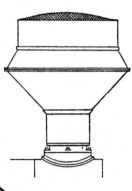

Lima three-truck Shays usually came from the factory with straight, or "shotgun," stacks; but this cross between a "diamond" and a "balloon" appears on several, including #5 built for the Diamond & Caldor, a northern California narrow-gauge line, in 1912.

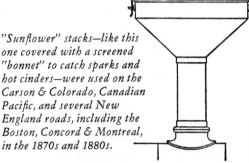

"Sunflower" stacks—like this one covered with a screened "bonnet" to catch sparks and hot cinders—were used on the Carson & Colorado, Canadian Pacific, and several New England roads, including the Boston, Concord & Montreal, in the 1870s and 1880s.

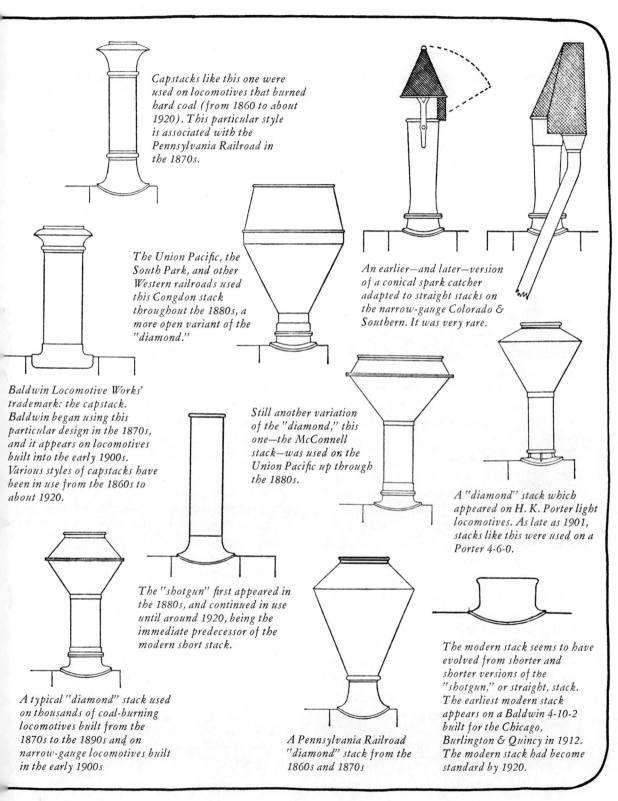

Capstacks like this one were used on locomotives that burned hard coal (from 1860 to about 1920). This particular style is associated with the Pennsylvania Railroad in the 1870s.

The Union Pacific, the South Park, and other Western railroads used this Congdon stack throughout the 1880s, a more open variant of the "diamond."

An earlier—and later—version of a conical spark catcher adapted to straight stacks on the narrow-gauge Colorado & Southern. It was very rare.

Baldwin Locomotive Works' trademark: the capstack. Baldwin began using this particular design in the 1870s, and it appears on locomotives built into the early 1900s. Various styles of capstacks have been in use from the 1860s to about 1920.

Still another variation of the "diamond," this one—the McConnell stack—was used on the Union Pacific up through the 1880s.

A "diamond" stack which appeared on H. K. Porter light locomotives. As late as 1901, stacks like this were used on a Porter 4-6-0.

The "shotgun" first appeared in the 1880s, and continued in use until around 1920, being the immediate predecessor of the modern short stack.

A typical "diamond" stack used on thousands of coal-burning locomotives built from the 1870s to the 1890s and on narrow-gauge locomotives built in the early 1900s

A Pennsylvania Railroad "diamond" stack from the 1860s and 1870s

The modern stack seems to have evolved from shorter and shorter versions of the "shotgun," or straight, stack. The earliest modern stack appears on a Baldwin 4-10-2 built for the Chicago, Burlington & Quincy in 1912. The modern stack had become standard by 1920.

on other western railroads as well. "Cowcatchers," as they were originally intended, or "pilots," as they were later known, also came in distinctive designs identified with a particular locomotive builder or railroad. There were many other distinctive modifications, too—in firebox shape, cab windows, valve gear, tenders—but the smokestack remains the most important clue to a locomotive's vintage, the kind of fuel it burned, and the probable manufacturer, when the identifying builder's plates are missing.

The spirit expressed in the colorful names and regional styles America's little railroads chose for themselves extended, oddly enough, to basic engineering and construction, including a multiplicity of rail weights, shapes, and track gauges that varied from road to road. But so meaningful and distinctive were these variations that the track hiker unable to find locomotives, cars, or other clues to a particular line's use can tell about it from just what's on the ground: rails, rusted tie plates, switches, a splice, or an old tie. This is where the real archaeology begins.

The size and weight of the rails found on an abandoned roadbed are clues to the maximum weight of the locomotives that once rode those rails, and even allow us to estimate the traffic. Once rail weight is known, in fact, we can make some reasonable guess as to the kinds of locomotives used on that railroad, even though none remain *in situ*. We can do this because, throughout the 1800s and early 1900s, locomotives grew in size and weight (and thus in greater tractive force) in response to increasing traffic. Each time a new series of locomotives carrying more weight on its drive wheels was acquired

by the railroad, heavier rails would have to be laid to accommodate the heavier use. Ties might have to be replaced, or more closely spaced, and eventually the entire roadbed made more substantial. These changes occurred mostly on the mainline, or "high iron," while lighter rails continued in service in yards, around shops, on sidings, and in terminals where only lighter switch engines were used and rails were not subject to the pounding of high-speed traffic.

Rail weight is the most important index of use. First, we need to know whether the rail is made of iron (not after 1883, when the price of steel fell below iron) or steel, and our best clue here is the shape shown in the accompanying drawings. Using the table, opposite, we convert rail dimensions to rail weight. The most accurate measurement to use for this purpose is the width of the base of the rail, measured by holding a ruler or tape measure (an indispensable item in the aboveground archaeologist's tool kit) under the rail. Although they may be needed to corroborate other measurements, rail height and the width and depth of the railhead are less accurate because they may be heavily worn, particularly on curves and gradients. In practice, mainline rails were allowed to wear ¼ inch to ½ inch in depth and width before being replaced.

Once we know the weight of the rail from its dimensions, we can then conjure up the kinds of locomotives that once used it. This is possible because of a coincidental relationship between rail and locomotive weights throughout the 1800s. There were no formulated rules or standards in the early days, but still the average weight of rails maintained a nearly fixed relationship with the average weight of locomotives. Once engineers be-

A Closer Look at Rails

Those rusty rails you have found on an abandoned right-of-way hold clues to a railway line's past. Make a tracing or rubbing of the end of the rail and compare it with the cross sections to the right. Then, by taking a measurement, you can determine their weight. Start by measuring the width of the base—the dimension least likely to have been changed by wear. The charts show rail weight, in pounds per yard, for rails of different dimensions. Even if no rail remains, where you've discovered an old line, you can get the base width of the rail from tie plates, impressions of the rail base in old ties, or even from the space between the spike holes in a rotted tie. Look at the guide on pages 26–30 to see a few of the locomotives which might have worked here.

Iron Rail

Pounds/ Yard	Height of Rail	Width of Base	Width of Head	Depth of Head	
70	$3\frac{3}{4}$	$3\frac{7}{8}$	$2\frac{1}{4}$	*	Measure-
65	$3\frac{7}{8}$	4	$2\frac{1}{4}$		ments from
60	$3\frac{3}{8}$	$3\frac{7}{8}$	$2\frac{1}{8}$		rail sections
56	$3\frac{1}{2}$	$3\frac{3}{8}$	$2\frac{3}{8}$		of 1855

Steel Rail (ASCE Standards, 1895)

Pounds/ Yard	Height of Rail	Width of Base	Width of Head	Depth of Head	
152	8†	$6\frac{3}{4}$	3	$1\frac{27}{32}$	
131	$7\frac{1}{8}$	6	3	$1\frac{3}{4}$	1933
100	$5\frac{3}{4}$	$5\frac{3}{4}$	$2\frac{3}{4}$	$1\frac{45}{64}$	
95	$5\frac{9}{16}$	$5\frac{9}{16}$	$2\frac{11}{16}$	$1\frac{41}{64}$	1905—heavy
90	$5\frac{3}{8}$	$5\frac{3}{8}$	$2\frac{5}{8}$	$1\frac{19}{32}$	traffic, 27
85	$5\frac{3}{16}$	$5\frac{3}{16}$	$2\frac{9}{16}$	$1\frac{35}{64}$	or more
80	5	5	$2\frac{1}{2}$	$1\frac{1}{2}$	trains a day
75	$4\frac{13}{16}$	$4\frac{13}{16}$	$2\frac{15}{32}$	$1\frac{27}{64}$	Light traffic,
70	$4\frac{5}{8}$	$4\frac{5}{8}$	$2\frac{7}{16}$	$1\frac{11}{32}$	10 trains a
65	$4\frac{7}{16}$	$4\frac{7}{16}$	$2\frac{13}{32}$	$1\frac{9}{32}$	day or less
60	$4\frac{1}{4}$	$4\frac{1}{4}$	$2\frac{3}{8}$	$1\frac{7}{32}$	Standard
55	$4\frac{1}{16}$	$4\frac{1}{16}$	$2\frac{1}{4}$	$1\frac{11}{64}$	narrow-
50	$3\frac{7}{8}$	$3\frac{7}{8}$	$2\frac{1}{8}$	$1\frac{1}{8}$	gauge
45	$3\frac{11}{16}$	$3\frac{11}{16}$	2	$1\frac{1}{16}$	weights for
40	$3\frac{1}{2}$	$3\frac{1}{2}$	$1\frac{7}{8}$	$1\frac{1}{64}$	1870s and
30-35	$3\frac{1}{2}$	$3\frac{1}{2}$	$1\frac{3}{4}$		1880s

*The radius of the curve under the head makes it difficult to come up with a meaningful measurement.

†The rail width at the base and the height are equal in ASCE standard so that the amount rail height is less than base width is some indication of the amount of wear on rails after 1895.

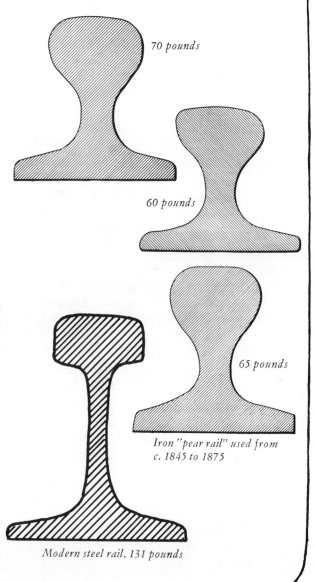

70 pounds

60 pounds

65 pounds

Iron "pear rail" used from c. 1845 to 1875

Modern steel rail, 131 pounds

came aware of this, a neat rule of thumb could be applied: The average weight of the rail in pounds per yard corresponds fairly closely to the average weight of locomotives using that rail in tons. In other words, 30-pound rail was considered safe and adequate for 30-ton locomotives. Later, 50-, 60-, 70-, 80-, 90-, and 100-pound rail came into general use (and intermediate weights as well) to meet corresponding increases in locomotive heaviness.

Assume for the moment that you've come upon an abandoned track. It's an easy matter, first of all, to determine if the rails are of iron or steel. Iron rail will be smaller and have an irregular, rounded head. The web curves inward from the head to the base. From these two characteristics comes the name "pear rail." Steel rail, on the other hand, will be taller, more massive. The surfaces of steel rail—the sides of the head, the web, and the sloping top of the base—are flat and more regular. The radii of the curves connecting these surfaces are much smaller than in iron rail. The weight of this rail can be determined by its dimensions. Suppose the base of the rail measures 3⅞ inches . . . Looking into the table on page 25, you'll find that rail of this width weighs 50 pounds per yard (you should check the other measurements too, for, as we'll see later, there were some variations even in standard rail). From this we can conclude that the locomotives that once plied this route weighed about 50 tons, that traffic was light, and that we've found a real antique railroad. The "Moguls . . ." table tells us that among the locomotives in this weight class were small Americans, Atlantics, Prairies, 4-4-4s, and four- and six-wheel switchers with simple cylinders. Whether Shays, tank

Locomotives for Rails of Iron and Steel (1870—1900)

With this guide you can exercise your historical imagination and bring an abandoned railroad back to life. Once you know the rail weight (see table on page 25), you can place some of these locomotives on it. Here you'll find—grouped by their usual rail weight—a small sampling of narrow- and standard-gauge locomotives in service from c. 1870 to the turn of the century. This isn't the whole story, of course; many of these locomotives were manufactured in different weights, such as Baldwin's Consolidation (2-8-0) for narrow-gauge 36-pound rail. The next step beyond this guide is to pore through builders' catalogues and early editions of the *Locomotive Dictionary* for locomotives run on particular railroads. You will notice in the examples varying arrangements of tank, boiler, and cab. For example, the locomotive at top left has its tank on the boiler; the one at top right has its tank back of the cab; etc. There are two double-ender locomotives at the bottom of the page.

KEY

EXP	Express passenger
F	Freight
H	Heavy
L	Logging
LF	Local freight
LS	Local service
M	Mixed service (passenger and fast freight)
P	Passenger
SW	Switching
T	Tank on locomotive

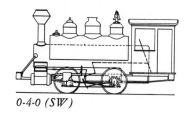

0-4-0 (SW)

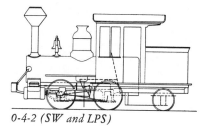

0-4-2 (SW and LPS)

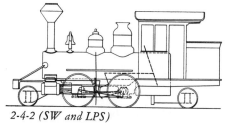

2-4-2 (SW and LPS)

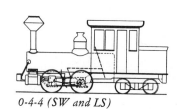

0-4-4 (SW and LS)

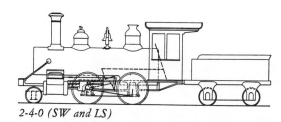

2-4-0 (SW and LS)

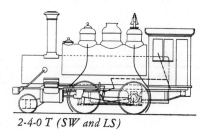

2-4-0 T (SW and LS)

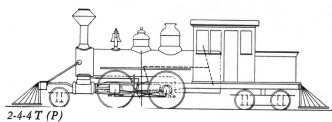

2-4-4 T (P)

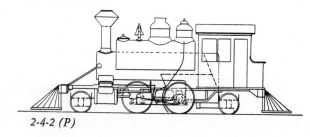

2-4-2 (P)

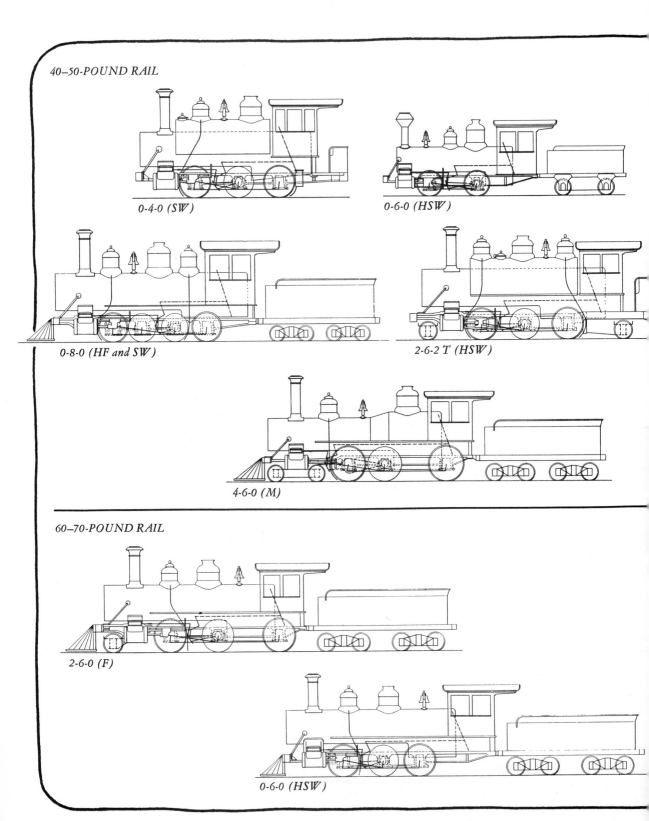

40–50-POUND RAIL

0-4-0 (SW)

0-6-0 (HSW)

0-8-0 (HF and SW)

2-6-2 T (HSW)

4-6-0 (M)

60–70-POUND RAIL

2-6-0 (F)

0-6-0 (HSW)

2-4-2 (EXP)

4-4-0 (EXP)

0-6-4 (HSW and LF)

0-6-4 (HSW and LF)

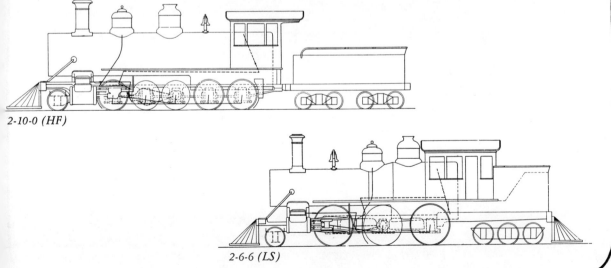

2-10-0 (HF)

2-6-6 (LS)

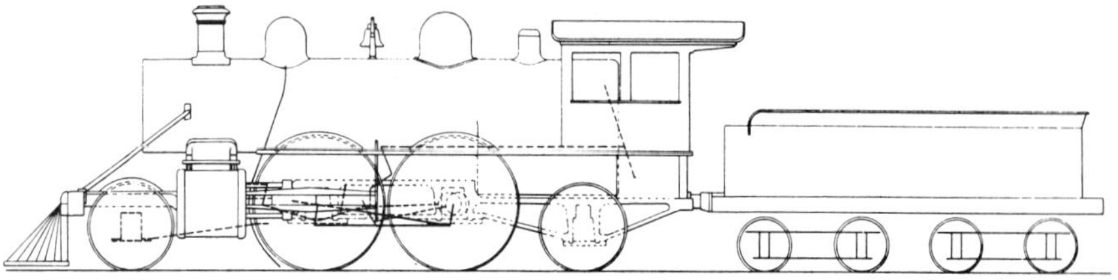

2-4-2 (EXP)

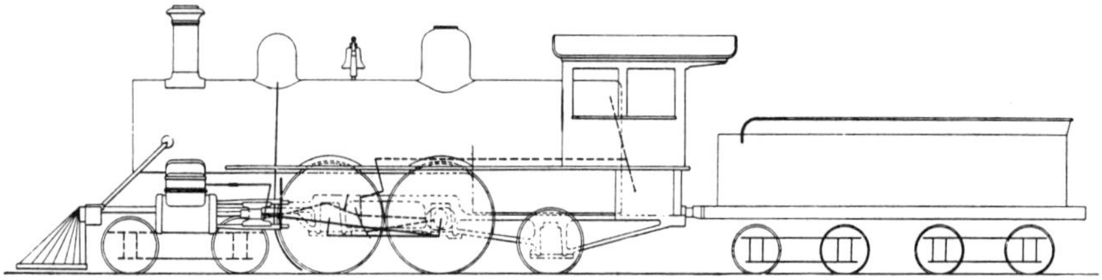

4-4-2 (EXP)

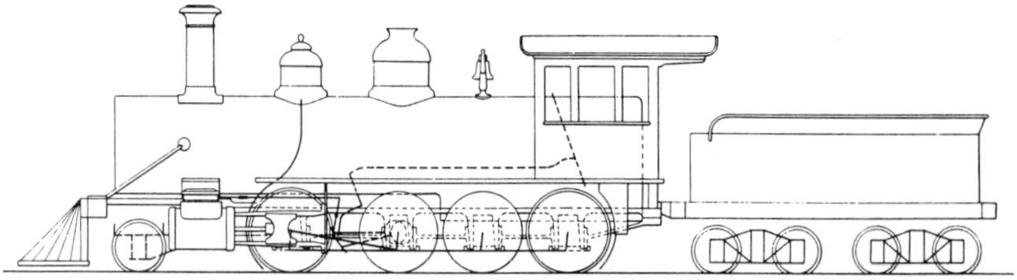

2-8-0 (HF)

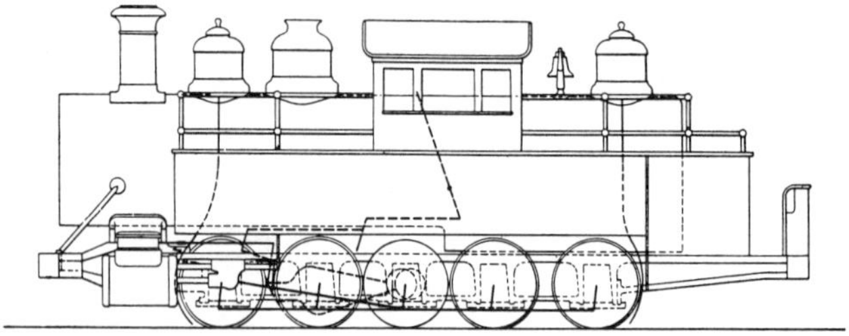

0-10-0 T (HSW)

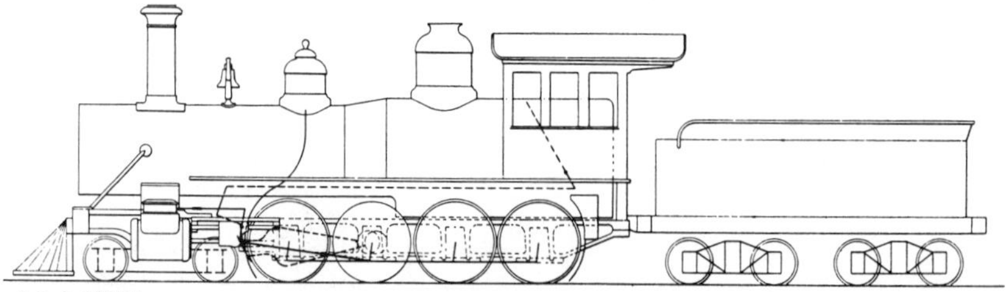

4-8-0 (HF)

locomotives, and other specialized equipment might have been used here can also be determined, for example, from the presence of steep gradients and switchbacks, sharp curves, narrow or low clearances, and, most important, the work of the road—logging, mining, quarrying—determined by what's along the line.

It should be noted that this correspondence, particularly for large, standard-gauge railroads, works only up to about 1920. From then to the late 1940s, locomotives began to reach gargantuan proportions while rail weights increased in smaller increments, and in the 1930s reached a maximum 152 pounds, used to this day. It was also during this period that railroads began laying heavier rail than their locomotive rosters would seem to justify, in anticipation of heavier traffic and locomotives that would certainly come in the near future. During the first decade of our century, 75- and 80-pound rail was considered standard for lines of heavy traffic. A check of locomotive builders' catalogs for the period shows that, with the exception of the Decapod type, then considered the heaviest motive power (over 100 tons), most locomotives weighed between 70 and 90 tons, as the rail weight would indicate. By the 1930s, however, larger lines like the Pennsylvania Railroad were already adopting 131-pound rail as standard, and even began laying what was to be the heaviest rail ever produced. Rails weighing 152 pounds per yard became the standard by the early 1940s, and this is what you'll find on most mainlines today. Locomotives during this period weighed from about 175 to 275 tons and, in a few instances—the massive articulated locomotives—385 tons.

The shape and cross section of a rail tell us little if anything about use, but as artifacts they reveal a great deal about particularistic aspects of early railroads. Rails varied considerably throughout the last century until 1893, when the American Society of Civil Engineers first established a standard cross section and 50-pound weight increments. Within ten years seventy-five percent of the railroads were using rail that complied with ASCE standards. Before this happened, there were about as many different kinds of rail as there were railroads.

Much of this variation can be attributed less to style and individual expression than to a lack of any coordinated research and industry standards. Yet, along with locomotive and car design, depot architecture, and regional styles, rails were also shaped in very personal ways. During the late 1800s, especially, the designing of rail sections, as one contemporary civil engineering study reported, had become something of a fad. Each railroad had its own engineering department, whose engineers felt called upon to get up an original design for their railroad. Nearly every railroad had its own "standard" rail section, which might be modified as often as there were changes in the personnel of the engineering department. The result was an almost endless variety of designs, which reflected the ideas of individual engineers and railroads—all practically identical except for slight and usually unimportant differences in dimensions. Most of the debate centered around the relative proportions of the head, web, and base. What percentage of the metal should be in each of the three parts? Does a wide, shallow head wear better than a narrow, deep head? What is the proper angle for the shoulders of the base, and what should be the ratio of base to height? Should the head be flat, inclined, or rounded and, if the latter, what is the radius to be? If the head is to be inclined, should it slope to match the coning of the wheels? Some webs had straight sides, others concave sides with the same thickness at the head and flange, and still others had concave sides thicker at the flange than at the head. Some rails were unsymmetrical, leading to the idea that they were meant to be used as "lefts" and "rights." The radii of the corners of the head and the fillets between the web, the base, and the head were still other topics in this esoteric debate. The bolt holes in the old iron rails were made oblong, to allow the rail to expand and contract without straining the fishplate bolts. In steel rails, provision for expansion and contraction was made by drilling round holes larger than the diameter of the bolts.

All this creativity must seem marvelous if you are an aficionado bent on "collecting" all manner of rails. But if you operated a steel mill in the 1870s, your feelings would be very different indeed. Each rail manufacturer was obliged to have on hand numerous different rolls to produce rails for his various customers. At the height of this trend in rail design, rail mills had no fewer than 188 different patterns considered to be "standard" and regularly manufactured 119 patterns in 27 different weights per yard, or 3213 possible combinations. Some of this variation was justifiable in that it allowed a railroad to adopt its track to local conditions. Railroads, for instance, tried whenever possible to manufacture ties from local sources of wood, sometimes making it necessary to modify rails and tie plates in order to be used with

certain woods. It is for just this reason that the base of the 80-pound rail laid on the Grand Trunk Railway in Canada is 6 inches wide rather than the 5 inches specified by ASCE standards. The increased bearing surface was necessary to accommodate the softer cedar ties then in use there.

Rail sections do make for interesting collecting, and there are at least a couple of ways of recording shapes of rails you find on your walks. If an exposed rail end is available, as might be the case with rails lying alongside the roadbed stacked up on rail stands, or exposed at the end of a siding or spur, it's simply a matter of placing a piece of paper against the end of the rail, backed by your clipboard or whatever, and tracing the outline with a pencil. A rubbing could be made, too. If no rail ends are exposed, measurements could be taken for a sketch or, better yet, an accurate profile can be arrived at with a carpenter's template former (another neat little tool for the archaeologist) and then traced on paper. Rail tracings and rubbings, especially from older rails, are attractive reminders of the time when even the design of something as mundane as an iron or steel rail was approached with a craftsman's care.

The standard track gauge throughout North America is 4'8½" measured from the inside of the railheads. So it has been in the United States since 1863. The problem of finding a standard gauge had become a concern of the federal government when the decision was made to build the first transcontinental railroad. The California railroads were built on a gauge of 5'0"; the most common gauge throughout the East was 4'8½". One gauge would have to be agreed upon, of

A rare harp switchstand and stub switch near Orbisonia, Pennsylvania, recalls the old days of the East Broad Top Railroad. Stub switches have no "points"—long, tapered rails—but are cut off squarely and meet the rails end to end. The stub switch disappeared from mainline service about 1910, but many, like this one, have been kept in use on sidings.

course, and that decision, according to the Pacific Railroad Act of July 1, 1862, was to be made by the President. After much consulting and discussion, Lincoln decided on a gauge of 5′0″. (This was a gesture toward the California group, whose participation Lincoln wanted to encourage. He knew that Congress would make 4′8½″ standard.) The railroad interests of the East and Middle West, however, were committed to the "standard" gauge and resolved not to accept the President's decision but to use their influence in Congress. The railroads won. When the law was passed, it really didn't change much; it was more a formal recognition of a trend already moving through the country. The "Battle of the Gauges" (an English historical term) has left its mark upon the land, and remains for the railroad archaeologist one of the most incredible episodes in American history. But to really understand, let's take a journey back in time to the year before the Civil War.

Place yourself for the moment in Pilot Knob, Missouri. The year is 1860, and you own the Iron Mountain & Pilot Mines, a small smelting operation and a forge, at the foot of a mountain said to be solid iron. The building of a railroad in Monroe, Louisiana (about 350 miles south of Pilot Knob) has begun, and you've orders for small iron-bridge truss parts to be shipped there. Checking the current *Burgess' Railway Directory,* you would find the following shipping arrangements necessary if you were to ship by rail. For the first sixty miles or so to St. Louis, your shipment would be carried by the St. Louis & Iron Mountain Railway (gauge: 5′6″). It would then be unloaded, ferried eastward across the Mississippi River to East St. Louis, and loaded on an Ohio & Mississippi Railroad boxcar bound for Sandoval, Illinois (gauge: 6′0″). At Sandoval it would be unloaded again and placed aboard an Illinois Central train to Cairo, Illinois (gauge: 4′8½″). Unloaded again in Cairo, the shipment would be loaded onto a barge for the ten-mile trip down the river to Columbus, Kentucky, there to be loaded on the Mississippi Central Railroad (gauge: 5′0″) bound for Jackson, Mississippi. Once in Jackson, it would be unloaded and carried across town to the freight depot of the Southern Mississippi Railroad (gauge: 4′10″), where it would await the next train to Vicksburg. Unloaded in Vicksburg, your shipment must be placed on a ferry to go back across the river to DeSoto, Louisiana, and the Vicksburg, Shreveport & Texas Railroad to Monroe (gauge: 5′6″). In 1860s America, markets followed railroads of the same gauge, and such "long distance" shipment by railroad, particularly north to south, would not have entered your mind; you would have chosen the river instead.

The maze of differing gauges that covered the country was a reflection of facts of American life already mentioned: the dominance of local interests and merchant capitalism, and the fact that when the railroads were being constructed, there were several gauges to choose from. Engineers for each railroad could select the one they thought best suited their needs.

In 1861 no fewer than six gauges were considered "standard": 4′8½″ and 4′9″ (in practice considered one gauge, as equipment was interchangeable), 4′10″, 5′0″, 5′4″, 5′6″, and 6′0″. Gauge differences presented fewer problems generally within geographical regions, but became a very serious problem indeed if, as in our example, shipment was to be made from north to south or from the Gulf States to New England. Railroads in New England and the Atlantic Seaboard states had a standard gauge almost from the very beginning. The "Stephenson gauge"—4′8½″—ran from Charlotte and Wilmington, North Carolina, all the way north to Vermont, New Hampshire, and Maine. It was not, however, a conscious act of integration. The uniformity was due in part to the tendency in New England and the Middle Atlantic states to follow the British example (a tendency certainly noticeable in other aspects of life in these states), and partly because the first railroads built in New England—among them the Boston & Lowell, the Boston & Worcester, and the Boston & Providence—imported their first locomotives from Robert Stephenson and Company in England.

For the archaeologist/trackwalker there is the challenge of finding examples and artifacts of these earlier gauges. The work of changing over to the standard gauge was not complete until around the turn of the century. After Congress adopted the 4′8½″ gauge in 1863, there was no dramatic change, although in the histories of individual railroads are found some incredible conversion records. When the Grand Trunk Railway converted from 5′6″ to 4′8½″ gauge in late 1873, Baldwin turned out forty-five new locomotives in three months, all delivered to the Grand Trunk within a five-week period. In 1885, the Mobile & Ohio Railroad changed over 500 miles of track in less than twelve hours, causing the delay of only one passenger train and but a few freight trains. A year later, over 1,800 miles of mainline and sidings on the Louisville & Nashville were changed from 5'0" to 4'9" gauge on a single day, May 30. There are many such stories, and the trend was clearly toward a standard gauge and the integration of all of the railroads into a truly national system. Still, it would take the next forty years or so for the work of conversion to be completed.

The changeover was an expensive and complicated process, particularly when locomotive conversions had to be made from the broadest to the standard gauge—from, say, 6'0" to 4'8½". In the meantime all manner of devices of interest to railroad archaeologists were tried in order to make transshipment possible until full conversion could be accomplished. One such temporary measure was the laying of a third rail, and sometimes a fourth, so that trains of two gauges could be used on the same tracks. Although trains operating over these tracks were usually made up of locomotives and cars of the same gauge, mixed trains were not uncommon. The general manager of a Canadian fast-freight line reported in 1867 that "the third rail from Windsor to Suspension Bridge, which enables the Great Western . . . to run their Broad Gauge cars [5'6"] in the same train with 'Blue Line' or Narrow Gauge cars [4'8½"] has . . . proved a perfect success."

Other alternatives for this awkward period of changeover involved modification of cars, the use of hoists to change trucks, and "compromise wheels."

Car hoists that enabled trucks of different gauges to be interchanged at transfer points were apparently familiar sights to travelers throughout the 1880s. Vestiges of these devices might still be found by the observant trackwalker using good archaeological techniques. One such steam hoist is described at Cincinnati, Ohio, where the Indianapolis & Cincinnati (4'8½") and the Ohio & Mississippi (6'0") entered the city from the west on double-gauge track, a group of small Ohio lines of 4'10" gauge came from the north, and the Marietta & Cincinnati (4'8½") entered from the east. Another is described by an early railroad traveler at Lynchburg, Virginia, where the Orange & Alexandria (4'8½") and the Petersburg & Lynchburg (5'0") met. We could expect to find at least traces of hoists—stationary steam engines and transverse tables used to move trucks between storage sidings and cars being outfitted—wherever interchange points are indicated on the map. This list is not complete, but contemporary sources reported the operation of hoists in Cairo, Illinois; in Louisville, Kentucky; and along the route of the Louisville & Nashville in Rowland, Nortonville, and Henderson, Kentucky; Evansville, Indiana; Milan, Tennessee; Mobile, Alabama; and New Orleans, Louisiana.

A real find for the trackwalker would be a pair of wheels or trucks from a "compromise car," recognizable by its wide wheel treads, which allowed the car to be used on three gauges: 4'8½", 4'9", and 4'10". The wheels of compromise cars had 5-inch-wide treads (measured from the wheel face to the base of the flange). The standard tread width at the time was a little over 4 inches. Thousands of these cars were in service beginning about 1860 and continuing up through the period of integration and changeover in the 1880s. It is quite likely that some are still around on sidings somewhere (forty-five hundred compromise cars were operated on two subsidiaries of the Pennsylvania Railroad in the late 1880s; namely, the Empire and Green Fast Freight lines).

Still another experiment was with sliding-wheel cars, which also appeared in the early 1860s. The wheels on these cars could be unlocked, leaving them free to slide in or out on the axle as the car was moved over rails that narrowed or widened to the new gauge. Although the Grand Trunk Railway operated about a thousand sliding-wheel cars over connections in Canada and the United States throughout the 1860s and 1870s, these were involved in a large number of accidents and mishaps. Eventually this concept was abandoned in favor of changing the gauge or using car hoists, though it's certainly possible that the trucks or connecting tracks still remain for our discovery (and, now, recognition).

The gauge maze continued in operation throughout the remainder of the century. As late as 1880, the North Carolina Railroad and other Southern lines were still laying track of 5'0" gauge, but during the decade the last of the Southern broad-gauge lines began the changeover to standard gauge or, more accurately, one of the two "standard" gauges of the time, 4'8½" and 4'9". The latter was the gauge of the Pennsylvania Railroad and its subsidiaries, with whom the Southern lines had most of their interchange business and which connected them most directly to markets in the East. By 1899, though, most of the railroads had completed their conversions.

There were still in service some twenty-five thousand miles of 4'9" gauge track, but during the years 1899 and 1900 the changeover to 4'8½" was virtually complete. Baldwin's *Record of Recent Construction, 1900* shows that all the locomotives delivered to the Pennsylvania Railroad that year were built to standard gauge, as were those delivered to all their other customers. Well, *almost* all. There still were some holdouts. Locomotives delivered to the Norfolk & Western; Charleston & Western Carolina; Atlantic Coast Line; Southern; Chattanooga, Rome & Southern; Chesapeake & Ohio; and Virginia & Southwestern—all continued to be 4'9" gauge!

What is most likely to remain of all this is evidence of the changeover on individual roads, or on the tracks (still not converted) of railroads, abandoned during what was a costly, often financially disastrous period. If rails are not still in position, look for evidence of gauge changes in the ties. Much of the work of changing gauges was completed before the widespread use of tie plates. Before tie plates, the usual practice was to lay rail directly on the ties and then secure the rail with two spikes, one on the inside, one on the outside at each tie. Weeks in advance of the changeover, track crews began pulling the inside spikes of one rail—every other spike on curves, two out of three spikes on straight track—allowing traffic on the line right up to the changeover day. The new gauge would be set out and a new inside spike driven every third tie along this new-gauge line. When the appointed day came (often the Fourth of July), track crews working in teams pulled the remaining inside spikes, shoved the rail over until the inside flange was under the new spikes, and then secured the rail with spikes at the outside flange.

This standard-gauge East Broad Top locomotive has an extra coupler (*lower right*)—smaller, lower, and offset so that it can also pull narrow-gauge cars. At this yard in Mt. Union, Pennsylvania, trains were switched to the Pennsylvania mainline.

This line of extra spike holes running down the ties outside one rail is almost certain evidence of a gauge change; another is the off-center position of the rails on the ties. Numerous spike holes and rail-wear marks *inside* the rails might well mean that you've discovered a line which once had laid a third, maybe a fourth rail to become, during the interim, a double-gauge railroad.

Whatever you find—hoists, compromise cars, sliding wheels, or the telltale line of spike holes in a roadbed of old ties—it will recall one of the most fascinating chapters in American railroad history.

An extra, offset coupler is unnecessary on the Denver & Rio Grande Western locomotive operating at Salida, Colorado, because the narrow-gauge rails are on the same centerline as the standard gauge.

A most important episode remains to be told in this brief industrial archaeology of American railroads: the story of the narrow gauge. This story began in Wales with Robert F. Fairlie and his *Little Wonder,* an articulated double engine he designed to replace the horses that pulled empty slate cars to the quarry over the 1'11½" Festiniog Railway. Fairlie became the protagonist for the narrow gauge, or "The Gauge for the Railways of the Future," as he referred to it in a paper read before an annual meeting of the British Railway Association. Not long after, Fairlie was assisting in the design and construction of the original mainline for what was to become the longest narrow-gauge railroad in America, the Denver & Rio Grande.

Any reasonable newcomer to railroad history would assume this chapter to be a flashback to pre–Civil War America and the days before the gauge question had been settled. The subtitle of Fairlie's subsequent book, *Narrow Gauge, Economy With Efficiency Versus Broad Gauge, Costliness With Extravagance,* seemed aimed at heating up the Battle of the Gauges, and we might guess that it was published, oh, sometime in the 1850s. That would be reasonable. But the facts are that *Little Wonder* made its Wales trial run in 1869; Fairlie's widely acclaimed paper was presented in 1870; the work on the Denver & Rio Grande began in 1871; and the book appeared in 1872. Building a new railroad of 3-foot gauge when all the established railroads of the time were converting to the 4'8½" gauge would seem to be more the building of an anachronism than a railroad for the future.

What occurred, instead, was the "narrow gauge fever" of the 1870s, as other railroads began to follow the example of the Denver & Rio Grande. Three-foot gauge was unknown in America in 1870; yet, by 1878, there were 2862 miles of new narrow-gauge track, and 5200 miles just two years later. The most track laid in any twelve-month period occurred in 1882, when some 2000 miles of mostly 3'6" gauge were built. Locomotive builders began scaling down some of their broad-gauge locomotives to 3'0" and 3'6" gauge (the more common gauge). The first, a Consolidation-type manufactured by Baldwin and delivered to the Denver & Rio Grande in 1877, was light enough to operate on 35-pound rail!

Again, history and geography are at the bottom of it all. The most significant statistic of narrow-gauge history is that well over half of all narrow-gauge track in America was laid *west* of the Mississippi. By the 1870s, railroads were pushing westward, a major force in opening up the remote, sparsely populated territories. Looking again at the historical

atlas, we find that in 1870 there were by now extensive railroad systems throughout Minnesota, Iowa, and Missouri. But aside from the transcontinental line the only line west of Missouri went to Sheridan, Kansas. Nine states had no railroads: the Dakotas, Montana, Idaho, Washington, Oregon, Arizona, New Mexico, and the Indian Territory that was to become Oklahoma. The map of 1880 shows a dramatic change. There is at least one railroad in each of the above-mentioned states and territories; railroad mileage had increased by 40,374 miles in a single decade, and by the end of 1888 another 62,785 miles had been added.

"Light iron" railways are the railroad archaeologist's joy. They could go from nearly anywhere to everywhere, and usually did. While many people think of the narrow-gauge railroad as an Out West phenomenon, they've been built in every state. Within a few years after work had begun on the Denver & Rio Grande, there were twenty-three railroads operating over 271 miles of track in Ohio, which, for a short time, took the lead in narrow-gauge railroad building. Pennsylvania was second with 261 miles of light-iron roads, and Illinois third with 202 miles. At the height of the fever, there were eighty-five of these little railways in California and over 350 miles of track in Colorado. There were, in 1876, 200 miles of narrow-gauge track on Prince Edward Island out of a total of over 2000 all over Canada.

But though they were numerous, narrow-gauge railways were also very short, the Denver & Rio Grande being the longest in the United States with 150 miles of track. Some of the shortest lines in the country were the Martha's Vineyard Railway, 9 miles; the Lawrenceville & Evergreen (Pennsylvania), 2¾; the College Hill Railway (Ohio), 3; the Summit County (Utah), 9; the Tuskegee Railway (Alabama), 6; and the Eureka & Ruby Hill (Nevada), 6. When passenger service began in 1898 on the White Pass & Yukon, Alaska's first railroad, there were 4 miles of track! Eventually the 3-foot gauge tracks stretched 110 miles between Whitehorse, Yukon Territory, and Skagway, Alaska—where it ran right through the downtown area on Broadway. This little railroad runs to this day.

Much of what has been said about the archaeology of broad-gauge railroads is true for the narrow-gauge, though if we've become sensitive enough to see individual elements of style in these larger roads, then the little narrow-gauge lines will seem quite eccentric. There were road names such as Peachbottom, the Bodie & Benton, the Bullfrog & Goldfield Railroad; the names of countless lumber companies, quarries, and mines such as St. Louis & Big Muddy Coal Company, Lehigh Coal & Navigation Company, Toms Creek Coal & Coke Company, and the United States Government Engineer Department. Rails were tiny—20, 25, 30, 35, 40, and 45 pounds per yard, the most common being 30 and 35 pounds. Apparently rails of from 40 pounds and up were steel, the lighter rails iron. Rail shapes were numerous, as were the gauges, the most common being 3'0" and 3'6", though many roads were 3'4", 3'8", and even 2'0", especially in Maine. Narrow-gauge cross ties usually measured 5" × 7" × 7' long and were usually laid 2 feet apart center to center (though there were no narrow-gauge standards for rails—some railroads simply threw down logs).

A footnote for the railroad archaeologist is that the building of these little railways was so hurried that there was a considerable amount of improvising when materials were not available. Some companies, unable to afford rails at the outset of construction or unable to get iron in time, actually laid wooden rails made of hard maple set into notches cut into the ties, and made fast with wooden keys. These were usually 3½" × 6", spliced with a lap joint and two bolts.

Many of the little narrow-gauge lines somehow kept going right into the twentieth century, the last logging and lumber lines in the Sierra Nevada disappearing as recently as the 1960s. More and more of these are reappearing each year, now, carrying railroad enthusiasts instead of logs over the old tracks. But the narrow-gauge fever subsided almost as quickly as it had appeared on the scene, the enthusiasm and financial support gone by the mid-1880s, just over a decade after it all began. By 1884 the forerunner, the Denver & Rio Grande, had laid a third rail between Denver and Pueblo to allow continuous service with standard-gauge lines from the East. It was all over. The spirit of these little railways, something of what they had hoped to be, is reflected in Fairlie's 1870s description of a narrow-gauge passenger car:

The finest quality of poplar is used on the outside, while the richest and best varieties of hard wood, such as cherry, walnut and ash are used with well selected profusion on the inside, and with its cushions of scarlet and green and its hooks and lamps and knobs, hinges, etc. of silver mounting give it the appearance of some fairy boudoir rather than a temporary convenience for the traveling public. The coloring is all very fine, and though not gaudy, it is yet bound to attract and please the dullest lover of the beautiful.

2. MAPS TO THE PAST

For most of us the search for old places and things is a pastime, the finding of an abandoned wood-burning locomotive, an iron bridge, or a stone blast furnace being more the surprise of an afternoon walk than the calculated end to our pursuit. You may prefer it this way, and continue such an enjoyable diversion for some time to come. But it is also possible that your curiosity will become a compulsion, that you will no longer be content with coming upon interesting things but will want to find them. It is at this point that we become historians. We've begun to plan, to anticipate where we might go and what we might find there, to pursue a personal interest in the past. When we've arrived at this stage, we'll want to look at some maps.

There are maps to the past as well as to the present. Happily, they are numerous, and while none of those I mean was originally intended for the historian's use, they are readily available in public libraries, county offices, university collections, government map reference libraries, and local and state historical societies; we can even own them, or copies of them anyway.

The first stop for the historian in search of maps is the library and its local history collection. Check the subject catalog for books about your city and state, but rather than spending a lot of time there, note the section in the stacks where the books are, and go there to get acquainted. For this kind of

work there's just no substitute for browsing. Unfortunately many old books do not have indexes, but they probably do have a list of illustrations somewhere toward the front. Don't forget to look at each book's end papers—the insides of the front and back covers—a favorite place for large maps. Here, too, you might find attached a foldout map or a pocket containing loose maps. Thumbing through, you could find a reproduction of a map like the one on page 42 from Charles S. Boyer's *Early Forges & Furnaces in New Jersey,* showing a portion of New Mills (Pemberton), New Jersey, in 1787. The original purpose of the map was to record the transfer of a piece of property. It shows the parcel for sale—"a Forge, Grist-Mill, Saw-Mill and Dwelling House, with Workmen's Houses, etc., together with the land and improvements belonging to the same—the works having lately been put in complete order"—and fixes the locations of several other small industrial sites nearby. There is a bridge, a "Cole House," a "Blacksmith's Shop," and a "Forge Race" carrying the water needed to power the hammers from Rancocas Creek to the forge.

A map such as this one is called a "land plat," which is prepared whenever property is subdivided, sold, or deeded. They are required in most states today and have been ever since the 1700s, forming a continuous history of the land and its use. They reside among county records and will usually show

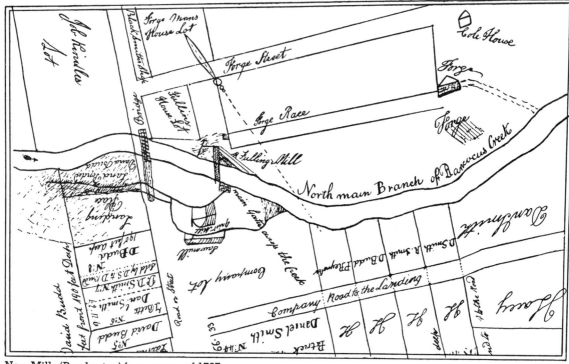

New Mills (Pemberton) from a map of 1787.

all the natural and man-made features of the area, including roads, springs, ponds, dams, footbridges, fields, fences, dwellings, out-buildings, wells, and barns. Sketched and hand-lettered, they are a joy, a simple and direct expression of early American life. But old land plats can also present some real problems. Notice that there are no coordinates, benchmarks, or other references that would help us locate this place. The roads might still be there all right, but creeks are notorious meanderers, and ponds become overgrown, dry up, and turn into meadows. We would have to know the immediate area well or have the help of someone who

does—which suggests the collaboration of amateur local historians, aboveground archaeologists, and old-time residents who would surely enjoy the journey back. In any case, make a copy of the plat map. You can try to match it with one of the other kinds of maps available and fix its present location.

Topographical maps are of larger scale than land plats, but they offer other advantages in locating historical sites. Back in 1879 the United States Geological Survey was established by Congress to collect topographic and geologic information to be recorded on base maps covering the entire country. For this purpose, the country was divided into

42

Topographical Map Key

Railroad: single track and multiple track . . . .

Railroads in juxtaposition . . . .

Narrow gage: single track and multiple track . . . .

Railroad in street and carline . . . .

Bridge: road and railroad . . . .

Drawbridge: road and railroad . . . .

Footbridge . . . .

Tunnel: road and railroad . . . .

Overpass and underpass . . . .

Small masonry or concrete dam . . . .

Dam with lock . . . .

Dam with road . . . .

Canal with lock . . . .

Buildings (dwelling, place of employment, etc.) . . . .

School, church, and cemetery . . . .

Buildings (barn, warehouse, etc.) . . . .

Power transmission line with located metal tower . . . .

Telephone line, pipeline, etc. (labeled as to type) . . . .

Wells other than water (labeled as to type) . . . .

Tanks: oil, water, etc. (labeled only if water) . . . .

Located or landmark object; windmill . . . .

Open pit, mine, or quarry; prospect . . . .

Shaft and tunnel entrance . . . .

Elevated aqueduct . . . .   Aqueduct tunnel . . . . . .

Mine dump . . . .

Tailings . . . .   Tailings pond . . . .

Exposed wreck . . . .   Sunken wreck . . . .

43

small squares, or quadrangles, bounded by meridians of longitude and parallels of latitude. In a similar way Canada has been divided and mapped by the Canadian Department of Lands, Forests and Water Resources. The result of this work in both the United States and Canada is a remarkable series of small-, medium-, and large-scale maps showing considerable detail. Here is the series most useful for our purposes. Since the largest-scale maps are most useful to us, we'll want to get the USGS 7½-minute quadrangle or the Canadian equivalent whenever we can. At this scale, as the table on page 43 shows, 1 inch on the map equals 2000 feet on the ground and the quadrangle covers about 60 square miles. This scale is sufficiently large to show bridges, railroads, dams, mines, quarries, trails, roads, buildings, and even small footbridges.

The first step in getting a topographical map for a certain area is to write to the Map Information Office, United States Geological Survey, Washington, D.C. 20242, and ask for an "index map" for your state or any other state you might be interested in. You can also request a copy of the information sheet "Topographic Map Symbols," a key to the language of the map and the meaning of its colors. Canadian "key maps" are available from the Director, Surveys and Mapping Branch, Department of Lands, Forests and Water Resources in each provincial capital. You'll receive a large map showing major cities, boundaries, and some natural features (rivers, mountain ranges, bodies of water) for points of reference, upon which the quadrangle grid has been overlaid. You'll understand that while each of the states and much of Canada is covered by the small-scale (larger-area) so-called "fifteen-minute series" maps,

there is only partial coverage by the large-scale (smaller-area) index map you've received. You will need various fifteen-minute maps. Each quadrangle is designated by a name, such as "Castle Butte," "Humphrey's Station," or "San Marcos Pass"—taken from a prominent natural feature, city, or town within the quadrangle (Canadian maps are numbered)—and which you must use for ordering. The date of the latest survey reflected on the map is also given. On the reverse of the index map are the names and addresses of topographic map dealers, geological survey sales offices, and map reference libraries (usually college and university, but also some public, libraries).

If you've not seen one, topographical maps are quite attractive, though a bit confusing at first. Elevations are shown with contour lines, which vary in density to give an almost pictorial view, and on some maps the cartographer has simulated the effect of sunlight and shadow, which is so convincing that you can almost feel the mountains and hills. Some familiarity with cartographic conventions and a bit of imagination are all you need to visualize the sheer face of a cliff into which a coal mine has been dug, the steep ravine spanned by a timber trestle, mills arranged along the banks of a swiftly flowing canal, or a heap of mine tailings. Old roads are there, too, leading us to bridges perhaps as old. Following the railroad tracks across the contours, we just may find a sawmill atop a series of switchbacks, tunnels, train sheds, and a water tower with its nearby spring. Topographical maps have an uncanny way of evoking a historical scene, allowing us to "see" sites we may never visit, encouraging the less ambitious among us to ease into armchair archaeology. Since each map is based upon aerial photographs and field surveys, there is very little that escapes recording.

Once we learn to interpret them, topographic map symbols become little pictures. Two classes of buildings are distinguished by symbols: dwellings and work buildings. Smaller buildings, up to 40-feet square, are shown with a conventional symbol, which does not reveal size or shape. But larger buildings such as mills, railroad roundhouses, factories, power plants, gasholders, and grain elevators are precisely drawn not only to scale but to shape as well. Groupings of small, closely spaced structures are dealt with in a special way. The outer buildings are plotted accurately, but the inner structures might be omitted, the object being essentially to preserve the outline of the group. We won't be able to tell exactly how many little buildings might be tightly clustered around a stone furnace or in a mining complex, but the accurate placement of the outermost structures allows us at least to estimate the extent of the site.

By the way, when you get around to looking for that site, you'll find that it is known in the area by its name on the map. USGS is quite careful with names, preferring to use terms long established in local usage and keeping as close as possible to the historical spelling. Conflicts between traditional and more recent usage do arise and, when they do, a decision is made by a Board on Geographical Names. Such changes in name, as well as the appearance and disappearance of artifacts, can be checked by going to an earlier edition of the map.

When you buy a topographical map, it will include the most recent revisions (made in the 1950s and 1960s). While some of the revised maps were originally plotted in the early 1900s and still carry that date, most will be more current. To find older maps that have not been revised (which include structures not present at the time of the revision), you'll need to visit one of the map reference libraries. Addresses can be found on the index maps of each state. Generally, revisions have not been made frequently enough to allow dating the appearance of a railroad line or bridge, for example; but if you have the older maps available to you and there's no better way to get a date, it is certainly worth a try.

Even the large-scale topographic maps cannot provide all the details we would wish, especially not in cities and large towns. But there is another map for cities and towns. Sanborn maps are large-scale city maps—50 feet to 400 feet to the inch—which allow us some exciting historical sleuthing. Their original purpose, as conceived by engineer D. A. Sanborn in 1866, was to provide information on city buildings needed by insurance underwriters. In fact, the very thing that makes these maps valuable to insurance companies makes them equally valuable to the urban historian. Sanborn maps show not only the size and floor plan of each building to accurate scale, but, through a system of color coding and symbols, indicate what kind of structure is hidden in the walls and under the floors, the primary materials used in construction, and even something of the style of the building as it was originally built. On these maps we can locate buildings with cast-iron structural members and fronts, roof trusses and arches, iron and brick chimneys, and architectural details such as mansard roofs, cornices, and

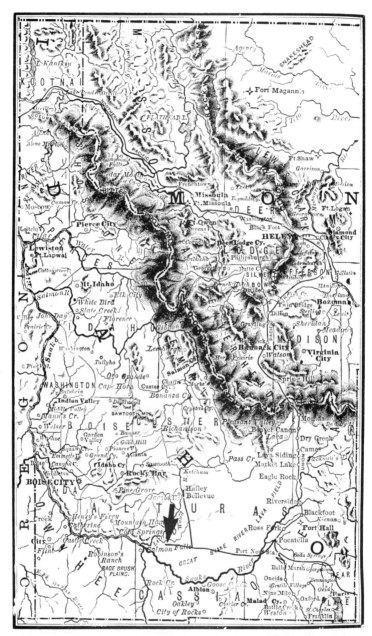

Maps to railroad growth are to be found in Poor's *Manual of Railroads*. Volume I covered the years 1868-69, but maps showing railroad trackage for each state did not appear until 1883; after that, new maps were included each year. These maps of Idaho for 1863

(*left*) and 1864 (*above*) date the building of the Northern Pacific line between a point just northeast of Salmon Falls to Weiser. The maps also date bridges, trestles, depots, and other structures constructed along the way.

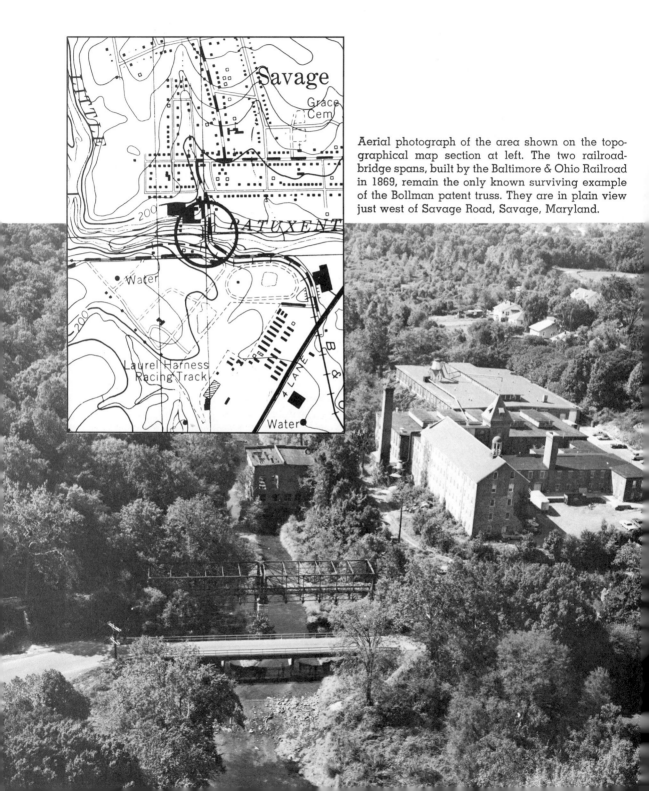

Aerial photograph of the area shown on the topographical map section at left. The two railroad-bridge spans, built by the Baltimore & Ohio Railroad in 1869, remain the only known surviving example of the Bollman patent truss. They are in plain view just west of Savage Road, Savage, Maryland.

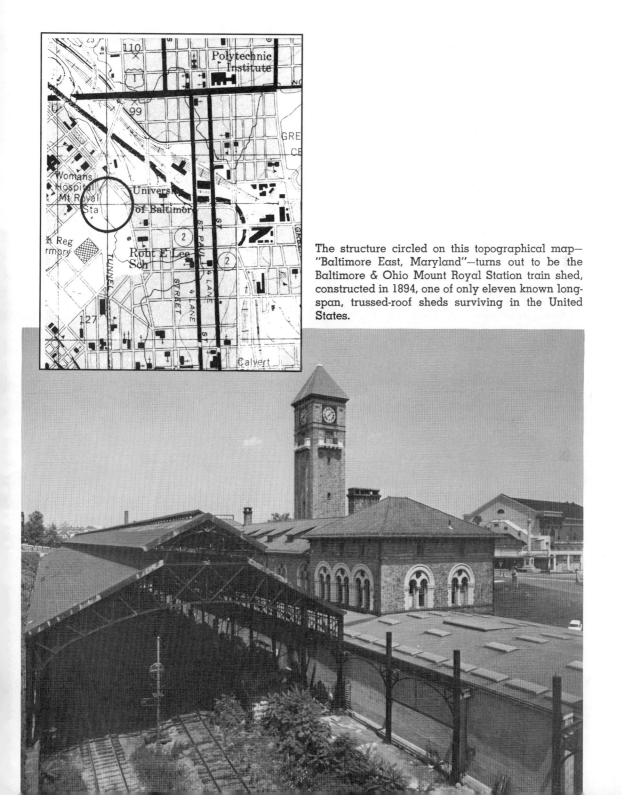

The structure circled on this topographical map—"Baltimore East, Maryland"—turns out to be the Baltimore & Ohio Mount Royal Station train shed, constructed in 1894, one of only eleven known long-span, trussed-roof sheds surviving in the United States.

apets. The original use for old buildings is noted as a "wagon shed," "carpenter shop," "blacksmith," and "japanning works." A note on the japanning works will even allow us a look around inside at the "wood posts" and "3 drying ovens." The code tells us if the building is made of adobe, stone, brick, tile, or various kinds of concrete construction. Lofts are noted, as well as skylights and stacks, and, where they've been changed, the old and new house numbers. Streets, alleys, railroad yards and sidings, water mains, fire hydrants, stables, boilers, and furnaces—all are there. Sanborn maps are updated constantly by pasting revisions over the section of the original map that has changed. Only the most up-to-date maps are available from the company. To get more information about specific maps, you can write to the Sanborn Map Company, 629 Fifth Ave., Pelham, N.Y. 10803. They are accustomed to receiving queries from amateur historians.

Historical Sanborn maps can be found in public libraries, the offices of city engineers and urban planners, and the Library of Congress, which maintains a complete file of over eleven thousand volumes of maps.

Aerial photographs are not, of course, maps, but they contain a great deal more information than maps and thus have become an indispensable tool for the archaeologist. On an aerial photograph, for example, you may be able to see abandoned locomotives and other rolling stock which will not show up on a topo map. Old cemeteries are clearly visible on photographs—assuming they are not shaded by trees—telling us more than the conventional symbols on maps. Until a few years ago, aerial photographs could be produced only as large, expensive photographic prints. Today there are ways of reproducing aerial photographs that bring the cost close to that of maps. Over the past twenty or thirty years, many American cities have been photographed from the air—some, several times. City engineers and urban planners called for aerial surveys in the 1950s to obtain information for planning freeways and urban-renewal projects. These were low-level surveys that produced pictures filled with the most minute details. In the city engineer's office in your community, you might find a reference set up on the wall. On one corner of each sheet is probably a number, which corresponds to a negative number in the file—a large city being covered by thirty or forty individual photographs. Reproductions from these individual sheets can be made on an Ozalid machine or similar copier at a cost per square foot that is quite reasonable. The engineer's office probably contracts its copy work to a local blueprint and copy service, and will arrange to have the prints made for you. The procedure will no doubt vary from city to city, but in most cases when aerial surveys have been done, reproductions are available to the public. Few people are aware of this, but some exciting historical discoveries are to be made by those who are.

3. BRIDGES OF TIMBER AND IRON

The history of bridges in America has two beginnings. The first goes back to the late 1700s and early 1800s, when the carpenter-engineers Timothy Palmer, Theodore Burr, Lewis Wernwag, and Ithiel Town conceived and built the original American truss forms. The second occurred about mid-nineteenth century, when, within just a few years, one Squire Whipple changed bridge building from an exacting but uncertain craft to a science.

The earliest bridges were made of wood. Details of construction were predicated on lifetimes of empirical information passed from builder to apprentice, a few pragmatic rules of thumb, and considerable intuition. Careful observation throughout the bridge's construction allowed changes to be made along the way.

Squire Whipple changed all this. In *A Work on Bridge-Building,* which he published himself in 1847, Whipple showed how to analyze the stresses in a bridge truss (the framework of wooden beams or metal bars that supports the bridge), using simple but accurate calculations. Working out the magnitude and direction of the forces acting on each member in the truss, and then referring to Whipple's tables on the tensile and compressive strengths of wood and iron, Whipple's reader could calculate the size of individual members and the truss depth needed to safely sustain a bridge's load. Aware that

his readers were practical men, most of whom had learned arithmetic well enough to do their own work but nothing more, Whipple avoided the use of algebraic equations and trigonometric functions and explained each step in as simple terms as possible. So important was this first book that its publication date is used by historians to mark the beginning of the era of scientific bridge design in America.

But Squire Whipple was first of all a *builder* of bridges. His iron bowstring truss, patented in 1841, and the trapezoidal truss of 1847 launched a new American industry, the manufacture and erection of iron bridges. He was by no means the first American to build bridges of iron. But with the founding of S. & J. M. Whipple, one of the first bridge companies specializing in metal structures, and by the selling of his patent designs to numerous licensees, he became the first to do so on such a large scale. Between 1850 and 1860 over a hundred Whipple patent arch and trapezoidal truss bridges were built to span canals and rivers, mostly in New York State. Then, when his patent finally expired in 1869, hundreds more were fabricated, copied right down to the last detail, by a number of bridge companies and contractors as late as the 1880s. Whipple's graceful little bridges of cast and wrought iron had proven themselves over the years to be marvelously practical. But where have they all gone? As David

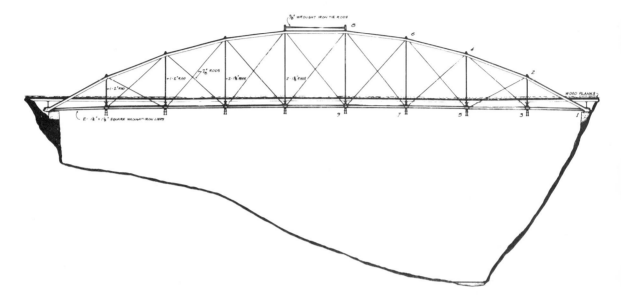

Whipple cast- and wrought-iron bowstring truss bridge at Normans Kill near Albany, New York. The general design of the bridge was patented in 1841 by Squire Whipple, a civil engineer of Albany. It was the first all-iron bridge trussing system to find wide use, hundreds of examples having been erected by Whipple and licensees over the Erie Canal and other waterways, mostly in New York State, all for highway use. Only two are known to remain. This span was fabricated by S. DeGraff of Syracuse for an unknown location and moved to the present site around 1900. Its private ownership, good maintenance, and remote location are responsible for the survival of one of the earliest iron bridges in the United States.

The Whipple bridge at Normans Kill.

Steinman, bridge engineer and historian, lamented in 1957: ". . . many Whipple truss bridges, for spans of less than two hundred feet, were built throughout the United States and lasted for decades, having disappeared from the American scene only recently."

Disappeared? So numerous and large an artifact as a heavy iron bridge 200 feet long? A fortunate axiom of history suggests not. Rather than having disappeared, much of our early history remains in evidence on the land, even on busy city streets, unnoticed or, more likely, unrecognized. Reduced to a rule, it might be expressed something like this: The more repetitive our encounters with an object throughout our day-to-day life, the less aware we are of it; it simply disappears. Squire Whipple's bridges didn't really disappear; they just fell subject to our rule.

Proof of this rule would be the reappearance of Whipple trusses under fairly ordinary circumstances, and this is just what happened. When the Historic American Engineering Record (HAER) survey of the Mohawk-Hudson area was completed in 1969, only two Whipple bowstring-arch trusses were known to have survived. Then, in 1974 a 75-foot cast- and wrought-iron Whipple bowstring was discovered spanning the Sugar River in Talcottville (Lewis County), New York. All but the wooden decking had survived. That's three. Again, in 1975, a bridge built on the patent design of Squire Whipple appeared in Ohio. This one, a 101-foot span across Wills Creek on Linton Township Road 144, was built in 1872 at the Coshocton Iron Works. That's four. Within the year *four* more bridges were found in New York State, including a 65-foot span near Johnstown, Fulton County, bearing cast-in legends acknowl-

edging the Whipple patents and giving the name of the builder, Shipman & Son of Springfield Centre, New York.

Whipple, or, more accurately, Whipple-type spans, are reappearing in Canada, too. The Blackfriar's Bridge over the north branch of the Thames River in London, Ontario, with its low parabolic top chord and characteristic bowstring lines, looks for all the world like a Whipple bowstring-arch truss. This one was of U.S. manufacture. One problem that not even Squire Whipple could solve was that the bridge companies were always "improving" on his design just enough to avoid both payment of royalties and patent-infringement litigation. For this reason then, even though the beginner bridge finder will easily recognize the familiar configuration and construction details of a Whipple bowstring-arch truss, he will search in vain for any acknowledgment of the bridge's paternity on a builder's plate or cast into one of the members, as was the usual practice. Seven more were built in London, Ontario, replacing all of the city's wooden bridges. How many have survived is yet to be known, but it is interesting to note that when the Blackfriar's Bridge was first opened, it was outside the city, on the route to the northwestern suburbs in Middlesex County; when it was discovered, it was over a century old and stood in the very heart of London!

Squire Whipple's bridges are interesting to us here because of the lessons of history they offer. That such historical structures as these could be "lost" in the first place is a lesson to those who would scoff at the idea of American historical archaeology. But although only a few spans have been found, there is already enough information gathered from them to allow us to anticipate the circumstances under which other old bridges might be rediscovered.

Certain patterns appear fairly consistently. The bridges, of course, are not really lost but merely unrecognized. When we do recognize them finally, it's usually with the astonishment that we've taken so long to "see" what has been there all along (How many bridges do you cross each day?). It may also be that we attach little importance to something like a bridge, so utilitarian, particularly if it is not in a prominent place. Whipple trusses, like other old trusses, have often literally been moved to the country or just out of town, where they now carry the light loads of country roads (as at Coshocton, Ohio) or private roads (as at Normans Kill, near Albany, New York), over small creeks and ravines. At least one was found abandoned. But most are still in service even after a century or more, though their use may have changed from railroad bridge to highway or footbridge. Comforting to the archaeologist is the fact that not only were all the bridges found to date intact, but, except for their movement from their original location and the replacement of the wood decking (originally oak planking on pine joists), the structures have not been altered in any fundamental way. The original elements—top and bottom chords, verticals and diagonals and connecting blocks—make positive identification easy.

Many historical bridges will show clear signs of having been moved at least once or twice. One of the most obvious signs is that the span is longer, sometimes considerably longer, than the present location would seem to require. Another clue, subjective as it is,

comes from the observer's feeling that somehow the bridge doesn't fit, perhaps because the bridge is too heavy for the loads it is now carrying, or that it is in some way anachronistic in its present setting. Don't ignore intuition; it's a valuable historical tool.

Abutments, too, show signs of the bridge's having been moved. The original abutments of bridges built in the early 1900s were masonry and would be concrete only if of more recent construction. Concrete abutments under a Whipple bowstring-arch truss, say, should alert the archaeologist to the possibility of relocation and start the search for further confirming signs. The original specifi-

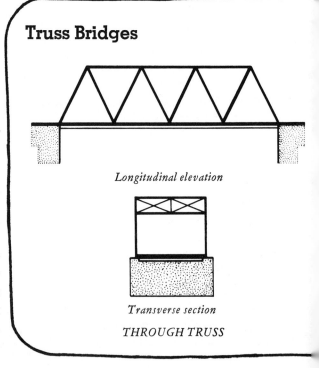

Truss Bridges

Longitudinal elevation

Transverse section

THROUGH TRUSS

The Parts of a Truss

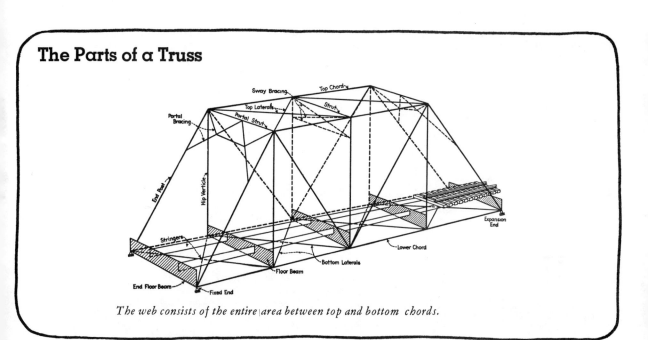

The web consists of the entire area between top and bottom chords.

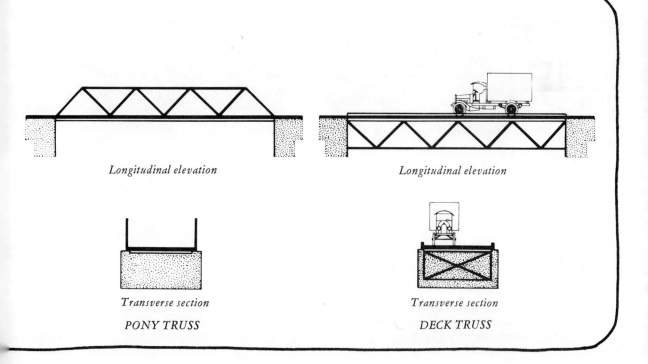

Longitudinal elevation

Longitudinal elevation

Transverse section

Transverse section

PONY TRUSS

DECK TRUSS

Bollman suspension and trussed bridge carrying an abandoned Baltimore & Ohio Railroad line across the Little Patuxent River just south of Savage, Maryland; it was built in 1869.

Iron binder used on the abutments of the Laughery Creek bridge near Aurora, Indiana; the bridge was built in 1878.

cations for the Whipple trusses did not call for metal bearing plates (between the top surface of the abutment and the ends of the lower chord), only that the extremities of the arches were to be "formed into feet resting on the abutments." Presumably, any metal bearing plates and certainly expansion devices like rollers would suggest a newer installation.

But why were they moved? The several reincarnations of the bowstring-arch truss help us to understand why bridges were relocated and thus "disappeared," and to see that it is entirely logical that they should someday reappear.

One of the Whipple cast- and wrought-iron bowstring trusses recorded by the His-toric American Engineering Record survey in 1969 was then over a hundred years old. It was found spanning a deeply wooded ravine north of Normansville, about two miles west of downtown Albany, New York. Through the ravine flows a small tributary of Normans Kill, which long ago supplied waterpower for woolen mills, sawmills, and a paper factory along its banks. This particular bridge is of interest, because it is a composite bridge—with components made of cast and wrought iron— representing an intermediate stage between bridges of timber and cast iron and bridges made almost entirely of wrought iron. The 109′ × 10′ span was fabricated by Simon DeGraff, a contractor who eventually specialized in bridge work. As was often done by small contractors, DeGraff assembled the castings, which he ordered from a Syracuse foundry. DeGraff did not, of course, build the bridge for its present owner, Mark W. Stevens, nor did he build it for Normanskill Farm's previous owner, Amanda Lightbody; he built the bridge, most likely, on order from the state of New York.

By the time the bridge reached its present location at Normanskill Farm, it had already been moved once, perhaps twice, and therein lies the story of the peripatetic Whipple truss and a lot of other bridges as well. As a young engineer, Squire Whipple worked first for the railroads and later the New York State canal system. As plans were being readied to widen the Erie Canal from 40 to 70 feet at the surface and to increase its depth from 4 to 7 feet, he must have realized how many new bridges would be needed to span the enlarged waterway. He had managed to save about a thousand dollars, and decided to invest it on a prototype of his yet unpatented and untried bowstring-arch truss, to be built over the canal, at Utica, New York. It was the first of hundreds that would be built throughout New York and the Northeast over the next thirty years or so. "Whipple's Patent Iron Arch Truss Bridge" was adopted by the State Engineer and Surveyor of the Canals as the standard bridge for the state's waterways.

Contemporary engravings depicting the canal show Whipple bowstring trusses on masonry abutments at Frankfort, New York, and Clinton Square in Syracuse, all with sidewalks and the specified "iron railing three feet high on the outside of each sidewalk." Just how many Whipple trusses were built across New York State canals is not certain, but in an old engraving of Clinton Square there is one very prominent in the foreground. As your eyes follow down the canal, receding into the distance between the tall buildings of Syracuse, you can count one, two, three, four more, one at each block.

It is more than likely that the little bridge over which Mark Stevens has traveled these many years is one of these Syracuse bridges. The state of New York was, initially, the sole builder or buyer of Whipples and built literally hundreds of them. The Normans Kill bridge was the same kind of bridge used on the state canals and was the right length for the canals. And, of course, proximity is a factor. Subsequent events confirm our hypothesis. The old Erie Canal underwent still another change in 1905, when it was renamed the New York State Barge Canal and again widened and deepened. By the time the work of enlarging the canal had been completed, in 1918, hundreds of Whipple trusses had been dismantled and sold off to

be used on small public and private roads. This would explain both the bridges' dispersal from along the canal and their current backcountry habitat. The job was done by numerous New York–based bridge companies who advertised in the business directories that they dismantled, moved, and re-erected small iron bridges.

We'll probably never know for sure just where Mark Stevens's bridge came from, but we do know the bridge began its life somewhere in Syracuse, either in Simon DeGraff's ironworks at 35 East Onondaga St. or his later location at 107 West Onondaga. After that, it becomes quite unclear where the span traveled. People around Normansville say the bridge was brought over the old Delaware Turnpike "from Schoharie," an area about twenty-five miles west of the site where it now stands—a clue that the bridge was erected and then dismantled at least twice before arriving at Normanskill Farm.

More Whipple spans will be recovered soon, as will all kinds of other historical bridges scattered about the countryside. Most, I suspect, will be found by amateur historians whose principal resources are simply curiosity, the patience to look a bit closer at the commonplace, and an operating knowledge of the history of American bridge design.

So far we've looked at bridges as artifacts in the landscape, without much inquiry into their workings. Trusses are fascinating objects in themselves, appearing in a variety of basic forms giving the beginning bridge finder considerable satisfaction in just "collecting" trusses as intriguing historical objects. It doesn't take long, however, before this awareness of bridges leads to the question of how they work. To answer that question does more than just satisfy an impulse of curiosity, for even the most basic understanding of how trusses work advances one from casual observer and "bridge spotter" to working historian—who can not only classify newly encountered truss forms, but also place them in their historical context and see how they fit into the evolution of modern designs.

When Ithiel Town patented his lattice truss in 1820, he had none of the equations that would enable bridge builders just thirty years hence to analyze accurately all the forces acting on a bridge. He could not calculate the stresses, wind forces, axle loads, vibrations and tractive forces, the compressive and tensile strengths of his materials, or the elastic limits of structural members. His only guide was an empirically derived "factor of faith," or safety factor, as we would say today; and through experience he had developed a sense of proportion. Town lattice trusses can still be found at work, after more than a century, beneath the roofs and sidings of many New England covered bridges. Used extensively throughout the northeastern United States for railroad bridges, the lattice truss was based on the most fundamental element of bridge design: the triangle. But let's read Ithiel Town's own explanation, expressed in the nonmathematical language of the early architect/builder:

... all plain figures of more than three sides are susceptible of having their angles and areas varied, as also the relative position of their sides so ... diamond work would be insufficient to resist power properly applied to it ... without other

timbers or other substances running horizontally, vertically or otherwise so as to serve as diagonals to a suitable number of diamonds and thereby dividing them into triangles, figures which are not susceptible of the change before stated ...

Town's explanation of the reaction of four-sided and three-sided figures to externally applied forces helps us to understand just how a truss works, to see the function of the various vertical, horizontal, and diagonal members, and to decide whether they are in tension or compression. Here's a simple way to visualize how the forces are distributed through a truss panel:

Cut eight 1-inch-wide strips from a piece of cardboard, seven of them about 6 inches long and the eighth piece about 9 inches long. Arrange the seven pieces of equal length into a rectangle and a triangle (as below) and put them together with a tack, push-pin, or paper

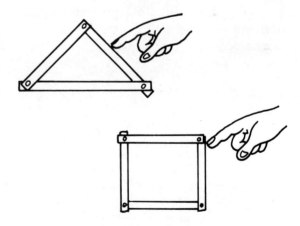

fastener. Stand your triangular and rectangular "truss panels" on edge and push against the sides and corners of each one and see what happens.

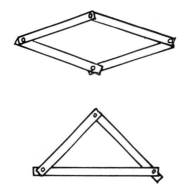

The square becomes a parallelogram and eventually collapses under the horizontal and diagonal forces. The triangle, on the other hand, remains rigid no matter how forces are applied to it horizontally, vertically, or diagonally. Now you understand Ithiel Town's preference for triangles, and perhaps you see already what you can do with that last cardboard strip to strengthen the rectangle so that it becomes a rigid panel, too.

That diagonal brace made two triangles of the square, just the way diagonal members brace a rectangular truss panel.

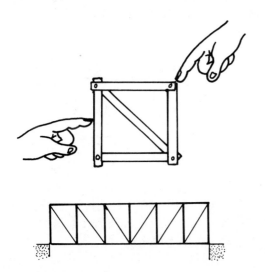

Simple? Well, maybe so, but it's so fundamental that every bridge and roof truss, transmitting towers, the supporting framework for the Statue of Liberty, the Eiffel Tower, and Buckminster Fuller's geodesic domes have triangular structural elements in them somewhere.

It all began with an ingenious but anonymous carpenter of the Middle Ages who discovered that the very same triangles of timbers with their vertical "king post" supporting the roof of a building could be used, again side by side, to make the first "through truss" for spans up to about 60 feet.

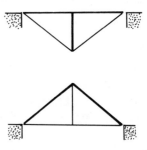

Any weight (even its own) out toward the center of the horizontal beam causes it to deflect and pull down on the king post, placing it under tension. The post, in turn, pulls down on the two diagonals, placing them under compression and transmitting the force out toward the abutments. Inverting the truss works as well, only now the vertical king post is in compression and the two diagonals are under tension. When spaces too wide for a bridge with a single post were encountered, a second post was added. The dotted lines in the drawings do not represent members, but help you to see that this "queen post" truss is actually two king post

60

trusses end to end. The queen post was useful for spans up to about 80 feet.

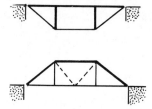

The simple little king- and queen-post spans embrace all of the basic elements of truss design. Every truss we will encounter will be composed of triangles, the only geometric shape that resists changes in its form. Ithiel Town realized, for example, that if two king-post trusses in the form of a queen post become stronger and can span greater distances, then ten, twenty, thirty, or forty together can span proportionally longer distances. The Town truss, then, became an *overlapping* series of king posts (vertical posts are no longer needed) made of planks—which could span up to 200 feet. But you have to look carefully to see all the triangles superimposed one upon the other, instead of a lattice. The design worked so well that, later on, Town lattice trusses were made of iron straps and used for the heaviest railroad loads.

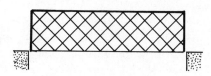

The same problem was approached a bit differently by James Warren and Theobald Monzani, who lined up single triangular panels in a row between parallel top and bottom chords, increasing the span of their trusses to about 400 feet.

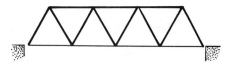

Albert Fink's suspended truss, patented in 1854, seems quite a departure until you realize that it's formed of seven king-post elements: one long king post, under which are two smaller king posts whose diagonals reach from each abutment out to mid-span, and which segments have each been further divided into two still-smaller king posts.

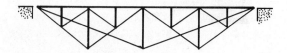

Variations on this basic theme would enable the bridge to carry heavier loads or span greater distances, such as this Fink suspended truss consisting of fifteen inverted king-post elements.

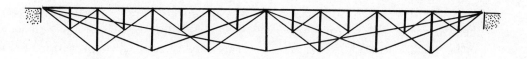

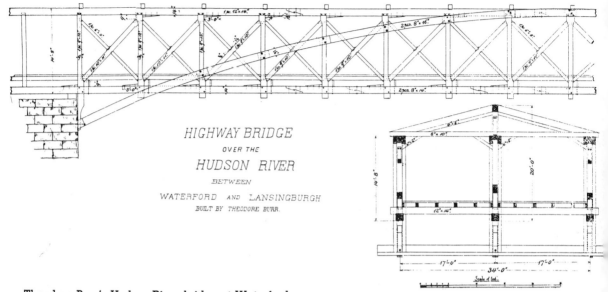

HIGHWAY BRIDGE
OVER THE
HUDSON RIVER
BETWEEN
WATERFORD AND LANSINGBURGH
BUILT BY THEODORE BURR.

Theodore Burr's Hudson River bridge at Waterford, New York, was an early experiment in combining truss forms—in this instance, an arch and a Howe truss, 1804.

Remember that all these designs were arrived at much as we've described them here—by simple experiment and combination of basic elements. Some early bridge builders built models of trusses to scale and added proportional loads until the little members gave way. Those that broke were replaced with ones of larger dimension and then loaded as before, the steps being repeated until the model would support scaled loads equivalent to the expected live loads plus some safety factor.

This empirical approach to design led to other means of increasing a bridge's loading and span. One alternative consisted of elaborating on the king post, arranging new combinations to come up with a new form, and then increasing the size and number of members to meet specific span and loading require-

ments. Another alternative of special interest to the bridge finder was the practice of combining truss forms, leading to designs with names like "arch truss" and "suspension truss." The idea behind this, largely discredited by bridge engineers later, was that one form would support the deadweight of the bridge and the other would come into play when live loads were applied. One of Theodore Burr's first bridges, built over the Hudson River at Waterford, New York, and completed in 1804, is an example of an attempt to increase loading capability and span by combining forms, in this instance an arch with a Howe truss. Built entirely of timbers, Burr's arch truss remained in continuous service over a century, until destroyed by fire in 1909. The Burr design is, in engineering terms, redundant, a combination of two sound structural forms, either of which would have worked alone. Redundant or not, throughout the last eight years of its life, the four wooden arches—with some strengthening—carried 25-ton interurban railroad cars!

The combining of truss forms was a common practice throughout the 1800s, giving rise to what at first seem to be new designs, but which are actually two bridges in one. Wendell Bollman's patented "suspension truss bridge" is actually a (Thomas Willis)

Pratt truss with counters and vertical end posts upon which has been superimposed a system

of wrought-iron rods radiating diagonally from the vertical end posts to the foot of each king post. These support the floor beams and deck, much as the hangers of a suspension bridge would:

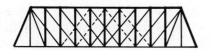

The Whipple, Whipple-Murphy, and Linville double-intersection trusses are actually two single-intersection Pratt trusses

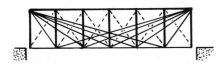

with inclined end posts transposed so that the vertical posts of one truss fall at the midpoint of the panels of the other truss. The following illustration makes this clear:

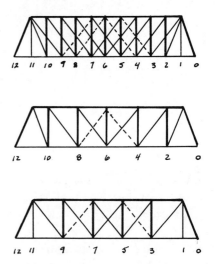

In this way bridge builders of the last century experimented freely with various combinations of structures, the most common being the arch beam in combination with Howe, Long, Pratt, and Town trusses.

Occasionally, the alert observer will find bridges constructed of two different but separate trusses, one type in the middle between the two traffic lanes, another type used for the two outside trusses. One such bridge originally spanned Jones Falls in Baltimore, carrying Lombard Street vehicular and pedestrian traffic. Designed by Bollman, the bridge's two outer trusses are conventional Pratt-type of cast and wrought iron. But the center-line trussing is a bowstring with the bottom chord and arched top chords formed by 30-inch water mains, bifurcated at the

Bollman's "waterpipe truss" in its original position over Jones Falls in Baltimore, Maryland; it was constructed in 1877.

ends and carrying the municipal water supply! Throughout the history of bridges it has been common for spans to carry water and gas mains, and circular (as well as rectangular) tubes have been used as structural members; but a combination of the two is unusual.

Until you get to know them, most bridges are not very pretty. One would have to possess an exceptional receptiveness to be able to love some old bridges, historic and interesting maybe, but undeniably ugly. For many, the bridge, like dingy brick factories and mine structures, is a symbol of the harsh and seamy underside of America's Victorian elegance. I think it's the girders and rivets. Old bridges have a way of evoking the days when the rush toward industrialism and wealth left scars upon the cities that are still not healed.

Bridges were not intended to be pretty. Early trusses of rough timbers and iron, particularly old-time railroad bridges, were primarily utilitarian structures. For the railroads, time and cost to erect a bridge were the paramount considerations. In the United States and Canada, railroads rushed across the continent to open lines to areas so distant and sparsely populated as to offer little expectation of return on their investment for years to come. Further construction was dependent on quickly erected structures that would allow work trains and supplies up to the railroad. The usual policy was to complete the railhead and commence service as soon as possible, at the lowest possible cost. Timber trestles and trusses went up first. Then, as traffic and loads increased, wooden structures were replaced with iron. The railroads chose as replacements the least expensive metal bridges and those easiest to erect—even a large span might be put up in one workday—those with parallel chords, like Pratt's and Whipple's trapezoidal trusses, Bollman's, and Fink's.

Bridges abound in the landscape suggesting factors tending toward their survival. For the industrial archaeologists these factors are of more than just historical interest, for understanding something of the changes that have taken place helps not only in the finding of old bridges but in tracing their background. The history of the railroad locomotive, for instance, tells us a lot about bridges. It would lead us to conclude that railroad truss bridges had a rather short life. As a matter of fact they were changed frequently and their life was short—as railroad bridges. But many of them show up again. We'll expect to find them moved to sidings and lines carrying lighter loads. What may not have occurred to us is that many were also given a new task, carrying roads. Track walking will still lead us to many old railroad bridges, but driving the secondary and dusty backcountry

roads nearby may lead to finding even more. Let's look for a moment, then, at some of the changes that have affected back road and highway bridges.

The loadings and traffic over road bridges—in distinct contrast to railroad bridges—did not increase significantly during this time. Travel was light and seasonal. The heaviest traffic was in the late summer and fall, when farm products were carted over local roads to nearby towns to be sold there or to be taken to the freight depot for markets farther away. Heavy, long-distance freight hauling was by railroad.

Bridge 129, a Bollman deck truss on the old Valley Railroad of Virginia, no longer carries Baltimore & Ohio traffic but might still be in use on some country backroad.

The automobile changed all that—in a way. The pace of highway travel would quicken, but still the weight of the vehicles had not changed all that much. Dusty, rutted roads were graded and covered with oiled crushed rock. The busiest among them would eventually be widened and, perhaps, resurfaced with macadam. In this whole progression from cart road to "highway," little happened to affect bridges along the way.

By the 1920s a nationwide system of roads was in the offing. The Federal Highway Act of 1921 imposed national standards on highway design and construction. It was during this period that many roads were widened and the first two-lane highway bridges appeared. There remains today on many secondary roads an artifact from this period: the "Narrow Bridge" and "One Lane Bridge" signs. Few drivers have not had the experience of coming to an unexpected full stop at the approach to a little one-lane bridge and waiting for traffic to come through from the other direction. Even fewer, I'm sure, have stopped to think about the history in those signs. The bridge was probably there long before the second road lane was added. Or perhaps sometime in the 1920s or 1930s the little span was removed from what was to become a primary road and placed here. In either case, the bridge and thousands like it survived progress, hidden away in the backcountry. Even the freeway construction spree of the 1950s seemed to have little effect on the old bridges. An entirely new network of highways was superimposed upon the intricate web of the old road map, leaving old roads essentially intact. A new concern, the desirability of moving traffic around, instead of through, towns and cities meant new roads. For the first time, on such a large scale, roads were supplanted instead of widened and resurfaced to sustain increased traffic.

The pattern of development varied, but in each instance seemed to preserve the old bridges. Sometimes the old two-lane road and its structures were obliterated by the new divided freeway, but usually not for its entire length. Traveling on freeways, we often see old macadam roads overgrown with weeds come to an abrupt and ragged end a few yards from the freeway. Some end there, but others continue after the brief interruption, to disappear over a rise on the other side of the freeway. Follow one of these roads if you've never done so. They take us to another day of farmhouses and fields; hand-lettered signs inviting the traveler to buy tomatoes from the garden, honey, or homemade sausage; gambrel-roof barns; Aeromotor Chicago windmills, and, perhaps, an old Pratt pony truss with timber deck planks that rattle as you drive across. Sometimes the older road was widened and incorporated into the new highway, it being necessary then to build only one road on the other side of a median strip. If this has happened, you may find that the original bridges on the "recycled" lanes are still in place. Elsewhere, the new highway takes off in an entirely new direction in search of an easier mountain pass or less populated right-of-way, leaving the old road where it has been all along. For the historian, great numbers of old green, silver, gray, and Rust-Oleum–orange trusses—Pratt, Warren, Parker, Howe, camelback—through pony and deck trusses dating from the late nineteenth and early twentieth centuries are still out there. Discovering and sketching or photographing them is one

Pratt through truss over Honey Creek near Burlington, Wisconsin. Built in 1877, this is the earliest metal truss bridge recorded to date in Wisconsin and is still in use for vehicular and pedestrian traffic.

joy of exploring the myriad roads of yesterday.

The transfer of roads from county to state and federal jurisdiction had other effects of interest to the bridge historian, too. It marked the end of an era in the history of American bridges. Prior to this time, in most states the construction and maintenance of roads were the responsibility of individual communities and counties. So it was, also, with the construction and maintenance of bridges needed within the county. Since each county had contracted individually for bridge work, and there were many bridge companies to choose from, the result was often a grand array of bridge styles and types from state to state. At least 170 bridge-manufacturing firms are known to have been operating from 1875 to 1935, mostly in the Midwestern and Eastern states and in New England, but also in Kentucky, Virginia, Maryland, Georgia, and Ontario, Canada. The bridge companies themselves were local firms; few were large enough to reach out beyond their own and surrounding states.

The discovery of local and regional styles of bridge design is one of the joys of acquiring an awareness of truss types and detail, especially those close to home. Individual variations in style and ornamentation are more noticeable in bridges built in the 1800s, but surprising touches occasionally appear on bridges manufactured as late as the 1930s. Bridges have been moved (though often to places within a short radius of the original site). It's difficult to generalize about

This little bridge over the Rock River in Washington County, Wisconsin, appears to be just another Pratt pony truss. In fact, it is a truss-leg bedstead—the sole example of this kind of construction to be uncovered in a recent survey of metal truss bridges by the State Historical Society of Wisconsin.

the style of bridges in a particular area, since the historical inventories have really just begun. Still, there are compelling historical reasons, aside from the local nature of bridge firms, for expecting differences in bridges—preferred designs, ornamentation, construction details, and setting—in different areas of the country.

Geography is a persistent factor contributing to differences in bridge design. As the railroads encountered new kinds of terrain, new geological imperatives had to be met with either wholly new bridge designs or, as was most often the solution, adaptations of "standard" designs. The truss leg, or "bedstead," bridge originated this way. It appeared in the 1880s, when the railroads, hav-

ing reached the open prairie and plains, found that there was little of the hard rock needed for the customary masonry abutments. The problem was met by extending the vertical end posts of a Pratt down below grade, where they were attached to a "dead man," a heavy timber buried in the ground, the weight of which, combined with weight of the soil and roadbed above, were sufficient

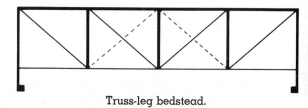

Truss-leg bedstead.

to keep the bridge from moving. Similarly, bridge builders, who were used to spanning the gently sloping wide river valleys of the Midwestern prairies, found themselves out West peering down into seemingly bottomless steep-sided ravines. This required spectacular feats of bridge building and resulted in the now-familiar timber trestles hundreds of feet high.

Geography also combined with the fragmented, discontinuous transportation lines of the 1800s to create regional economic interests as well. If you recall the great adventures of the iron parts shipment in the first chapter, you'll understand why bridges had to be built by nearby companies. For most of the nineteenth century no means existed to haul heavy, unwieldy freight like bridge timbers and tons of cast- or wrought-iron bridge

parts. A survey and photographic inventory of metal truss bridges in Virginia built between 1865 and 1932 shows that even in the 1920s, bridge trusses and parts were still expensive to ship long distances. Hundreds of bridges have been recorded in this fascinating survey by the Virginia Highway and Transportation Research Council, and hundreds more are yet to be recorded. But it is already clear that more than half of all the bridges in the state were built by manufacturers, contractors, and engineering firms in Virginia, mainly in Roanoke and Richmond. Of those spans not fabricated in Virginia, almost all were from cities—Bethlehem and Pittsburgh, Pennsylvania; Wheeling and Charleston, West Virginia; Wilmington, Delaware; and Cincinnati, Ohio—all within a two-hundred-mile radius. In one region, Fredericksburg,

Humpback covered bridge in the vicinity of Covington, Alleghany County, Virginia; it was built in 1835. Under the roof of this oldest surviving covered bridge in Virginia is to be found an adaptation of Burr trusses with curved upper and lower chords.

the builders of thirteen of the fourteen bridges found could be identified, and all were made by either the Roanoke Iron and Bridge Works or the Virginia Bridge and Iron Company, also of Roanoke. Incidentally, twelve of the fourteen were half-hip and full-slope Pratt pony and through trusses. The other two were Warren trusses.

Which last is to be expected, too. Not only did each bridge company have its own territory, but each company usually specialized in one type of truss. Usually this came about in one of several ways. First of all, there was the company, formed by the bridge designer himself. Squire Whipple was among the first to start his own company to manufacture and sell his own designs. Another very common arrangement occurred when the patentee of a bridge design licensed manufacturers to specialize in his truss in return for royalties. A new generation of companies appeared when patentees of improvements on existing truss forms then manufactured and marketed *their* patent designs. Each bridge company, then, had its own specialty, either by virtue of a patent, a license from a patentee, or, after patents expired, familiarity with a design or local preference. Companies advertised in the directories their own particular form of truss, such as Bollman, Fink, Linville, Post, Whipple, or their particular patented variation in posts, diagonals, or other details, such as Phoenix, Austin, or Herthel. Here's a list of just a few bridge companies of the 1880s, their location, and the truss in which they specialized:

The result of all this was considerable variation in style, cast-iron ornaments, fluted or octagonal posts, masonry abutment patterns, filigree builder's legends, finials gracing each

Austin Bridge Co., Chicago, Ill.	Austin
Berlin Iron Bridge Co., Berlin, Conn.	Lenticular
Cincinnati Bridge Co., Cincinnati, Ohio	Whipple
Hawkins, Herthel & Burral, Springfield, Mass.	Herthel
Kellogg Bridge Co., Buffalo, N.Y.	Kellogg
Louisville Bridge & Iron Co., Louisville, Ky.	Fink
Canton Bridge Co., Canton, Ohio	Post
Chas. Kellogg & Co., Detroit, Mich.	Bollman
S. & J. M. Whipple, Utica, N.Y.	Whipple

end post, ornamental-ironwork handrails, and sculpture. Colors were limited; there were a few considered traditional for bridges or called for in county and state specifications. But like everything else on a bridge, paint color, too, was expected to be functional. One of the bridge-building manuals of the day recommended that "the final coat or coats had better be of such a tint as will show the first indication of rust. All tints bordering on cream buff, and different greys, answer this purpose excellently well." Nevertheless, bridges were truly distinct. Theodore Cooper, who at the turn of the century was the most eminent of America's railroad bridge builders, once recalled that during this period, up until about 1890, "of a thousand bridges of which no two would be alike, a practical bridge engineer could almost invariably determine the designer and manufacturer, either by the general

Baltimore & Ohio bridge at Benwood, West Virginia, dated about 1890. The builder's legend atop the portal strut reads: "Keystone Bridge Co., Pittsburgh, Pa."

Double-intersection wrought-iron highway bridge, c. 1880. Recommended by Waddell, this bridge became a standard for many years.

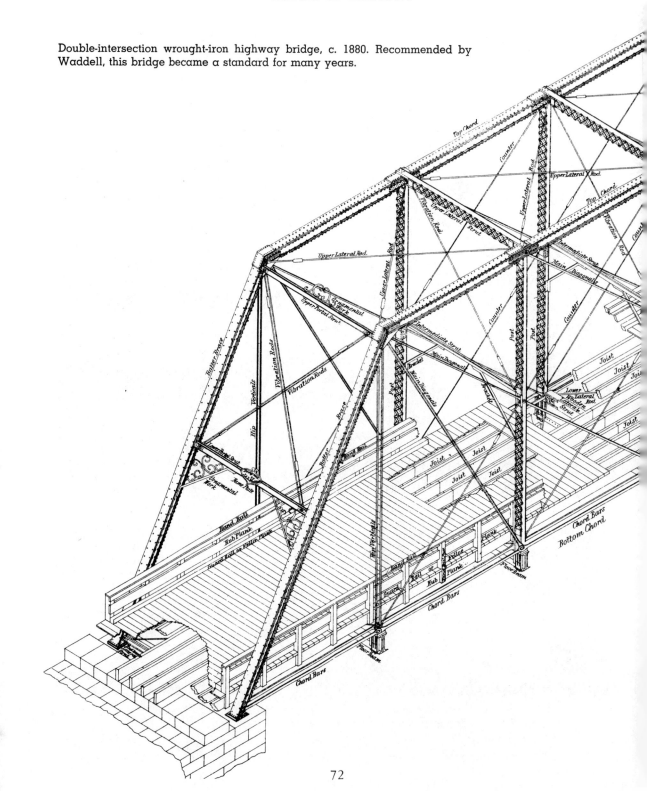

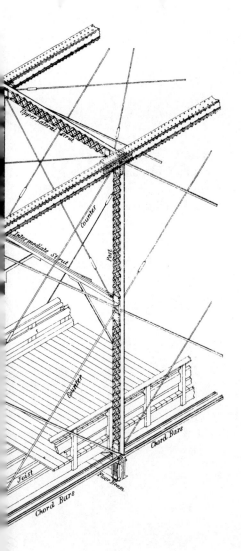

style of the bridge or by the use of some peculiar forms of member or detail."

The end of all this, just as with the railroads, was standardization. The culprit would seem to be state and federal agencies, who adopted and then imposed as standard designs the most dependable and economic trusses. But state and federal engineers were not themselves formulating the standards; rather, their decisions reflected engineering practices of the times. By the early years of this century, it was clear that both standards and construction practices arose from the writings of two engineers, Theodore Cooper and his counterpart in the world of iron highway bridges, J. A. L. Waddell. (Waddell is credited with designing and building the first vertical-lift bridge in the United States, a 130-foot span carrying South Halsted Street, Chicago.)

Waddell observed in 1884 that at least ninety percent of all American iron highway bridges then being built were either of Pratt or Whipple (trapezoidal) design, a trend which had apparently continued throughout the decades after the Civil War. Long years of experience had proven, Waddell felt, that the most practical and economic structures employed vertical web compression members (posts), the Pratt and Whipple being the most proven. (Note that in the Howe and Warren designs diagonals are in compression.)

Bridge finders involved in informal and official inventories will confirm Waddell's statement. The Virginia inventory has recorded several single-intersection (with verticals) and double-intersection Warren trusses and a few Whipple trapezoidal spans, but the individual counties and the state of Virginia clearly preferred Pratt's. In one of the construction districts, Culpeper, fifty-two of the seventy-five inventoried and recorded bridges (about seventy percent) were Pratt trusses—half-hip and full-slope pony trusses, and through trusses—and Pratt-type trusses,

including camelback and Pennsylvania designs. The beginning bridge finder will soon discover, no doubt with some disappointment, this unmistakable pattern of predominance of one truss configuration over all others: the Pratt and Pratt-derived forms. This is not a recent trend.

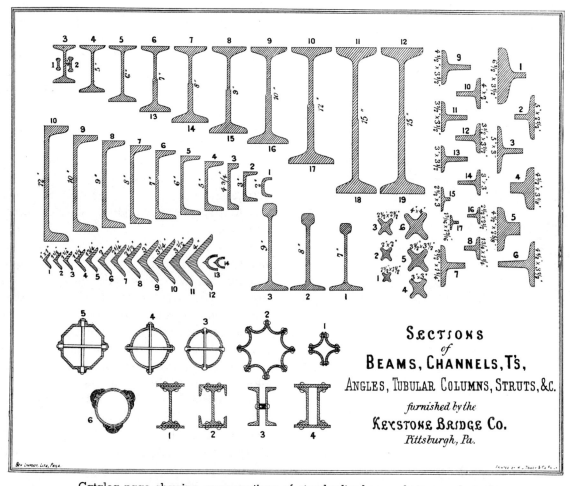

Catalog page showing cross sections of standardized wrought-iron and steel shapes manufactured by the Keystone Bridge Company. The proprietary columns 1–6 are now very rare. The names of the large iron and steel manufacturers such as Bethlehem, Carnegie, Jones & Laughlin, and Lackawanna also appear on bridge parts.

The trend toward standardization was fixed around 1900 with the mass production of standard shapes—posts, channels, angles, rods, Ts, and beams—in wrought iron and steel. These were manufactured by a few companies, such as the Phoenix Bridge Company, the New Jersey Steel and Iron Company, the Keystone Bridge Company, and the Union Iron Mills. Now, instead of ordering wrought-iron diagonal members made to their own specifications from a local forge or distinctive cast-iron details from the nearby foundry, bridge companies simply stocked standard structural shapes. When a bridge order was received and the stresses computed, a table provided the dimensions of the various shapes needed, which were then cut to length from stock, machined, and prepared for assembly. Top chords and posts were similarly fabricated from channels, plates, angles, and straps; struts and sway braces from angles and bars. Top chords and posts might also be formed of proprietary octagonal, round, and fluted sections like the patented Phoenix column and those made by Keystone. These consist of a series of vertical segments riveted together forming a cylindrical column. (These columns are, by the way, an identifying feature of Phoenix and Keystone bridges.)

The extensive use of standardized parts manufactured by a very few companies assured uniformity. As Waddell put it then, "the use of a peculiar form or truss, member or detail is due more to the special necessities of the case than to the idiosyncrasies of any particular individuals."

Up to this point we've been talking about bridges constructed of a combination of iron and timber and, later, both cast and wrought iron. By the turn of the century engineers were using more and more a new and stronger bridge building material, steel. Steel and steel alloys did more than just replace wrought and cast iron; their use brought about a fundamentally new approach to designing bridges and some new silhouettes as well. The first steel truss bridge in America had been built over the Missouri River by the Chicago & Alton Railroad in 1878–79 and, by 1900, steel was becoming the exclusive material for bridges, replacing wrought iron entirely by about 1910. Because of its greater tensile strength (about 16,000 pounds per square inch as compared with 12,000 for wrought iron), engineers could now design bridges of longer spans, using fewer though more massive members. This change in design resulted in one of the subtle differences between bridges of iron and of steel that may help us distinguish them. Again, it is a matter of experience with all kinds of bridges and our historical intuition. But there is in a steel bridge a definite first impression, the overall effect being that of a more massive and more ponderous and earthbound structure than the older ones of cast and wrought iron. Even the latticed and laced girders of iron bridges seem lighter than later ones of steel. This—combined with the characteristically tall, narrow proportion of the through trusses and the small-diameter ($1\frac{1}{2}$ or $1\frac{1}{4}$ inches) wrought-iron rods forming the diagonals, vibration rods, counter bracing, top lateral, and sway bracing—resulted in an elegant, weblike structure that fit in well with the styles of its day. Of course, clues as to whether the bridge is iron or steel are also to be found in cast-in legends or on bridge plates, which might read "Wrought Iron Bridge Co., Canton, Ohio"

A Closer Look at Iron Highway Bridge-Construction Details (c. 1880)

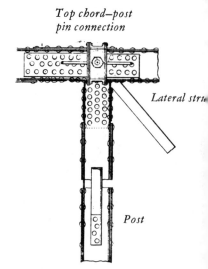

Top chord—post pin connection

Lateral stru

Post

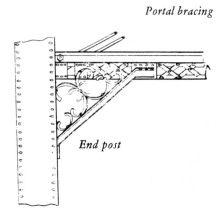

Portal bracing

End post

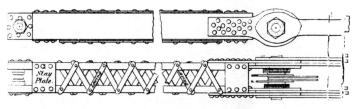

Stay Plate.

Bottom chord

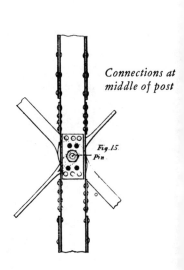

Connections at middle of post

Fig. 15. Pin

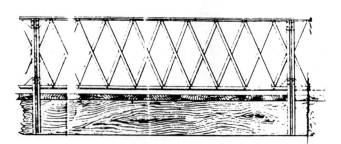

Hand railing

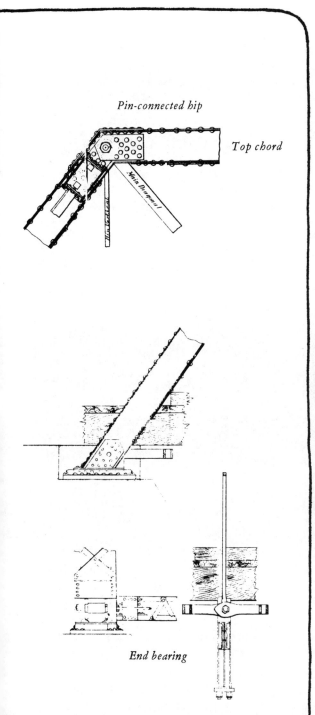

Pin-connected hip

Top chord

Main Diagonal

End bearing

Decorative cast-iron newel post and railing of curved cut pieces found on a Pratt through truss spanning the Chippewa River in Eau Claire County, Wisconsin. A name plate remains, to give the date—1899—and the bridge's builder, Milwaukee Bridge and Iron Works.

and even provide us with a date, or perhaps nothing more than "York Bridge Company, York, Pennsylvania." The latter does give us something to go on, though, especially if we're able to find the company's advertisement or listing in a business directory telling us what kinds of bridges it manufactured.

There *is* a way to arrive at a bridge's vintage and, possibly, even to guess whether it is made of iron or steel, and that is to determine which of two methods have been used to fasten its different members to-

gether: pins or rivets. From the 1890s to well into the 1920s is a period of transition separating two very distinct construction methods, both easily recognized. The changeover was too gradual for precise dating, during the transition period, but we would be able to give a "before" and "after" guess—rough but still useful.

Pin-connecting consists of simply fastening together two or more members meeting a joint or panel point with a wrought-iron or, later, a steel pin. The pin, secured with nuts, may be a square or hexagonal-head bolt or a length of rod threaded at both ends, called a "screw end." In the special case of the Bollman design, the diagonals are attached to the end abutment castings with unthreaded pins held in place by friction.

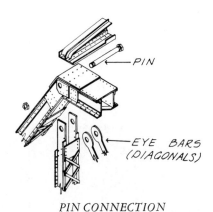

PIN CONNECTION

In the illustration, a single pin is used to connect the end post, top chord, hip vertical, and diagonals in one neat connection. Generally, trusses connected with square-head pins would predate bridges with hexagonal-head pins and nuts.

The use of pins goes back to the days of Squire Whipple, before rivets and at a time when not only metal-to-metal but metal-to-wood connections were necessary. Long after the use of rivets had become standard practice for British engineers, American builders preferred and continued to use pin connections exclusively. They had sound reasons for this preference. Pin connections were faster. It was not unusual for crews to assemble a 250-foot railroad bridge in sixteen working hours. Labor is expensive in America and has always been a prime consideration; but

safety, and integrity, of design seem to be even more important here. Bridges were constructed on falsework (wooden scaffolding) sometimes of prodigious heights over deep ravines and river beds. The longer the time the falsework was up, the greater the chances of destruction and deaths from flash floods, ice jams, and wind.

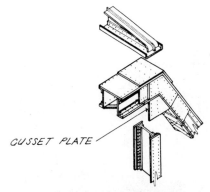

RIVETED CONNECTION

Riveting was slower and the results less certain. There would be no way of knowing if a rivet had a crack or some internal flaw or if the head had come loose (the usual "test" was to strike each rivet with a hammer). The shrinkage in cooling left rivets under high strain, some of them being said to snap off like a piece of glass with the first blow. Besides this, engineers could not readily calculate the distribution of stress throughout a riveted joint. The pin, therefore, was seen by engineers as one large "rivet," its tensile strength and qualities known, its application easier in the field with more predictable results, its single point of stress unambiguous.

By the late 1800s, pin connections had reached their practical limits. Inherently less

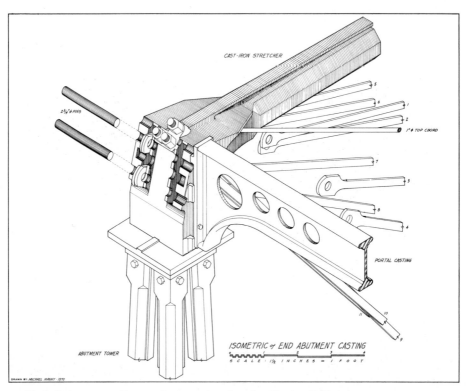

CAST-IRON STRETCHER

2¾"Ø PINS

1"Ø TOP CHORD

PORTAL CASTING

ABUTMENT TOWER

ISOMETRIC of END ABUTMENT CASTING
SCALE 1½ INCHES = 1 FOOT

DRAWN BY: MICHAEL MAHANY 1970

End-abutment casting and pin-connection detail of a Bollman iron suspension and trussed bridge. A wrought-iron tension rod extends from this abutment to the foot of each of eight posts in the truss.

rigid than riveted systems, pin-connected trusses required more web members—counters, vibration rods, and struts—for stability in winds and under increasing railroad axle loadings, which, in turn, meant more complicated assembly. The invention of the portable pneumatic riveter solved this dilemma; riveting could now be done in the field faster than before, and the resulting connection was stronger and more reliable. The advantages of pin connections had been met and, in the minds of most engineers, surpassed by riveted connections. From about 1890 to 1915, both kinds of bridges were built, but pin connections were now used generally for shorter spans. The conversion of minds and shops proceeded at an increasing rate. In 1890 the maximum recommended span for a riveted truss had been 100 feet, but within the same twenty-five-year period the maximum increased to 350 feet.

For the bridge finder, these transition years have considerable meaning as a turning point in American bridge-building practice and as a convenient historical bench mark. Before the 1890s, riveted bridge connections were rare in America. After about 1910, very few new bridges of pin-connected construction would be built. The conclusion reached by the Virginia⁴study—that the great majority of the bridges built after 1910 were of riveted construction—is certain to be confirmed by further inventories in other states.

Until you get to know them, all truss bridges look pretty much alike. There seems to be little in that maze of inclined and vertical posts, struts, stringers, chords, counters, lateral and sway bracing to distinguish one from the other. Still, after this brief introduction to some bridge history, you've probably become aware that bridges, too, have personalities.

King and queen posts remain staunchly the ancient rustics. Town lattice and Burr arch trusses have become recluses, to be sought out under roofs and splintered planks.

I find Mr. Whipple's bowstring-arch trusses endearing, poised, quite unpretentious. Warren, Pratt, and Howe strike me as unimaginative, straightforward, hardworking types. The Bollmans and Finks, well, they're a bit eccentric, ostentatious really, as when they appear as deck trusses without bottom chords. Once you can identify with an old bridge, you'll easily learn its name and be able to tell it from others.

There are a few problems. While some truss bridges remain in their original form, others—the ones that cause real identification troubles—have been altered over the years. An old Warren truss might acquire an additional vertical in each panel to provide more support to the bottom chords, which now carry heavier loads than they did fifty or seventy-five years ago. Yet it is recognizable as one variant of the characteristically triangular Warren truss panels. Other changes

At first glance, this Rall-type bascule bridge would seem to be a new truss form. A closer look, however, reveals that it is simply a through Warren span that lifts.

were made when problems unforeseen by the designer arose during the bridge's first few weeks of service. Swaying caused by the lateral loads of heavy locomotives often had to be corrected with top and bottom sway bracing. These are generally lighter members and rarely alter the characteristic patterns of verticals and diagonals, which allow us to distinguish one truss from another.

Even with these problems, learning to identify truss forms is simply a matter of awareness and a little practice, and soon you will be seeing a "Pratt," or a "Howe," or a "Weichert" where before you saw only a "bridge."

The bridge-finding section that follows is meant to help you identify bridges that you've found nearby or when you are traveling. Some of the bridges are historical—that is, dating to the early to mid-1800s—surviving examples of which might conceivably still be found. Others are of more recent design or are more recent forms of earlier trusses, as recent as the 1930s and 1940s, which means they'll be everywhere and easy to find. These are good to practice on. Anyway, the guide is certainly not complete; it is a beginning guide. Make sketches of unique or little-known spans, and make your own additions to the Hints for Bridge Identification.

The first step is to remember our "Rule of the Commonplace." You don't have to go on long expeditions to find interesting bridges; the ones down at the river or over the railroad tracks will do. Stop and think if there are any bridges you cross as you go about your daily activities. If you've been driving over a deck truss frequently, get out of your car next time and walk down the embankment a ways to see what's underneath. You may be in for a historical surprise.

When you've found a bridge you'd like to know more about, compare the arrangement of its members with the trusses shown in silhouette on the following pages, and choose the one which seems closest to it. Don't worry about length or proportions at this stage; just look for pattern. It helps to make a sketch of the truss. You'll be concentrating on the pattern of members as you draw, and you'll have a simplified plan that's closer to the identification silhouettes. Under the bridge silhouette is a number that refers to one of the boxes that follow. Bridge finder boxes give you more information on the bridge you've found, drawings of historical and modern examples, variations on the basic design, brief explanations on how the various members of the truss react to forces, and field notes pointing out details of construction and clues to identification. The goal is not only to help you identify your bridge, but to get you on your way to developing a repertory of clues and facts that will make looking at bridges more interesting. Included in the boxes are also drawings showing what the truss looks like as a half-through or deck truss, if it varies greatly from the through truss configuration.

Hints for Bridge Identification

Heavy members—cast- and wrought-iron posts, latticed or laced box girders—are generally in *compression*.

Light members—rods, bars, or channels and angles—are always in *tension*. Remember that a column is best suited to carry compressive forces; thin rods and bars could not.

Deck trusses are usually the inverted image of the through or half-through truss, the top chord of the through truss becoming the bottom chord of the deck form.

The deck form of a truss with inclined end posts may have inclined posts, too, but is more likely to have vertical end posts:

Trusses may have either an odd or an even number of panels. But when there is an odd number of panels, the center panel may get a redundant counter for visual balance:

Many of the truss forms shown here may appear with either *parallel* or *polygonal* top chord:

Panel width and depth will vary from span to span, but this *does not* alter the basic form. To make a bridge of given length stronger and more rigid, the engineer may increase the truss depth, the number of panels, or both. All of these are Pratt trusses:

Patterns may be reversed without altering the truss form. Both of these are K-truss bridges:

It is difficult to date design details in bridges, but the following may be helpful as rules of thumb:

are older than

cotter pins	nuts
square nuts	hexagonal nuts
looped bottom chord links	eyebars
tension rods of round section	tension bars of rectangular section
pin connections	riveted connections
vertical end posts on through trusses	inclined end posts

Bridge Genealogy

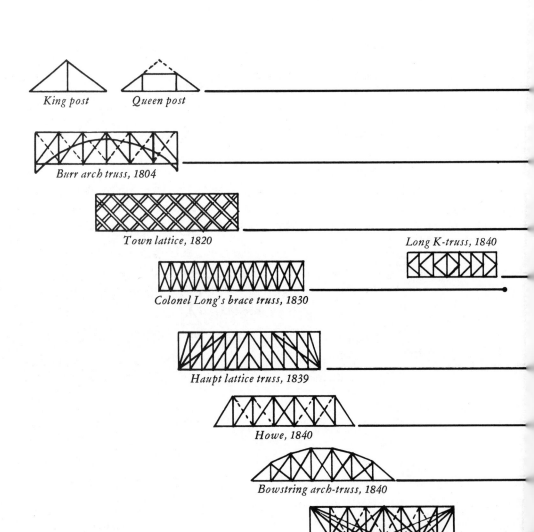

King post

Queen post

Burr arch truss, 1804

Town lattice, 1820

Long K-truss, 1840

Colonel Long's brace truss, 1830

Haupt lattice truss, 1839

Howe, 1840

Bowstring arch-truss, 1840

Fink, 1851

Bollman, 1852

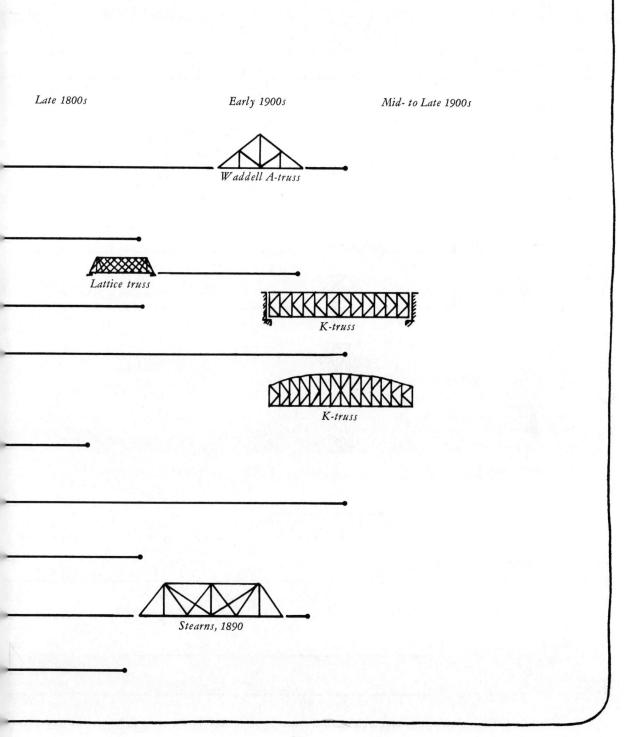

Late 1800s   Early 1900s   Mid- to Late 1900s

Waddell A-truss

Lattice truss

K-truss

K-truss

Stearns, 1890

85

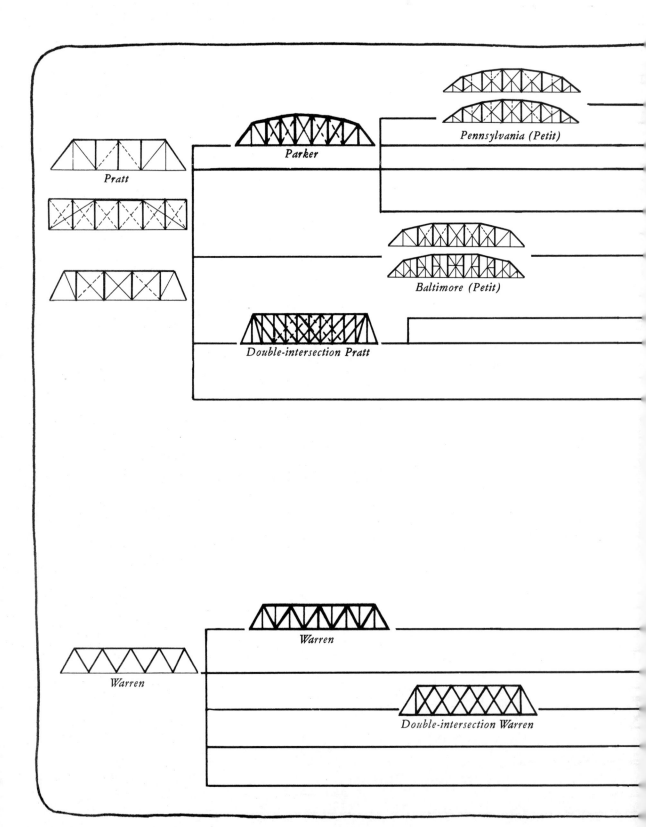

Pratt

Parker

Pennsylvania (Petit)

Baltimore (Petit)

Double-intersection Pratt

Warren

Warren

Double-intersection Warren

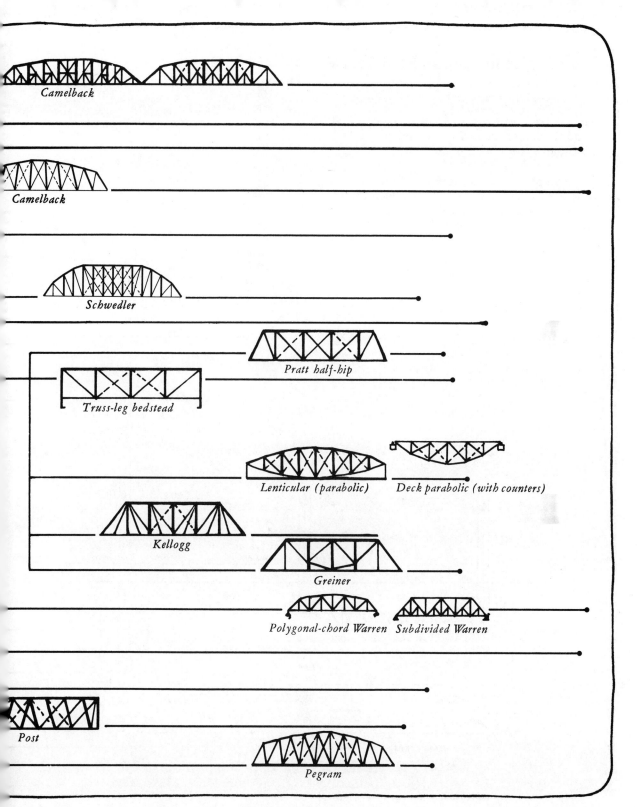

Camelback

Camelback

Schwedler

Pratt half-hip

Truss-leg bedstead

Lenticular (parabolic)   Deck parabolic (with counters)

Kellogg

Greiner

Polygonal-chord Warren   Subdivided Warren

Post

Pegram

King-Post and Queen-Post Trusses

Length: 20–40 feet (king post)
20–80 feet (queen post)

Many king- and queen-post trusses are to be found in Oregon and Washington, where timber bridges were built in recent times.

A queen-post truss is merely a king post to which one panel of top chord has been added between the end posts. This addition extends the maximum span to about 70 or 80 feet.

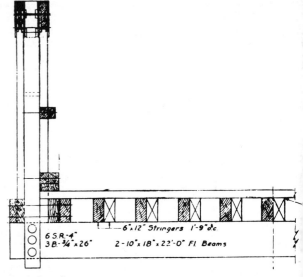

End elevation

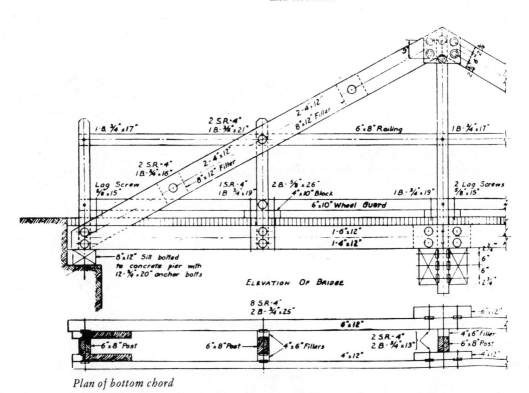

Plan of bottom chord

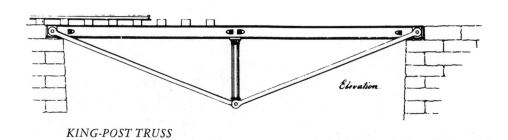

KING-POST TRUSS

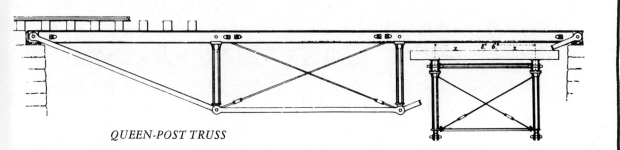

QUEEN-POST TRUSS

89

Town Lattice Truss
Length: 50–220 feet

Ithiel Town's wooden lattice bridge is considered one of the first steps in the evolution of the modern truss form. A great number of these trusses—some combined with an arch, most of them covered—were built all over America on turnpikes and railroads, and many are still in service today. Their popularity was due to the rigidity of their design, the ease of construction, and their low cost. Unlike the Howe truss, no huge timbers were required, the thin planks of which the truss was built up being readily available and easily handled. No iron bolts, straps, or rods were called for in the original design—all fastenings were of wood. Nevertheless, in later years the Town wooden lattice became the prototype for iron lattice trusses.

Spacing of the diagonal web members varied. They were placed very close together in long spans and in railroad bridges.

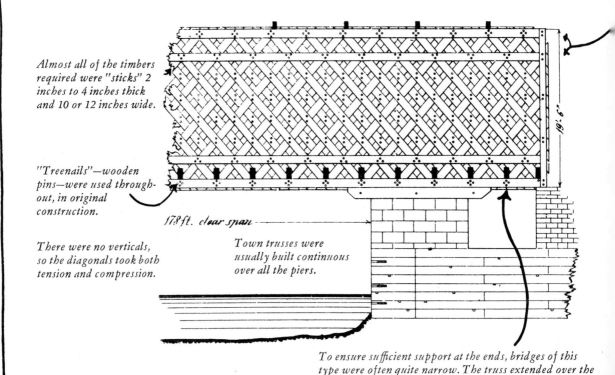

Almost all of the timbers required were "sticks" 2 inches to 4 inches thick and 10 or 12 inches wide.

"Treenails"—wooden pins—were used throughout, in original construction.

There were no verticals, so the diagonals took both tension and compression.

178 ft. clear span

Town trusses were usually built continuous over all the piers.

19' 6"

To ensure sufficient support at the ends, bridges of this type were often quite narrow. The truss extended over the abutments a distance about equal to the truss depth.

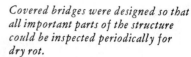

Covered bridges were designed so that all important parts of the structure could be inspected periodically for dry rot.

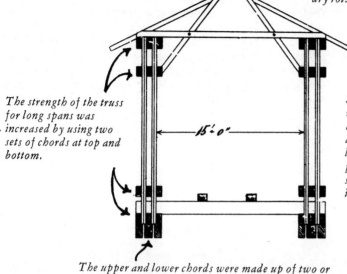

The strength of the truss for long spans was increased by using two sets of chords at top and bottom.

_15'-0"_

Some bridges were simply roofed over; others were roofed and covered with plank siding as well. Openings were often left in the siding to let the pleasing pattern of the truss show through and to let light into the bridge.

The upper and lower chords were made up of two or more sticks spaced so that wooden diagonal web members could fit between them and be nailed through.

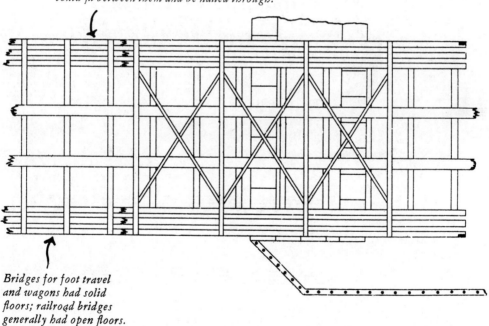

Bridges for foot travel and wagons had solid floors; railroad bridges generally had open floors.

Howe Truss

Length: 30–180 feet

The Howe truss has been popular in regions where timber is plentiful, and has all but disappeared except in the Pacific Northwest. There they are still common, the covered Howe truss having served as the standard 150-foot span of the Oregon State Highway Department up through the 1920s. Extravagant timber requirements are only part of the reason for the Howe's lack of general acceptance: American engineers have always preferred trusses with *vertical* compression members, as in the more popular Pratt. The through form of the Howe truss is more common than either deck or half-through forms. For heavy railroad loadings, the panels were made very narrow so that the diagonals were almost vertical. In a properly designed truss the timber is strained longitudinally only—along the fiber.

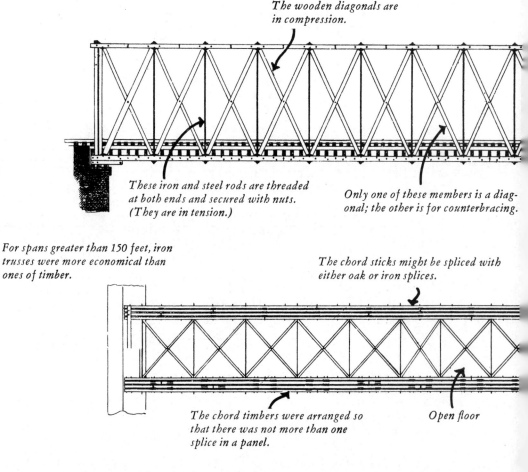

The wooden diagonals are in compression.

These iron and steel rods are threaded at both ends and secured with nuts. (They are in tension.)

Only one of these members is a diagonal; the other is for counterbracing.

For spans greater than 150 feet, iron trusses were more economical than ones of timber.

The chord sticks might be spliced with either oak or iron splices.

The chord timbers were arranged so that there was not more than one splice in a panel.

Open floor

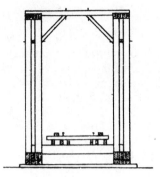

End elevation

There is either a vertical or inclined end post. Trusses with inclined end posts are more recent.

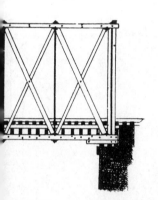

The wooden diagonals abut against hardwood (usually oak) or cast-iron angle blocks at the top and bottom chords, and are held in place with dowel pins.

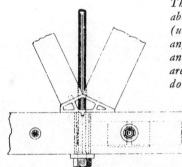

The top and bottom chords are both made up of the same number of timbers.

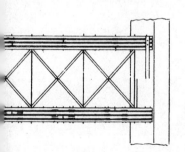

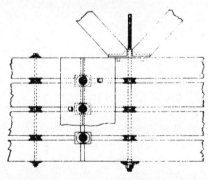

The nuts of the web rods bear on heavy iron "gib plates."

The chord sticks are spaced far enough apart to allow the vertical rods to pass through without having to drill holes and thus weaken the timber.

Fink Combination Truss

Length: 75–150 feet

Albert Fink's Blue River bridge is typical of the kind of spans that came into general use on many Southern railroads during the 1800s, especially the Louisville & Nashville Railroad. This is a combination bridge in which the compression members are of wood and only the tension members in the web and lower chord are of wrought iron. These bridges were looked upon by the railroads as temporary—they would be used until service on a particular line justified the expense of a wrought-iron bridge of more modern type. Thus, they were designed so that the iron members could be used again, in the construction of new iron bridges. It is likely that many have survived in backwoods areas, where, earlier in this century, they may have been put to use as road bridges.

The pin connections are through eyes at the upper and lower ends.

At first glance, this might appear to be a Warren with verticals. In this truss the verticals are in every other triangle, forming the characteristic Fink king posts.

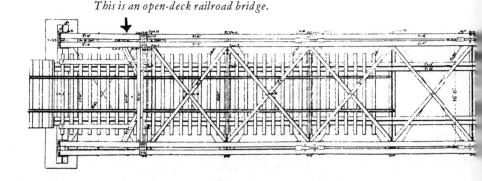

This is an open-deck railroad bridge.

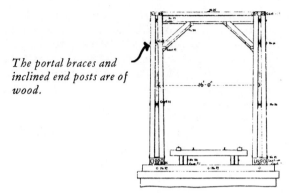

The portal braces and inclined end posts are of wood.

The compression members—chords and diagonals—are of wood.

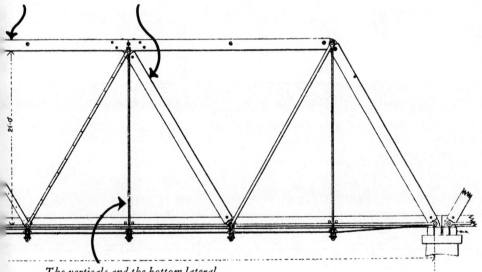

The verticals and the bottom lateral bracing—tension members—are of wrought iron.

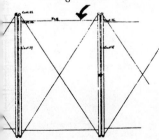

Fink Suspension Truss (Through)

Length: 75–206 feet

Fink trusses abound in a variety of forms, but most typical are the through truss with vertical end posts and the deck truss without a bottom chord. All forms, however, are recognizable by the repetition and enlargement of the basic king-post elements. Albert Fink and Wendell Bollman were assistants to Benjamin H. Latrobe, chief engineer for the Baltimore & Ohio Railroad. Latrobe preferred to use Bollman trusses when shorter spans were called for, and adopted the Fink suspension truss for new lines west of the Cumberland Gap. The through trusses over the Monongahela spanned 205 feet between abutments; the Green River deck truss, 206 feet. Long considered extinct, two Fink trusses were discovered just recently— one near Zoarville, Tuscarawas County, Ohio, and the other (a deck truss) in West Lynchburg, Virginia.

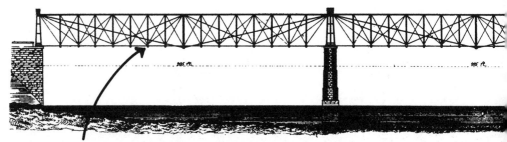

The truss is actually a series of king posts transferring loads from the smaller to the larger trusses until the forces reach the abutments.

The suspension diagonals run from the end posts to the center-panel points.

The cast-iron chords and posts are in compression.

The upper ends of the web diagonal are threaded for adjustment.

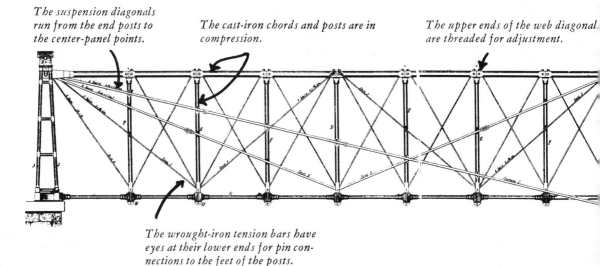

The wrought-iron tension bars have eyes at their lower ends for pin connections to the feet of the posts.

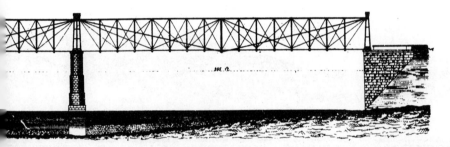

Fink suspension trusses always have vertical end posts.

Note the absence of portal bracing.

Top and bottom chords and posts are octagonal in section.

Heavy timbers are used for floor beams.

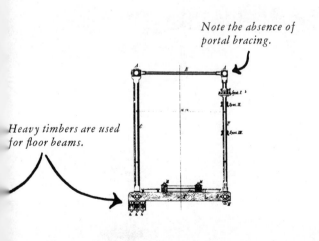

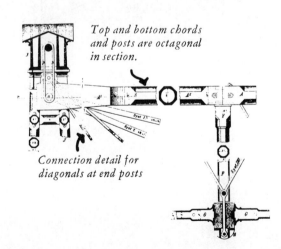

Connection detail for diagonals at end posts

Fink Truss (Deck)

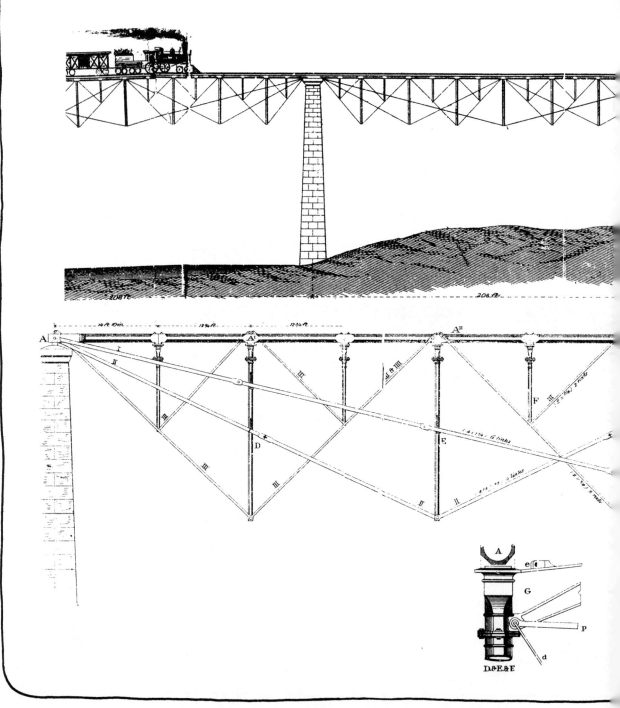

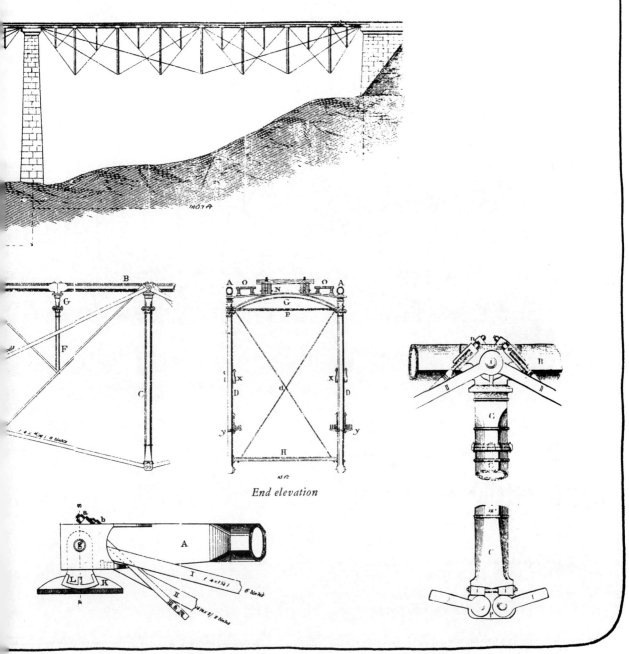

End elevation

Bollman Iron Suspension Truss Bridge

Length: 75–100 feet

Wendell Bollman's iron suspension truss bridges in through and deck forms were used extensively on the Baltimore & Ohio Railroad from 1850 to 1875. Several remained in service on the Valley Railroad of Virginia between Harrisonburg and Lexington until 1924.

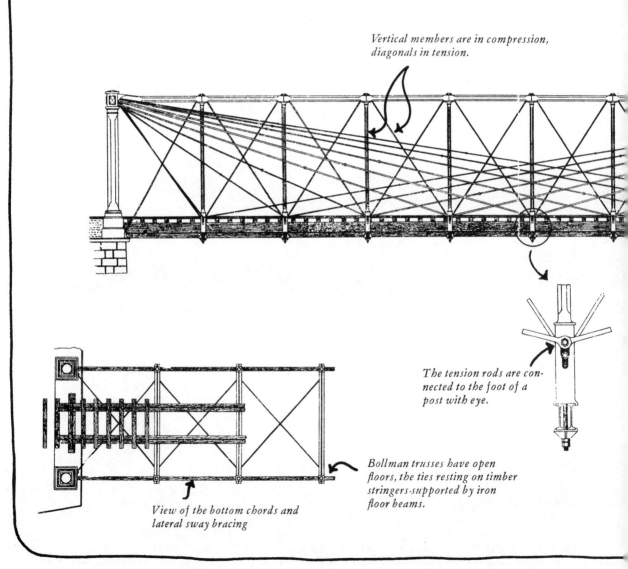

Vertical members are in compression, diagonals in tension.

The tension rods are connected to the foot of a post with eye.

Bollman trusses have open floors, the ties resting on timber stringers supported by iron floor beams.

View of the bottom chords and lateral sway bracing

Detail of the Bollman trusses at Savage, Maryland, showing the abutment castings and towers, portal castings, cast-iron top chords and diagonals.

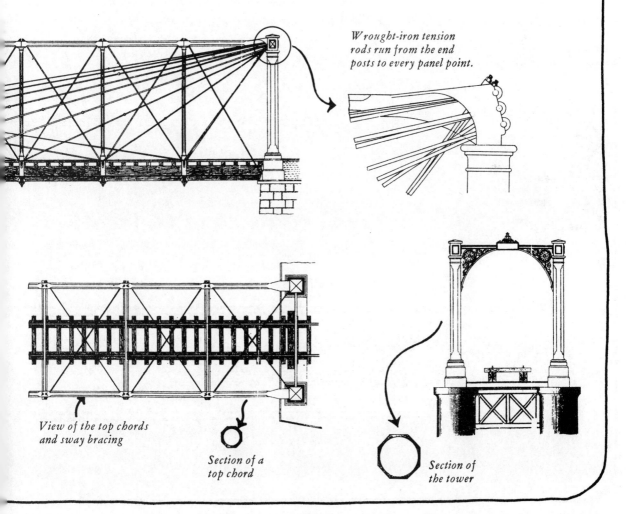

Wrought-iron tension rods run from the end posts to every panel point.

View of the top chords and sway bracing

Section of a top chord

Section of the tower

Post Diagonal Truss

Length: 100–300 feet

S. S. Post's first patent diagonal-truss iron bridge was built on the Erie Railroad in 1865, and many others were constructed over the next fifteen years. The lower ends of the posts were inclined half a panel length toward the ends that formed the characteristic single triangle at mid-span. These inclined iron posts formed one system; diagonals of iron bars and rods with eyes at each end running counter to the posts formed two more systems. The effect was the same as combining a Warren and a double-intersection Pratt. The stresses were ambiguous, but the truss's popularity as a railroad bridge stemmed from its stiffness under heavy moving loads. It was also used as a road bridge.

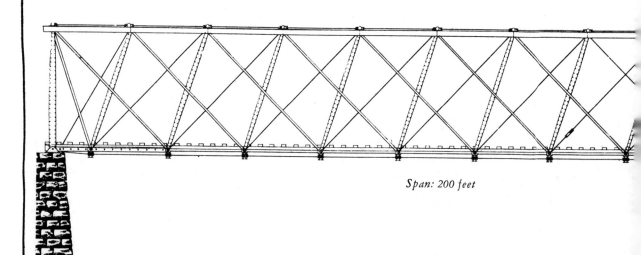

Span: 200 feet

C

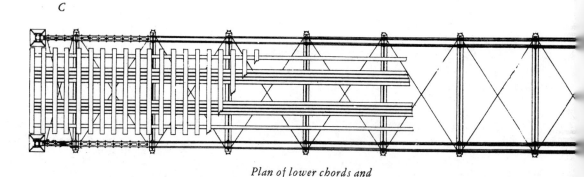

Plan of lower chords and lateral bracing

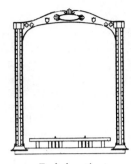

End elevation

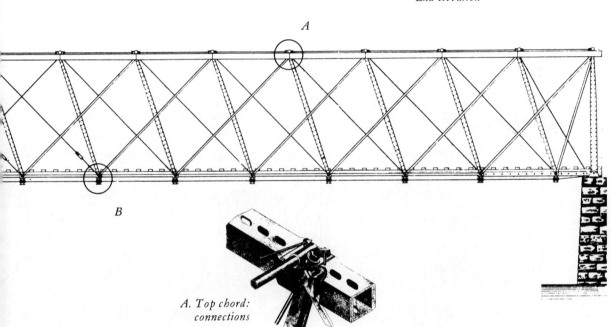

A

B

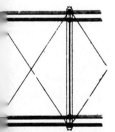

A. Top chord: connections

B. Lower chord: connections at center-panel point

C. End-post detail showing connection of end post, bottom chord, and counter

Whipple Trapezoidal Truss

Length: 70–300 feet

A double-intersection truss—or double-cancelled truss, as it is sometimes known—is actually two bridges in one. Faced with the need to span distances exceeding the practical limit of one system of triangles, Whipple combined two triangular systems. The trapezoidal truss is actually a double-intersection Pratt—the diagonals extending across two panels and intersecting—with inclined end posts: a form which later became known as the Whipple, Whipple-Murphy, or Linville truss. Each system works independently, carrying loads to the abutments. This particular bridge, below, built for the Rensselaer & Saratoga Railroad north of Troy, New York, was a clear span of only 146 feet, but trapezoidal trusses have been used for spans of over 400 feet. This truss was inverted, retaining the inclined end posts, and used in a deck form on the Baltimore & Ohio Railroad.

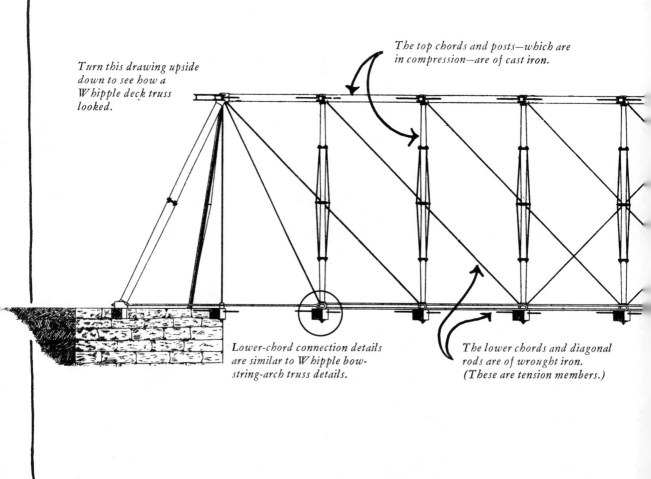

Turn this drawing upside down to see how a Whipple deck truss looked.

The top chords and posts—which are in compression—are of cast iron.

Lower-chord connection details are similar to Whipple bow-string-arch truss details.

The lower chords and diagonal rods are of wrought iron. (These are tension members.)

Upper end of a web diagonal rod, which fits into the upper chord and is secured with a pin

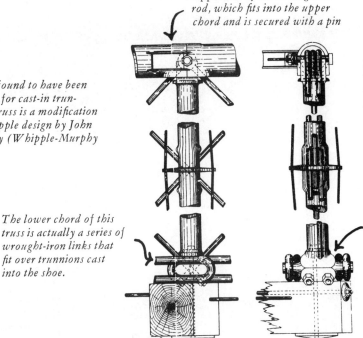

Some of these trusses were later modified with wrought-iron compression members.

If pins are found to have been substituted for cast-in trunnions, the truss is a modification of the Whipple design by John W. Murphy (Whipple-Murphy truss).

The bottom end of a web diagonal is threaded and passed through this cast-iron shoe at the bottom of the post. Tightening or loosening the nut adjusts tension.

The lower chord of this truss is actually a series of wrought-iron links that fit over trunnions cast into the shoe.

Timber floor beam

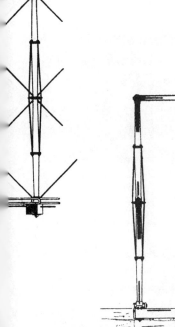

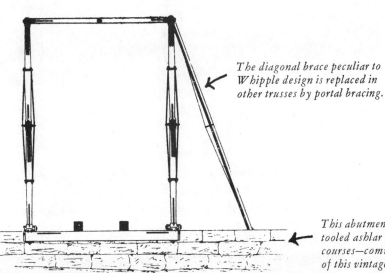

The diagonal brace peculiar to Whipple design is replaced in other trusses by portal bracing.

This abutment is random-tooled ashlar masonry laid in courses—common for bridges of this vintage.

J. H. Linville Double-Intersection Truss

Length: up to 500 feet

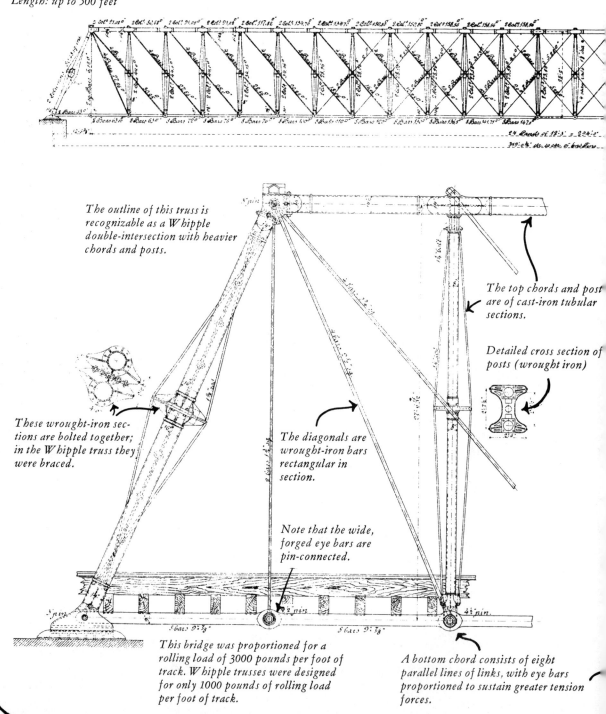

The outline of this truss is recognizable as a Whipple double-intersection with heavier chords and posts.

The top chords and post are of cast-iron tubular sections.

Detailed cross section of posts (wrought iron)

These wrought-iron sections are bolted together; in the Whipple truss they were braced.

The diagonals are wrought-iron bars rectangular in section.

Note that the wide, forged eye bars are pin-connected.

This bridge was proportioned for a rolling load of 3000 pounds per foot of track. Whipple trusses were designed for only 1000 pounds of rolling load per foot of track.

A bottom chord consists of eight parallel lines of links, with eye bars proportioned to sustain greater tension forces.

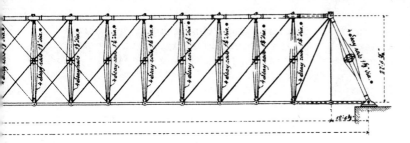

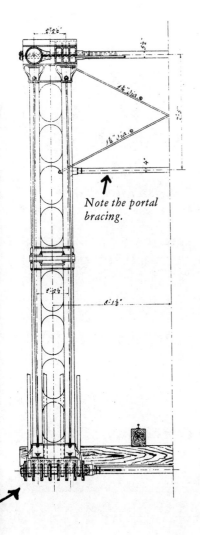

Note the portal bracing.

Jacob H. Linville kept breaking his own records for long-span railroad bridges throughout the 1860s and 1870s. His first was a 320-foot channel span for the Steubenville (Ohio) bridge, illustrated here; it was built over the Ohio River in 1863–64 and is considered by historians to have inaugurated the era of long-span bridges. At 515 feet, Linville's Ohio River bridge at Cincinnati, completed in 1870, was the longest single span of the time. He modified the Whipple trapezoidal design to increase its strength and rigidity, retaining the double-intersection principle.

Lowthorp Truss Bridge

Length: To 150 feet

F. C. Lowthorp receives little mention in the literature of bridges, but Theodore Cooper saw fit to include this drawing in his *American Railroad Bridges* (1890). The first of several bridges based on this patented design was built in 1857 for the Catasauqua & Fogelsville Railroad in Pennsylvania; it consisted of eleven spans totaling 1,122 feet. This pony truss suggests a cast-iron, pin-connected version of the Pratt truss—a form that is quite pleasing in its overall proportions and in the quality of the ironwork.

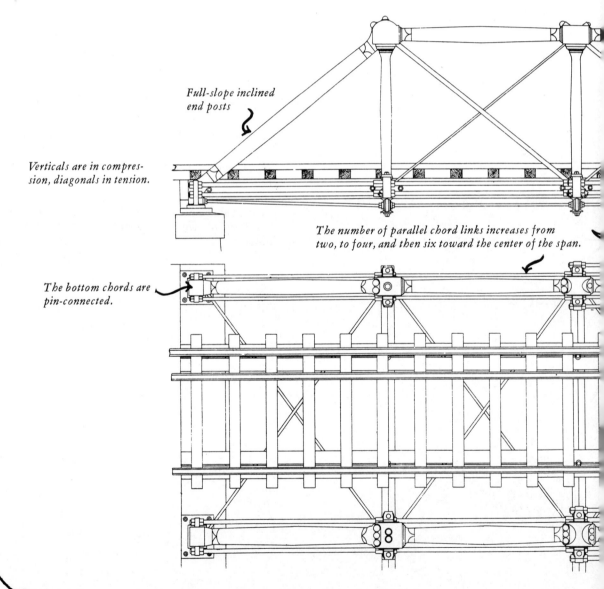

Full-slope inclined end posts

Verticals are in compression, diagonals in tension.

The number of parallel chord links increases from two, to four, and then six toward the center of the span.

The bottom chords are pin-connected.

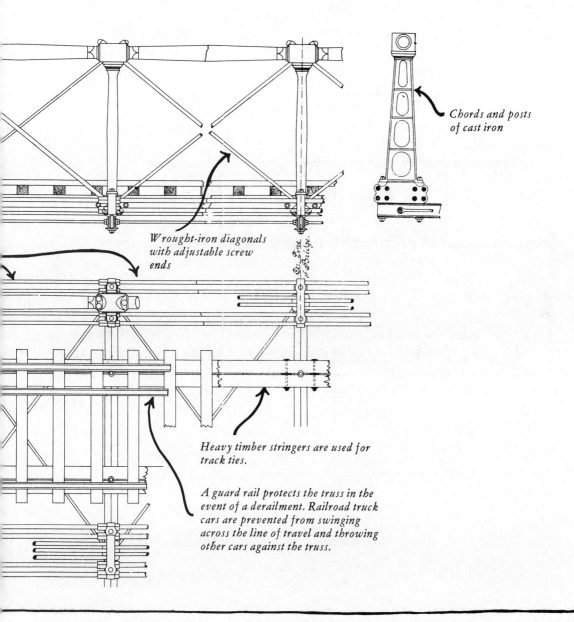

Chords and posts
of cast iron

Wrought-iron diagonals
with adjustable screw
ends

Heavy timber stringers are used for
track ties.

A guard rail protects the truss in the
event of a derailment. Railroad truck
cars are prevented from swinging
across the line of travel and throwing
other cars against the truss.

Pratt Truss

Length: 30–250 feet

Thomas and Caleb Pratt's original design of 1844 called for only one tension diagonal in each panel. It was discovered, however, that under certain conditions live loads can reverse the stresses in the truss members, causing the diagonals to come under compressive forces. For this reason, a "counter" was added in the center panels. Iron Pratt trusses began to appear in large numbers in the 1850s. The Baltimore & Ohio Railroad used Pratt trusses almost exclusively from 1880 until 1905, when they began using Warrens. A very high proportion of all the road spans in use today are steel Pratts and Pratt types with riveted connections, though engineers have preferred to use pin connections on spans over 200 feet.

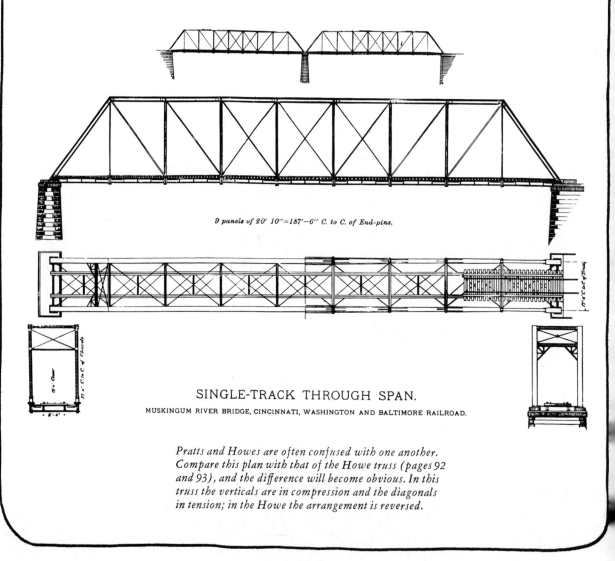

9 panels of 20' 10"=187'–6" C. to C. of End-pins.

SINGLE-TRACK THROUGH SPAN.

MUSKINGUM RIVER BRIDGE, CINCINNATI, WASHINGTON AND BALTIMORE RAILROAD.

Pratts and Howes are often confused with one another. Compare this plan with that of the Howe truss (pages 92 and 93), and the difference will become obvious. In this truss the verticals are in compression and the diagonals in tension; in the Howe the arrangement is reversed.

Warren Truss

Length: 50–450 feet

Warren trusses of riveted construction, modified with vertical members, became the standard long-span bridge on many railroads in the early 1900s and superseded the Pratt truss for short spans as well. Deck Warrens, which had vertical end posts, were a popular truss for elevated railroads in cities, and more recently this simple triangular form is often found in continuous bridges, cantilevers, and Weichert trusses. In its original form, with inclined web members only, the Warren was elegant in its use of equilateral triangles. This simplicity was practical too—considerably less metal was needed than in vertical post designs. The Warren was never as widely used for road bridges as the Pratt and Whipple double-intersection trusses were, but it survives today in more modern forms such as bascule and Scherzer lift spans. The double-intersection Warren, composed of two separate triangular web systems superimposed on each other, reacts to forces much as does the lattice truss.

Because of its design, the Warren is sometimes called a "triangular" truss.

The diagonal web members carry both compressive and tensile forces.

In a true Warren truss, each panel is an equilateral triangle.

When the Warren is used as a deck truss, the tension rods become posts and are heavier.

Most common form of the Warren truss

Added vertical members are in tension.

Vertical members do not transmit forces to the abutments. Their purpose is to provide intermediate support for the deck.

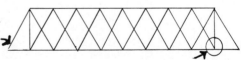

DOUBLE-INTERSECTION WARREN

POLYGONAL CHORD WARREN

A subdivided Warren is used in special cases where the floor must be shallower than normal.

As late as the 1940s, engineers recommended eye bar and pin connections for Warrens over 200 feet long. Riveting would have required very wide members as well as large joints.

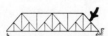

SUBDIVIDED WARREN

Girder Guide (c. 1880)

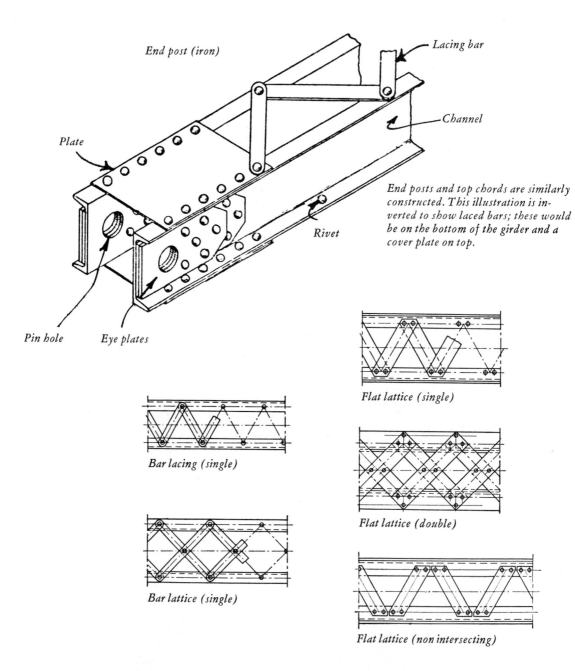

End post (iron)

Lacing bar

Channel

Plate

Rivet

End posts and top chords are similarly constructed. This illustration is inverted to show laced bars; these would be on the bottom of the girder and a cover plate on top.

Pin hole

Eye plates

Bar lacing (single)

Bar lattice (single)

Flat lattice (single)

Flat lattice (double)

Flat lattice (non intersecting)

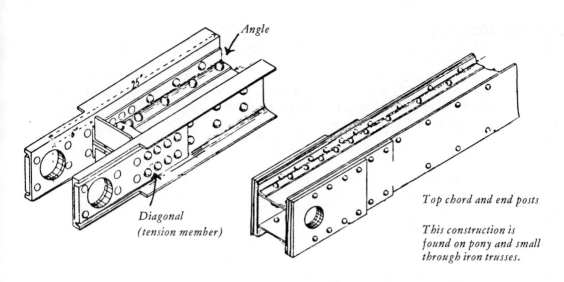

Angle

Diagonal
(tension member)

Top chord and end posts

This construction is
found on pony and small
through iron trusses.

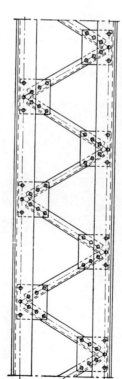

Single-angle lattice
with gussets

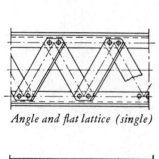

Angle and flat lattice (single)

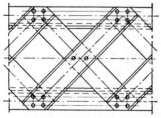

Channel and flat lattice (double)

Plate Girder Bridges

Length: 30–125 feet

Plate girder bridges were specified in American railroad standards of the 1920s wherever spans of 30 to 125 feet were required. Bridges of rolled beams were recommended for spans shorter than this and Pratt- or Warren-type trusses for longer spans. The most practical plate girder length was 30 to 70 feet; it could be fabricated at less first cost than any other type of bridge span. Girders longer than 125 feet were considered difficult to transport in one piece, and required splicing in the field.

Generally, plate girder bridges also proved less costly to maintain over the years. Solid floors were used when ballasted tracks were laid over the bridge, otherwise an open floor system was used. The use of deck or through girder construction was determined by how close the tracks would be placed (parallel deck bridges can be placed closer together) and how much clearance there was under the structure (through spans required less clearance).

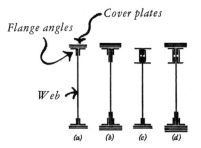

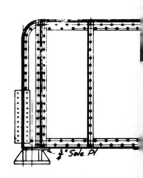

Open floors usually consisted of track ties laid about 4 inches apart, on which the rails were laid.

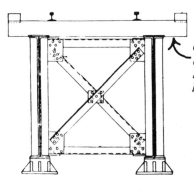

Cover plates

Flange angles

Web

(a) (b) (c) (d)

PLATE GIRDER SECTIONS

Of the sections, (a) is the most common, (b) is a strengthened girder with additional cover plates, (c) is a form sometimes used for deck bridges, and (d) is a heavy girder used for long spans carrying heavy loads.

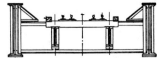

Base of Rail

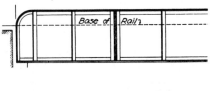

HALF-THROUGH PLATE GIRDER BRIDGE

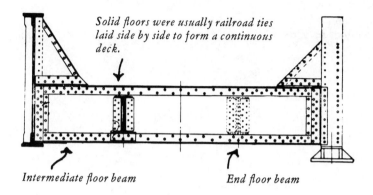

Solid floors were usually railroad ties laid side by side to form a continuous deck.

Intermediate floor beam   End floor beam

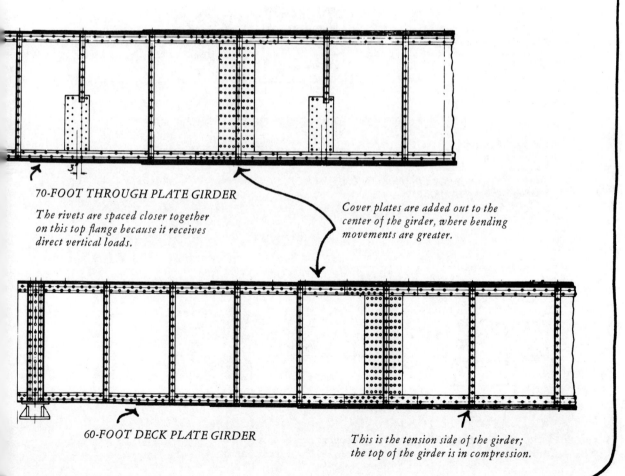

70-FOOT THROUGH PLATE GIRDER

The rivets are spaced closer together on this top flange because it receives direct vertical loads.

Cover plates are added out to the center of the girder, where bending movements are greater.

60-FOOT DECK PLATE GIRDER

This is the tension side of the girder; the top of the girder is in compression.

Bascule and Lift Bridges (c. 1930)

Movable bridges do not constitute a separate category of truss form. They are an adaptation of various truss configurations to a more recent development in bridge design. Single-leaf spans act like simple spans; double-leaf spans are designed to act like cantilevers.

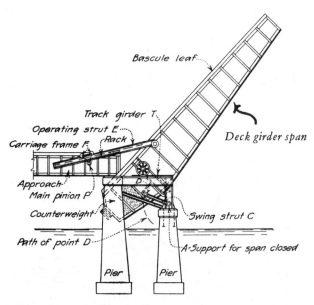

Bascule leaf

Deck girder span

Track girder T

Operating strut E

Carriage frame F

Rack

Approach

Main pinion P

Counterweight

Path of point D

Swing strut C

A=Support for span closed

Pier

Pier

SIMPLE TRUNNION BASCULE BRIDGE (DOUBLE-LEAF)

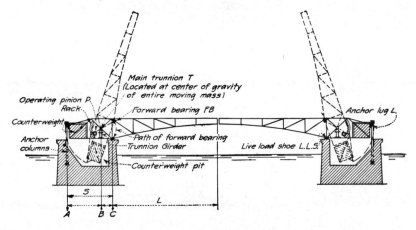

Operating pinion P

Rack

Counterweight

Anchor columns

Main trunnion T
(Located at center of gravity of entire moving mass)

Forward bearing FB

Path of forward bearing

Trunnion Girder

Counterweight pit

Anchor lug L

Live load shoe L.L.S.

S

L

A   B   C

In this "Chicago" type, the entire weight of the leaf and counterweight is carried by the trunnions.

116

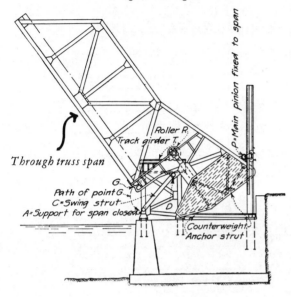

Rall and Scherzer bridges are types of roller-lift bascules. In addition to the trunnion motion, the bridge also rolls backward along the track girder.

D=Main pinion fixed to span

Roller R.

Track girder T.

Through truss span

Path of point G.
C=Swing strut
A=Support for span closed

G.

D

Counterweight.
Anchor strut

RALL DIRECT-LIFT SPANS

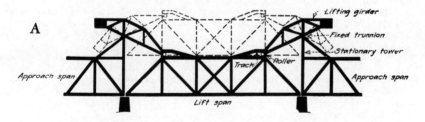

A

Lifting girder
Fixed trunnion
Stationary tower

Approach span

Track Roller

Approach span

Lift span

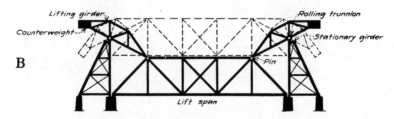

B

Lifting girder
Counterweight

Rolling trunnion
Stationary girder

Pin

Lift span

In type "A," the rollers are above the top chord of the lift span. The rolling motion in type "B" occurs atop the stationary girder.

Truss Bridge Survey and Inventory Form

STATE HISTORICAL SOCIETY OF WISCONSIN
    HISTORIC PRESERVATION DIVISION

TRUSS BRIDGE SURVEY AND INVENTORY FORM

Geographic Information

County: _JACKSON_

City or Town: _MELROSE_

Route: _STH 108_   Over: _BLACK RIVER_

USGS Quad.: _____

Recorded by: _G. DANKO_

Date: _8-6-77_

Affiliation: _____

Film Roll: _BRDG-13_

Negative No.: _32A-37_

UTM/KGS Coordinates: _____

Historical Information

Local and/or Technical Name: _PARKER TRUSS W/ SUB-TIES_   DOT No.: _B454_
Designer: _____   Basis: _____
Builder: _WORDEN ALLEN CO., MILWAUKEE, WIS._   Basis: _NAME PLATE_
Date: _1922_   Basis: _DOT INVENTORY_
Original owner: _____   Use: _____
Present owner: _PUBLIC_   Use: _VEHICULAR_

Historical or Technical Significance

    The Worden Allen Company was incorporated in Wisconsin in December, 1902. One of the largest twentieth-century bridge companies in the central states region, the firm had offices in Chicago, Illinois, and Houghton, Michigan, and controlled through stock ownership the Lackawanna Bridge Company of New York. In 1911, the firm could boast of a structural steel capacity of 12,000 to 15,000 tons per annum and a yearly business of one million dollars.
    This span, the sole Petit truss encountered in the survey, exhibits the uniformity of structural components which prevailed in the twentieth century. Shy of the minimum length of 220 feet recommended by some prominent engineers for a span of this design, the bridge is, nevertheless, the largest truss fabricated by the Worden Allen Company in the surveyed area.

Present Condition

Bibliographic References and Contemporary Photographs

Greater Milwaukee: Financial, Commercial and Biographical. Milwaukee: The Journal Company, 1911.

Ketchum, Milo S. The Design of Highway Bridges. New York: Engineering News Publishing Co., 1908.

Poor's Manual of Industrials. New York: Poor's Railroad Manual Company, 1911.

Design Information

No. of Spans: 7   Overall Length: 664'8"   No. Lanes: 2   Width: 21'

Span type(s):
1.) PARKER TRUSS _____ ; length: 200'9"
2.) WARREN TRUSS _____ ; length: 77'8"
3.) WARREN TRUSS _____ ; length: 77'3"
4.) WARREN TRUSS _____ ; length: 77'3"
5.) WARREN TRUSS _____ ; length: 77'3"
6.) WARREN TRUSS _____ ; length: 77'3"
7.) WARREN TRUSS   77'3"

Structural Information

Substructure:
    CONCRETE PIERS AND ABUTMENTS

Superstructure:
    Material: STEEL _____   Source: ILLINOIS·S·USA, ILLINOIS·G

    Connections: _____ pinned.   Field Connections: _____ bolted.
                 ✓ rigid.   ✓ riveted.
    Top Chords: 2 UP-RIGHT CHANNELS CONNECTED W/LATTICING,STAY & COVER PLATES
    Bottom Chords: 2 SINGLE ANGLES CONNECTED WITH STAY PLATES
    End Posts: 2 CHANNELS CONNECTED W/ LATTICING, STAY PLATES & COVER PLATE
    Intermediate Posts: 2 CHANNELS CONNECTED WITH LATTICING & STAY PLATES
    Diagonals: 2 SINGLE ANGLES CONNECTED WITH STAY PLATES
    Counters: SUB-TIES: 2 SINGLE ANGLES CONNECTED WITH STAY PLATES
    Top Lateral Bracing: SINGLE ANGLES PLACED DIAGONALLY
    Bottom Lateral Bracing: CYLINDRICAL RODS WITH UPSET ENDS
    Top Lateral Struts: PAIRED ANGLES RIVETED

Truss Configuration

Main Span Type: PARKER TRUSS W/ SUB-TIES

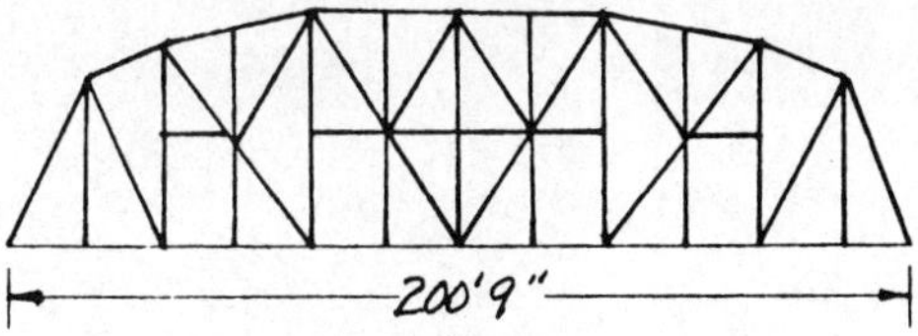

200'9"   21'

Secondary Span Type: WARREN PONY TRUSS

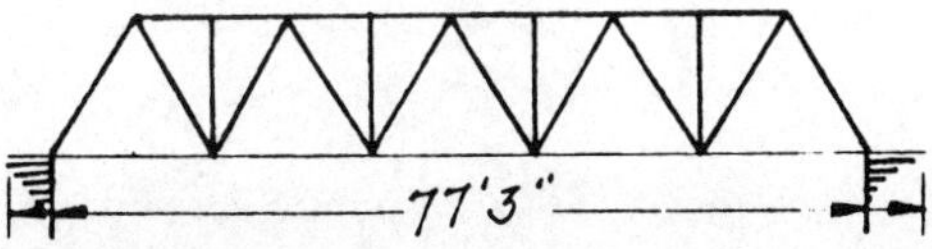

77'3"

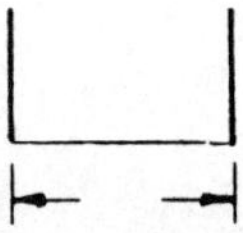

Left: Pier detail of a North Platte River bridge.

Right: The Smithfield Street Bridge in Pittsburgh is a beautiful example of the lenticular or parabolic ("pumpkin seed"), truss designed by Gustav Lindenthal. Built in 1883, it is the oldest known steel truss bridge in the United States.

Below: This bowstring truss bridge spanning the North Platte River near Fort Laramie is perhaps the oldest iron bridge in Wyoming. The three spans were built by the King Iron Bridge and Manufacturing Company, Cleveland, Ohio, in 1875.

Roof-truss connection details of the Union Station train shed in Montgomery, Alabama; it was built in 1897-98.

4. ROOF TRUSSES

Beginning sometime about the middle of the last century, the area of American work spaces—mill buildings, warehouses, railroad shops, factories, casting houses, foundries, forges, rolling mills—increased greatly as both the machines and their output got larger. Builders sought roof-support systems that would make possible long, clear spans. And the answer was already at hand; from the variety of wooden and iron bridge trusses that had appeared by then, similar forms could be derived to be used for supporting roofs. The roof truss, then, is simply a bridge-like framework designed to support a roof covering or ceiling over large spaces, thereby eliminating the need of interior columns. Once the amateur industrial archaeologist has become aware of the many different kinds of bridges in the landscape, the search for roof trusses is inevitable.

The truss works to support a roof in the same way it does to support a bridge. A simple framework composed of triangles spans the required distance between the walls of the building and supports the deadweight of the truss itself and the roof, as well as snow and wind loads. The members of the framework are usually arranged in such a way that they are in direct tension or compression. Roof trusses, like bridge trusses, may be composed of a single web system or a double web system, though the single is preferred since the stresses are more readily deter-

mined. Some of the same names applied to bridge truss forms—such as Howe, Pratt, Warren, and Fink—apply as well to the corresponding roof-truss form. Even the terms used in describing the structural members of a roof truss—top and bottom chords and web members—are much the same. The evolution of roof and bridge trusses are similar, too. The earliest forms were of wood with iron tension members, giving way eventually to trusses fabricated entirely of iron and then steel. The history of the roof truss, however, is compressed into but two or three decades.

Roof trusses, particularly in the form of an arch, found early and showy use in theaters, auditoriums, and exposition buildings. But the real impetus for building trusses of longer and longer spans came from the need for large, clear-span train sheds in metropolitan terminals.

The fierce competition among the many railroad lines was expressed, in part, in the

Single web system.

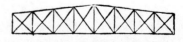

Double web system.

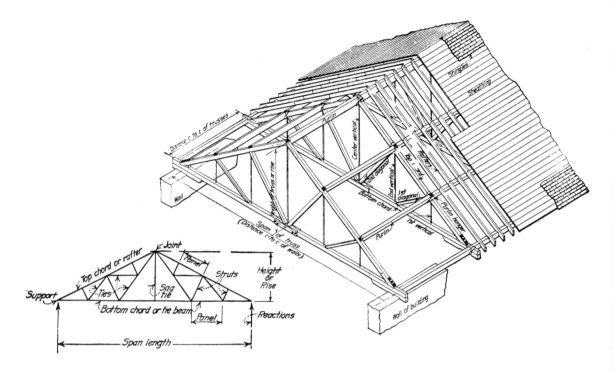

architecture of passenger facilities. As we've already seen, the various lines entering a city had their own separate terminal (as well as their own gauge), and each attempted to outdo the others. Terminals were built on a grand scale, beckoning passengers with architecturally extravagant concourses, waiting rooms, and dining halls—great vaulted spaces that bespoke the opulence of the era. Some railroad terminals incorporated the platform area in the station building itself. Elsewhere the platforms were enclosed in masonry walls covered over with a shed roof that formed a continuation of the terminal building. Later, as traffic increased and more and more tracks were added, the separate train shed with its vast open spaces, spanned by great soaring trusses, came into being. The effect of this, rather than standardization, was the appearance in any one city of a variety of

architectural styles embodying virtually every known truss configuration. Just as increasing locomotive weights and train speeds had challenged engineers in the decades before to build more substantial and stable bridges, the increased volume of passenger traffic in the years after the Civil War encouraged experimentation with longer and longer truss spans for terminals and train sheds. Even following the trend toward immense *union* stations serving many lines, which developed in the last quarter of the century, many of these interesting buildings of smaller scale survived and, what's more, remain in service to this day.

The truss system for train sheds went through three distinct and, for the historian, easily recognizable stages of development, from which emerged three general classes of roof trusses. One of the first consisted of rigid masonry walls upon which rested the roof trusses. The walls in this instance are directly analogous to the masonry abutments that support bridge trusses. The purpose of the abutments and the walls is to resist the vertical forces of the truss. Atop the masonry walls of an old train shed we might find a familiar Howe truss of wood and iron or wrought-iron Pratt trusses, still recognizable with their elegant, arched bottom chords. This kind of roof-support system—trusses on masonry or wood-frame walls—can be found everywhere, having been in continuous use over the years for all kinds of buildings. It derives, actually, from the medieval king post as did the bridge truss.

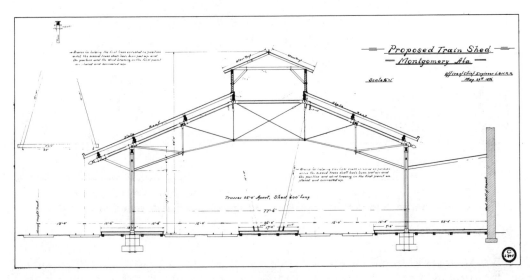

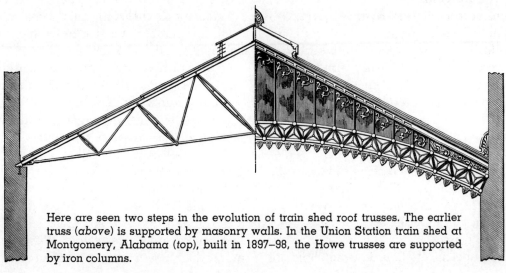

Here are seen two steps in the evolution of train shed roof trusses. The earlier truss (above) is supported by masonry walls. In the Union Station train shed at Montgomery, Alabama (top), built in 1897–98, the Howe trusses are supported by iron columns.

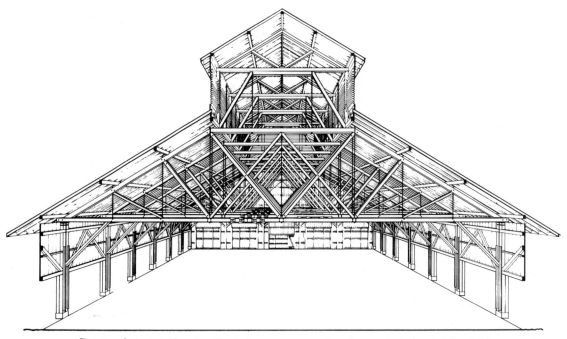

Section drawing showing Pratt trusses supporting the roof of the Baltimore & Ohio's Cumberland Rail Rolling Mill, built 1869–71, at Cumberland, Maryland.

The next step was to eliminate the need for heavy, costly masonry walls, using instead columns of iron or steel. By themselves, columns in such an arrangement could not resist lateral forces. So, to make them more rigid, they were joined to the truss with an additional member called a "knee brace." This formed the familiar useful triangle at the corner made by the lower chord of the truss and the vertical column. The several "knee-brace bents," or simply "bents," were tied together in a system of diagonal bracing similar to the diagonals, counters, and sway bracing of the bridge truss—all of which was covered by a lightweight curtain wall.

Roof trusses, again like bridge trusses, had fairly specific applications, the choice of a particular roof-truss configuration being based on a number of considerations. These considerations included the length of the span, the number and spacing of supporting columns, wind and snow loads, roof slope, type of roof covering to be used, lighting requirements, ventilation needs, and the architectural features of the structure.

Slope was an important consideration; the slope of a truss was determined by the type of roof covering called for. Tar and gravel, for example, will run under a hot sun if the slope is too steep. Wind will drive rain under the lap of slate or corrugated sheeting if the slope is too flat. For these reasons the slope of a tar-and-gravel roof is usually not more than one inch per foot, corrugated sheeting not less than 6 inches per foot, and slate 7 inches per foot.

Span length was the principal consideration in the choice of a truss form. Generally, roof trusses were designed so that there would be a panel point directly under each purlin (the wood or metal member running lengthwise tying all the trusses together and supporting the rafters). In a design rule that has evolved over the years, the maximum distance between panel points and purlins is 8 feet, making some roof-truss configurations

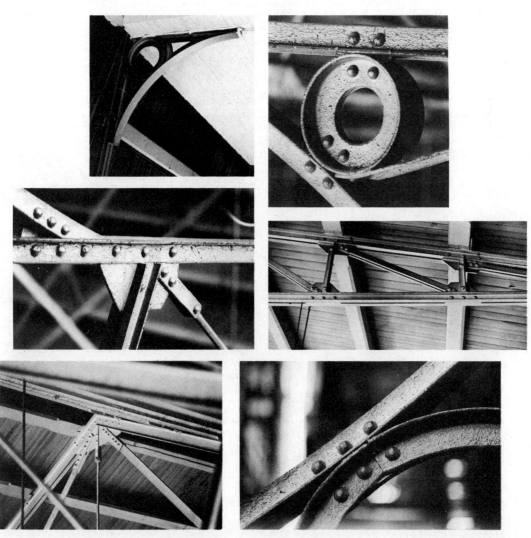

Cast-iron fluted column, capital, and bracket and riveted roof-truss members of the Market House (city market), Indianapolis, Indiana; it was built in 1886.

Roof Trusses

Queen rod

King post, or king rod

Two-hinged arch,
with tie rod

Howe, or English

Howe (top chord flat or
with slight slope)

HOWE
The diagonals are in
compression.

Pratt (steel or
combination of wood
and steel)

PRATT
The diagonals are in
tension.

Flat Pratt

WARREN

Flat Warren

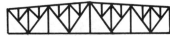

Subdivided Warren

FINK
This is a variation of the
Fink truss shown in the
bridge diagram.

Cambered Fink

Fink, or compound Fink

Fan

Fan, or compound fan

Fan Fink

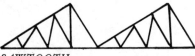

SAWTOOTH
This truss is generally
used to allow natural
lighting of large floor
areas.

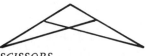

SCISSORS
This truss is usually used
for large, vaulted
ceilings.

*Three-hinged steel arch
(for spans of 125 feet
and over)*

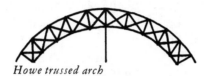

Howe trussed arch

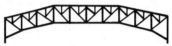

*Long-span subdivided
Pratt truss*

Howe (with counters)

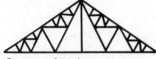

Warren with monitor

Bowstring

Compound Fink truss

Fink with verticals

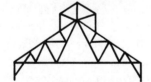

Fink with monitor

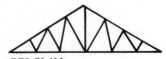

Crescent

*BELGIAN
The diagonals are
perpendicular to the top
chords.*

better suited to short, medium, or long spans. As a rule, the following maximum spans apply for various truss forms:

20 to 30 feet	king post (sometimes called "king rod") and queen rod
30 feet	Fink and cambered Fink
40 feet	fan and cambered fan
50 to 60 feet	compound Fink and cambered compound Fink
70 to 80 feet	compound fan and cambered compound fan
80 to 90 feet	Fink with subdivided panels

A few truss configurations—Pratt, flat Pratt, flat Warren, Howe (triangular), and flat Howe—could be used for spans from 20 to 80 feet by varying the number of panels. The cambered lower chord, incidentally, was used for the sake of appearance.

A long line of trusses with exposed horizontal chords appears to sag, an illusion overcome by cambering the lower chord. The cambered truss was used, also, for churches, railroad sheds, gymnasiums, and other structures where a more ornamental effect was desired. The chart above stops where it does because simple trusses were not considered practical for span lengths exceeding 100 feet. Longer spans called for a more economical alternative, and engineers turned their attention to the arch.

Some of the most dramatic and spectacular roof trusses are of the third roof-truss type: the arch. Great trussed arches, too, are to be found in huge train sheds of the nineteenth and of the early years of the twentieth century. Roof arches are designated in the same way as bridge arches, by the number of pins or hinges which support the arch at its abutments or fasten together arch segments. A hingeless arch is rigidly attached to its abutments without connecting pins, a two-hinged arch has one at each abutment, and a three-hinged arch has an additional hinge at the crown of the arch. Each of these may be classified, in turn, according to the construction, either as a "braced or trussed arch," which has open framework, or as a "ribbed arch," which is made of solid flat plates.

Many wooden arches are still extant. The great dome of the Salt Lake City Tabernacle (1864–67) is constructed entirely of lattice timber arches, providing a clear area 250 feet long and 150 feet wide. The intriguing fact about this arch is that while iron bolts are used at a few critical points, most of the connections are mortised, pinned, and wedged, and the timbers wrapped with rawhide ties to prevent splitting. Just recently, what is probably the earliest extant barrel-vault train-shed arch was discovered supporting the roof of the President Street Station in Baltimore. The arched

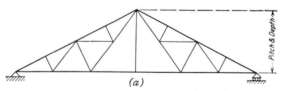

Fink truss with straight lower chord.

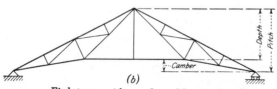

Fink truss with cambered lower chord.

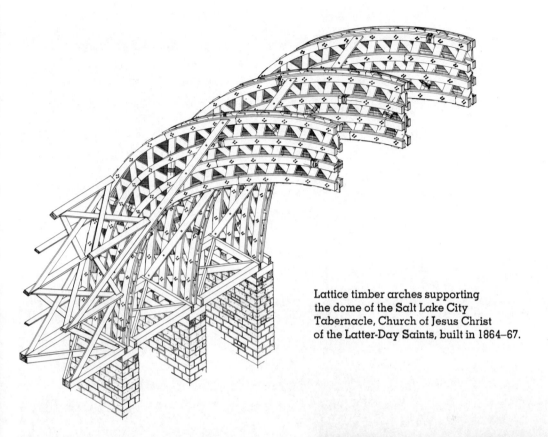

Lattice timber arches supporting
the dome of the Salt Lake City
Tabernacle, Church of Jesus Christ
of the Latter-Day Saints, built in 1864–67.

top and bottom chords are braced with
wooden diagonal struts and iron ties characteristic of the Howe truss. The two ends of the
arch that bear on the brick sidewalls of the station are tied together by a horizontal timber,
supported by vertical iron rods, or hangers,
coming down from the arch. This tie resists
the outward thrust of the arch and, in this case,
doubles as a girder, which carries the floor
joists of the attic. The arch would be interesting in itself, but it supports the roof of the earliest surviving (1849–50) metropolitan railroad station in all of North America.

Detail of Salt Lake City Tabernacle roof arch showing wedged pins (*center and upper right*), iron bolt
(*lower left*), and rawhide ties used to prevent further
splitting of the boards.

Atop the stack of the Nassawango Iron Furnace, Worchester County, Maryland, is a very early example of a hot-blast stove. This, furthermore, is one of the few bog-ore furnaces to be found anywhere in the United States and is probably the only such furnace in Maryland. The furnace was in operation from 1830 to 1849.

5. THE IRONMASTER'S GIFT

In the *New Jersey Gazette* of September 2, 1778, we read:

MOUNT-HOPE and HIBERNIA FURNACE
Are now in Blast;
Where all sorts of Hollow Ware, and other sand castings are made: SCYTHES, nails, cast iron kettles, pots, large and small skillets, small mortars, weights, griddles with or without legs, and-irons, smoothing irons, waggon, chair and cart boxes, close stoves, six and ten plate stoves, &c. &c. &c. To be SOLD for cash, or exchanged for any kind of country produce by me at Mount-Hope furnace, Morris County.
JOHN JACOB FAESH

Iron was once basic to American life. In the scarce-money days after the American Revolution, John Jacob Faesh and other ironmasters used iron as a kind of currency in exchange for the materials they needed to carry on business.

Iron was as much a part of the American scene of the 1800s as its derivative, steel, and a whole array of other metals are today. It provided entire communities with generations of livelihoods and names like Irondale, Washington; Iron City, Utah; Carbondale, Illinois; and Ironton in Minnesota, Wisconsin, Ohio, Missouri, and Alabama. Terms like "ironware," "iron horse," "iron clads," and, of course, "ironing" began to appear in conversations and new editions of dictionaries. Iron became the symbol of the American indus-

trial revolution—embraced, as Americans often do, as though it were our own. Now we think of it as a decorative metal, its usefulness in the American home confined to the kitchen and hearth. Yet well within memory of older generations of Americans is a world of iron, of storefronts and street lamps, bridges and school desks, steam tractors and plows, horseshoes and stoves, bathtubs and battleships.

If we could return to an early American city, village, or farm, we would rediscover the wonders of the furnace, foundry, and forge. Lifting our eyes to the rooftops, we would be greeted by a marvelous array of weathervanes—galloping horses, swans, trumpeting angels, roosters, peacocks, locomotives, birds, and fanciful serpents—cast in sand molds, cut from flat-iron sheets, or hammered to shape in iron molds or templates. Passing through the iron gate, fence, and trellis on one of the houses and announcing our arrival with the tap of an iron door knocker, our attention would certainly be drawn to the hand-wrought door strap hinges and footscraper. Inside, all the doors of the house and the hutches would be hung and latched with iron hardware. Giving warmth would be a ten-plate stove or perhaps a Franklin fireplace decorated with the popular cast-in patterns of the day: ships, flower and leaf motifs, peacocks, the shepherd, or the fox chase. Hanging from iron kettle hooks or sitting about the kitchen would be skillets, Dutch ovens, riddles (coarse sieves), waffle irons, bake plates, stew pans, and a teakettle—all of iron. Time was kept by iron clock weights; windows were counterbalanced with iron sash weights. Hollow ware and iron utensils filled the drawers and cupboards— and there, under the table, would be a child's toy horse and wagon reflecting in its every detail the molder's art. Iron binders steadied the brickwork of the chimney, and in the yard wheeled implements of iron would sit by the barn awaiting their turn in the fields.

The iron in the barn was hardworking. There were the familiar shoes for horses and oxen, the ox yoke with its iron fittings, and some unfamiliar blocks of wood through which passed an iron stirrup secured with wing nuts; these were "bog shoes," clamped onto the horse's hooves to act much like snowshoes, providing more support for the horse as it pulled the iron plow through soft, marshy soil. Iron hammers, knives, saws, a broadax or two, peat cutters, froes (cleating tools), splitting wedges, and a cow bell would hang on the wall. The iron letters and symbols attached to wooden handles would be sheep markers and branding irons for cattle, and the gracefully curved handwrought iron blades attached to wooden footholds, which hang from buckled leather straps in the corner, would be recognizable even today as ice skates.

At first, in the late 1700s and early 1800s, the articles cast at the furnace were mostly housewares like these and some anvils, hammers, wheels, and small castings for the farm and forge. But the records of the early ironworks began to reflect the quickening pace of American growth. In the 1820s and 1830s, the list of manufactures began to include more and more items for farm and industry, including mandrels, gudgeons (or trunnions), iron parts for windmills and pumps, wagon parts, plows, lathes, plaster mills, wheels and tires, "coulters" (or plow blades), rolling-mill castings, threshing-machine parts, and beams. A growing shipbuilding industry placed larger and more frequent orders for spikes, nails, rudder iron, and huge anchors weighing more than a thousand pounds. In the 1830s the first iron ships were built. In the next decade there would be orders for iron locomotive parts. Everywhere was the evidence of just how useful this most abundant of the earth's metals was to our ancestors.

Many of the furnaces, foundries, forges, rolling mills, and smithies from which these remarkable structures of iron came are still in the countryside, especially in the backcountry. The oldest, their foundations and casting floors buried and grown over long ago, await careful excavation by teams of trained archaeologists. But many others, built from the late 1700s on, are within the realm of the aboveground archaeologist. Hundreds of furnaces are known to have been built, and the number of forges and smithies must approach the number of small towns that there are in America. Virtually every little village had its blacksmith, who may himself have extracted small amounts of iron from ores gathered in nearby meadows and swamps. But the blacksmith, who wrought all manner of things from iron, and the farrier, whose specialty was shoeing, were usually consumers rather than producers of iron, obtaining pigs or bars from local furnaces and bloomeries. In his book *Pennsyl-*

Left: Wharton Furnace, built in 1839, repaired in 1962. Fayette County, Pennsylvania. *Below:* Valley Furnace, built in 1850 by L. C. Hall and Company. Westmoreland County, Pennsylvania.

Below: Mt. Etna Furnace, built in 1808 by Canon, Stewart and Moore. Blair County, Pennsylvania. *Right:* Castle Rock Furnace, built in 1836 by Cross and Hoge. Venango County, Pennsylvania.

Above: Ross Furnace, built in 1815 by Meason, Mathiot and Paull. Westmoreland County, Pennsylvania. *Right:* Buena Vista Furnace, built in 1847 by McClelland and Company. Indiana County, Pennsylvania.

vania Iron Manufacture in the Eighteenth Century, Arthur Bining lists the names and locations of over 170 ironworks, furnaces, and forges operating in the state between 1716 and 1800. Myron B. Sharp and William H. Thomas visited over 160 furnaces in nineteen Pennsylvania counties and described how to get to each one in *A Guide to the Old Stone Blast Furnaces in Western Pennsylvania.* In Clarion County alone they found 30 furnaces, in Venango County 25, and 20 in Fayette County, in which three counties most of the furnaces built before 1810, and the Alliance furnace— the first west of the Alleghenies—are to be found. The whereabouts of perhaps a hundred furnace and forge sites in New Jersey is known. Many more are scattered throughout New England.

But the mining, smelting, and working of iron were not confined to just a few coun-

ties in the Eastern states. In recent years we've come to associate iron- and, later, steel-making with one state in particular: Pennsylvania. It is true that more furnaces have been built there over the years than in any other state and that in the 1890s Pennsylvania, along with Ohio and Illinois, already produced most of the country's iron—ninety percent of it, in fact. But this can be misleading. The story of iron, in one or more of its aspects, is to be found in every part of the country.

The earliest dates in the history of American ironmaking will, of course, be found in New England and in New York, New Jersey, Pennsylvania, Delaware, and Maryland. But directories of ironworks and

Left: Victory Furnace, built in 1843. Venango County, Pennsylvania. *Above:* Laurel Hill Furnace, built in 1845 by Reed, Gallagher and Hale. Westmoreland County, Pennsylvania.

steelworks from the 1800s show that there were also furnaces in blast at one time or another in Virginia, West Virginia, Kentucky, Tennessee, North Carolina, South Carolina, Georgia, Texas, Ohio, Illinois, Indiana, Michigan, Wisconsin, Minnesota, Missouri, Colorado, Washington, and Oregon. At least two charcoal furnaces were built in Utah: a small one (19 feet high and 4 feet wide at the boshes) at Iron City, Iron County (1873), and a larger one at Ogden City (1875). California's first furnace wasn't built until 1884, but rolling mills producing rails, bar iron, angle iron, and shafting went into operation in 1868. In Arkansas, accounts dating to the time around the Civil War tell of iron ore being picked up off the ground in

Howard County, smelted in a blacksmith's forge, and hammered into horseshoe nails. There were early rolling mills at Burlington, Iowa (1885), and at Rosedale and Topeka, Kansas (1874–75); a cut-nail factory at Omaha, Nebraska (but the machinery was moved to St. Joseph, Missouri, in 1888); and the Union Pacific Railroad Company built a rolling mill at Laramie City, Wyoming (1874). The first furnace in Canada was erected at the St. Maurice, Quebec, works in 1737, and at the time of its abandonment in 1883, it was the oldest furnace still in blast in all of North America.

A second important center of ironmaking in the 1800s was at Birmingham, where extraordinary deposits of iron ore, coal, and limestone stretched through Alabama and eastern Tennessee. The first furnaces there were built by early immigrants from Scotland

Furnace and Cold-Blast Bellows (c. 1750)

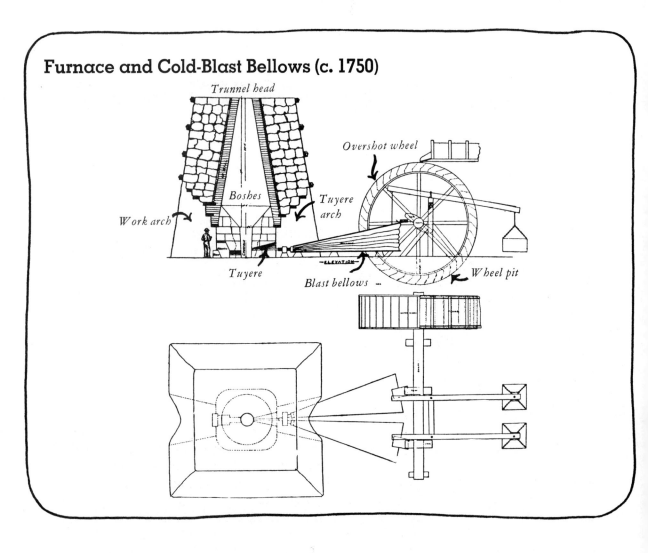

Trunnel head

Overshot wheel

Boshes

Tuyere arch

Work arch

Tuyere

Blast bellows

Wheel pit

and Ireland, and over the century the number of furnaces grew to meet the increasing demands of the agricultural South for blast-furnace products. The census of 1890 shows Alabama to be second only to Michigan in the raising of iron ore (Pennsylvania was third). That year there were twenty coke furnaces in Birmingham and others at Anniston (three), Rome, Georgia (one), Shelby (two), Ironton (five), Tuscaloosa (two), Montgomery (one), and three in the vicinity of what is now Gadsden along the banks of the Coosa River.

Eight more furnaces were clustered in the very northwestern corner of Alabama, where, in 1890, there were as yet no settlements large enough to appear on the map. Sheffield is there now. Just to the north and east of Alabama, at Chattanooga, Tennessee, were nine more furnaces. Ten years later, at the turn of the century, there were forty furnaces in blast at Birmingham. Today, one of the oldest of Alabama's furnaces, Tannehill Furnace Number 1, built in 1855, has not only been restored in its setting at Tannehill State Park southwest of Birmingham, but has been put into blast again on occasion (usually the Fourth of July) to produce iron for cannon and 12-pound shot just as it did in 1865, when it was captured by the Eighth Iowa Cavalry.

If the record of iron production in Alabama and the widespread distribution of furnaces and forges around the country surprise you, this might well be cause enough to start looking into the history of iron in your own state or community. In states where ironmaking or coal mining have been dominant historical and economic factors, there is no paucity of literature on the subject, and considerable awareness of the history there; the studies of ironmaking in Pennsylvania and New Jersey are one example. Other restorations, such as that at Tannehill Number 1, are beginning to happen more frequently now, one instance being the beautiful reconstruction of the Buckeye charcoal furnace and the nineteenth-century village which surrounded it near Jackson, Ohio, in the heart of the Hanging Rock iron region. But who will find the old furnaces and forges in *your* town and spark an awareness of their history? That chapter in the history of iron awaits a historian, who just might be you.

In the *Pennsylvania Journal* of January 11, 1743, we find:

TO BE SOLD A good substantial Furnace, for making Sows and Pigs of Iron, with Utensils fitting to work the same, and a large Forge with good Brick and Stone Chimneys, well compleated for two Finerys and Chaffert, for Manufacturing the Sows and Pigs into Bar Iron, with necessarys for carrying on the same; all Scituate and being about a Quarter of a Mile from a good Grist Mill, Saw Mill, and Fulling Mill: Which is in the Town of Mount Holly, in the County of Burlington, in the Western Division of the Province of New Jersey and is built on a good constant Stream of Water 27 miles from Philadelphia, and is Water Carriage within 3 or 4 Rods of the Furnace and Forge, with plenty of Wood at a small distance for making of Charcoal and good Coal Houses and Smiths Shop . . . Also a good Iron Mine which makes the Toughest and best Bar Iron, about 18 Miles Distance, all Water Carriage except one Mile and a Quarter, a good Road and a great Quantity of cold short Mine, about 4 Miles Distant from the Works; a good Road without Hill in the way, and this is exceedingly good for potting of any sort of Cast ware.

The furnace is the heart of the ironworks, and of all the structures there, it is the most enduring. It was there that iron was made in a simple operation, which remains essentially the same to the present day. Inside the stone furnace, iron ore is heated in burning charcoal until the metal becomes molten, separates from the earth and rock in which it is found, and trickles down into the hearth. There it collects and is kept molten until the founder lets it out. To this mixture of charcoal and ore is also added a "flux," usually limestone, which helps the liquid iron separate and flow freely from the rock, charcoal, and other impurities. These appear at the hearth as "slag," which, because it is lighter than iron, floats on the top of the molten mass, where it can be drawn off before the iron is let out. Oxygen for the burning mixture is forced in at the bottom of the furnace and exhausts through the open stack at the top. The ironmaster or furnace manager can adjust this "blast" to control the temperature inside the furnace. The pressure of the blast is created by a blast machine, originally nothing more than a huge fireplace bellows. Early blast machines were powered by waterwheels, later replaced by steam engines. Beginning sometime in the 1830s, the blast itself was heated to further increase the efficiency of the furnace. The usual method was to conduct the blast through iron pipes to a hot blast stove at the furnace exhaust, and then to the furnace. The blast entered the furnace through conical nozzles called "tuyeres," which could be moved to adjust the direction of the blast inside the furnace. Much of the work of ironmaking, therefore, was cutting wood, making charcoal, mining or collecting iron ore and limestone, crushing the ore and flux, and bringing the mixture together in the furnace in the right proportions and at an optimum temperature.

Around the furnaces were clustered entire communities, and in the early days these were actually called "iron plantations." Ironworks needed to be near water and raw materials, a forest for charcoal, limestone for flux and iron ore and, therefore, were more often than not built deep into the backcountry. Yet during the nine or ten months that the furnace was in blast, and while repair work was under way after the furnace had been blown out, hundreds of workers were needed. At Hopewell Village, Pennsylvania, in the 1850s, between two hundred and two hundred and fifty workers were on the payroll, who, with their families, made up a settlement of considerable size in the wilderness, perhaps five or six hundred. In addition to the woodcutters, colliers, miners, molders, founders, patternmakers and their helpers—all of whom were closest to the ironmaking—were many others who lived in the community. At Hopewell, besides miscellaneous laborers, we find listed on the company rolls: cabinetmakers, carpenters, masons, clerks, farmworkers, gardeners, makers of boxes and baskets, teamsters, wheelwrights, splitters of posts and rails, and a tutor. Lodging was provided for workers and their families near the furnace, and for others several miles away near their work at the mines, the charcoal "hearths" (or "pits"), or the woodlot. As part of the ironworks there were barns, company stores, springhouses, smithies, a school, a church, housing for itinerant and permanent workers, a carpenter's shop, forges, saw and grist mills, and the casting house. Life was complete here. Some of the workers at furnaces in the Hanging Rock region of Ohio lived there all their lives without ever visiting the nearest towns (which were usually some distance away), working forty-five, fifty-five, and, in the case of one man, sixty-five years at the same ironworks.

From these buildings we can reconstruct the home life and daily activities of the workers, wives, and children of an ironworks village. Of the work that was done here much is to be learned, too. Clues are everywhere; though, of course, not the same ones in every instance. We might find the charcoal house and other stone buildings. If the blast machinery and waterwheels long ago turned to dust, traces might still remain of the wheelpit, dam, millrace, and tailrace. A retaining wall at the top of the hill behind the furnace marks the charging terrace, or bench; a crumbling masonry abutment, the charging bridge. A roadbed of rotted ties and rusted rails or perhaps a tramway may be nearby. Cast-iron pipe that once carried the blast from the blast machinery to the furnace may be lying about.

Hot-Blast Furnace (c. 1851)

Blast air passed through the stove before it reached the tuyeres. The iron pipe carrying the blast air to the tuyere on the opposite side was usually laid under the bottom stone.

From blast engine

Hot-blast stove at base of blast furnace

Left and below: sections and end views of round- and flat-bottom water tuyeres

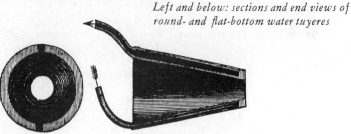

Round- and flat-bottom water tuyeres were made of boiler plate, forming hollow walls through which cold water circulated to cool the tuyere. Round tuyeres were used in anthracite, coke, and most charcoal furnaces. The flat-bottom tuyere was used for the Catalan forge, finery, German forge, and sometimes the charcoal blast furnace. Some tuyeres were fabricated of copper, brass, or cast iron.

Diameter of narrow end:
Anthracite and coke
4–4½"
Charcoal 2"

At the top of the Eliza furnace in Cambria County, Pennsylvania, can be seen—still in position—the iron heat exchanger, or hot-blast stove. Even the slag and cinder piles deserve our careful attention, for here we'll find clues to the fuel burned in the furnace (charcoal or coal) and the kind of iron produced in its hearth. The size of the slag heap gives us some idea of the length of a furnace's life—whether it was "blown out" after only a few years or after a century of operation. And there's always the possibility of finding dis-

Buckeye Furnace (1851)

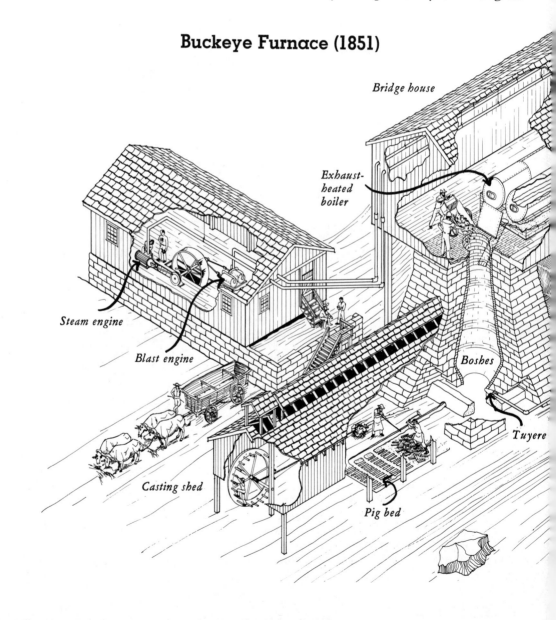

Bridge house

Exhaust-heated boiler

Steam engine

Blast engine

Boshes

Tuyere

Casting shed

Pig bed

*Heat exchanger,
or hot-blast stove*

*Charging terrace
(bench)*

carded pieces of the furnace product: a broken piece of a skillet, a stove plate with the founder's very special design cast in, or perhaps a pig (an oblong chunk of iron) into which has been cast the name of the furnace or even the date, as was often the practice.

Furnaces differ, one from another, in the details of construction, but not in any fundamental way. Because of this we can look at a typical furnace and use what we've learned as a means to interpret almost any other furnace we may encounter.

Our model is the Buckeye furnace, built in 1851 and typical of the furnaces of the mid-1800s. The furnace is shown at the center of the accompanying drawing. On top of the furnace and reaching across to the "bench" is the "bridge house," which provides shelter for the fillers working in inclement weather and for the heat exchanger, which uses the exhaust from the furnace to heat the blast. Below are the shed enclosing the steam-driven blast machines and the "casting shed" sheltering the "pig bed," or casting floor. These are the basic structures of any ironworks, and their position in this drawing helps us to locate at least their traces around an old furnace.

The iron furnace consists of an inner and outer wall enclosing the space in which smelting takes place. Any kind of stone would do for the outer wall, usually the closest at hand. We are most likely to find sandstone blocks; but granite, graywacke (from the German *Grauwache,* a kind of dark gray sandstone containing shale), and slate were also used a lot. The choice of materials for the "in wall" or "lining," however, was crucial. The early ironmasters preferred fine-grained white limestone. Later in the 1800s, furnaces were lined or relined with firebrick, but in either case the material chosen had to withstand the intense heat of the smelting process without cracking or crumbling. Firebrick was not always available and was more expensive than sandstone, but it could be easily molded into the required curvature and bevel. Stone, on the other hand, had to be painstakingly cut and dressed to shape. Between the lining and the rough outer wall there is a space of about 8 inches, which was filled with stone chips or broken furnace cinders. This space allowed

the lining to expand and contract with changes in temperature. One look inside a dilapidated furnace is all you need to appreciate the skills of the early American stonecutters and masons, who were hired to build the furnace walls and then stayed on to carry out necessary repair work on the lining after each period of blast.

The shape of the Buckeye furnace shaft is typical, too. At the top of the furnace is an opening called the "throat," or "trunnel head." Into this opening the fillers dumped

Charcoal Furnace Hearth and Ground Plan

A cross section through the work arch shows the construction of the hearth and boshes.

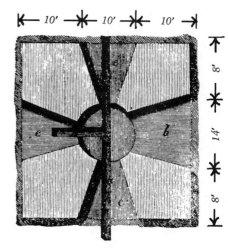

Ground plan for furnace foundation (three tuyeres)

(a) Bottom stone   Hearth:
(b) Damstone   Height (from base to boshes) 5'6"
(c) Side stones   Width at bottom 24"
(d) Tuyere stones   Width at top 36"
(e) Topstone
(f) Tuyere holes   Boshes:
(g) Timpstone   Diameter 9'6"
(h) Back stone   Slope 60°

(a, a) Channel for blast pipes
(b) Work arch
(c, c, c) Tuyere arches

basket or wheelbarrow loads of iron ore, charcoal, and limestone, as called for by the furnace manager. From the trunnel head the diameter of the shaft increases to a point about two-thirds of the way down, where it reaches its greatest diameter, and then tapers inward and downward to form a small opening just above the hearth. This area is called the "bosh," and its purpose is to support the furnace burden weighing many tons, at the same time funneling the molten iron and slag down into the crucible of the hearth. Below

is a section through the furnace hearth, showing its construction.

Determining the taper of the shaft, bosh, and crucible was part of the ironmaster's "gift," derived from years of experience with all kinds of ores, fluxes, and charcoal. The kind of ore to be smelted, whether the charcoal was made from hard or soft woods, and the kind of iron desired at the hearth—all influenced his decision. Where either hydrates or oxides of iron were to be smelted, as was most often the case in American fur-

Details of Two Charcoal Furnaces (c. 1851)

The proportions and dimensions of the hearth, boshes, and stack of a charcoal furnace depended on the fuel (hard- or soft-wood charcoal) and ore available. Here are the interiors of two typical furnaces. The charcoal consumption of these furnaces was considered good.

Other furnaces required as much as 300 bushels of charcoal to produce one ton of iron. Both of these furnaces produced gray pig iron.

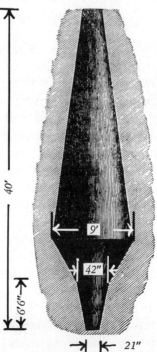

Local magnetic ores, brown hematite, and some bog ore were smelted in this furnace. To produce one ton of iron in this furnace required two and one-third tons of ore and 150 bushels of charcoal.

To produce one ton of iron, from rich ores, required two and one-half tons of ore and 180 bushels of charcoal. Furnaces like this one are also found west of the Allegheny Mountains, particularly in Tennessee.

Eastern Pennsylvania furnace

Cold Spring, New York, furnace

naces, a uniform, almost straight-sided stack was called for. Furnaces found to have round, concave boshes and generally oval interiors were probably built for smelting soft bog ores. If the charcoal was coarse and the ore was in large chunks, a stack as tall as 40 or 50 feet might be built; stacks for powdery charcoal and soft ore would have to be smaller. If gray iron was desired at the hearth (the kind of iron used for fine castings), the furnace shaft would be somewhat greater in diameter throughout in proportion to its height. White iron, used in the forge and rolling mill, might require a narrower, taller crucible. Generally, 40 feet was the maximum height for a charcoal furnace of this vintage, a figure based on years of experience. If the ironmaster wished to have a furnace of larger capacity, he would more than likely have increased the diameter of the stack and bosh rather than increased the height beyond this rule-of-thumb limit.

Atop Buckeye is a bridge house, or "top house" as it was sometimes called. The term "bridge house" reflects the evolution of this structure. In its earliest form it was indeed nothing more than a timber bridge between the top of the furnace and the bench. Here there might be a small shed built to hold the night and Sunday stock, as well as the straw pallets upon which the fillers might catch, as best they could, a few hours' rest as the furnace remained in blast throughout months of day and night shifts. The bridge eventually acquired a fence and still later a windscreen which, with the simple addition of a roof, became a bridge house, such as that at Buckeye.

Let's return in spirit to Buckeye and look in on the activities of the casting house (the shed covering the work arch) and the casting floor. It's five o'clock in the morning, about eleven hours since the cast last evening—six o'clock in the morning and six in the evening were the times customarily set aside for casting so that each twelve-hour shift had its cast. There is an air of expectancy about, heightened by the increased activity in the work arch and on the casting floor. The founder and his helpers are moving around quickly in the heat of the arch. The position of the tuyeres, those nozzles that carry the blast into the furnace, must be checked, as well as the blast, in order to make sure the crucible and hearth are just the right temperature. Against the furnace's roar can be heard the ringing of the cinder hooks striking the stone and iron plates of the hearth as slag is drawn off over the damstone. The time is near for the iron to be let out. On the casting floor, preparation of the pig bed is under way. The keeper and his helper, the "second keeper," have cut the runners into the sand casting floor leading from just in front of the hearth to large oblong depressions, each of which is connected to several smaller depressions. The large "sow" molds and smaller "pigs" are formed in the sand with a pattern of mahogany or some other hardwood. On the rounded pattern has been carved the name of the furnace and the year. These will appear in raised lettering on the iron pigs and sows, an early form of advertising that has become a help to historians. Again the founder checks the cinder, and a shout muffled by the din sends two helpers scurrying to the tuyeres and the blast machines. The iron must be let out at precisely the right time. If the molten metal stays in the hearth too long, its qualities can change and the furnace might be damaged.

It's time; the founder looks around to

make sure all is in readiness. Workers stand in their positions around the casting floor. The founder breaks out the clay plug, and a white-hot ribbon of molten iron darts across the bottom stone and into the runner, sputtering as it hits the damp sand. The workers urge the running metal along with iron rods. The iron seems to stop as the sows fill, but then it is moving again into each pig. The keeper has done his work well, for just as the glowing pigs and sows seem about to overflow the sand molds, slag appears at the taphole, riding atop the last of the iron leaving the hearth. In an instant the founder is working at the empty hearth, chipping the slag out of the corners and off the sides of the hearthstones with his long iron ringer. This done, he scrapes the nose, or lower end, of the burden protruding into the now-empty hearth and replaces the plug in preparation for the next casting.

If the blast is going well, the metal on the casting floor will be gray and remain liquid for some time yet. The pig bed would now remind the modern viewer of the plastic parts which come in various model kits (for airplanes, boats, cars, etc.), each little piece attached by a stalk to a central shaft, or "gate" as the founder would call it. After the iron has cooled, the pigs are broken off the sows, weighed, and placed in a waiting cart. The metal in the runners and whatever was spilled during the cast is gathered up, broken into small pieces, and thrown into a barrel. (The quality of this "gate metal" is as good as that in the pigs and sows, but it is less convenient to handle and, since it will require remelting at the foundry, it will sell for a bit less.) This done, the cinders will be loaded on a cart and dumped on the slag pile nearby. The sand of the casting floor will be dug up, wetted, and smoothed out with rakes in preparation for the next cast that evening.

Again and again, this scene will be repeated over the several months the furnace is in blast, until, finally, when the winter ice jams the waterwheel or the lining needs repair, the furnace will be blown out.

This scene changed little over the next few decades. Efficiency and furnace capacities would improve in later years, to be sure, but not necessarily quality; the well-designed and well-managed furnace of this era produced superb iron. Charcoal would be replaced almost entirely by coke and coal by 1910. Conveyors would replace the bench, charging bridge, and bridge house just as steam engines were already replacing the waterwheel. There would be refinements in hot-blast machinery, heat exchangers, and tuyeres. The shape and proportions of the stack, bosh, and hearth would change to suit the new fuels and to support heavier and heavier burdens. More tuyeres would be added, and a bell hopper at the trunnel head. Furnaces would grow to 80 feet and more by 1900, compared to the 30- to 35-foot stacks of the time. But even with these and more recent developments, the steel-shelled, refractory lined furnaces of today are easily recognized as direct descendants of the charcoal-fired stone and brick ancestors of the 1800s.

The form of the blast furnace is determined simply by its function, yet outwardly there is considerable variation in style. While it sounds strange today, it is perfectly proper to refer to the "style" of an old blast furnace. There is every reason to believe that America's early ironmasters and builders were con-

Development of the Hot-Blast Furnace

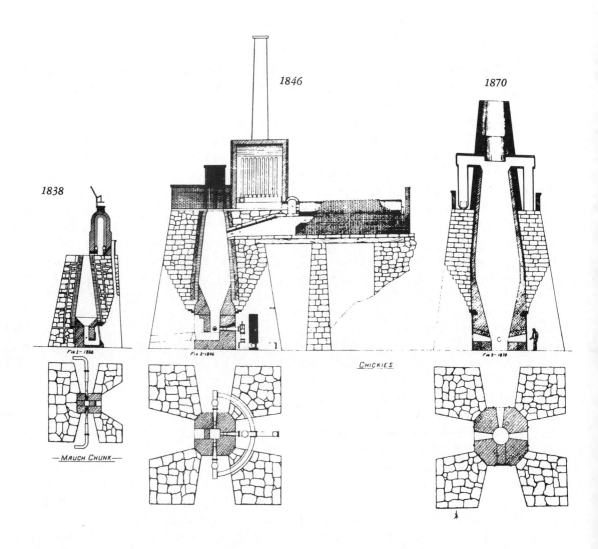

1838

1846

1870

Fig.1 - 1838

Fig 2 -1846

Fig 3 - 1870

CHICKIES.

MAUCH CHUNK

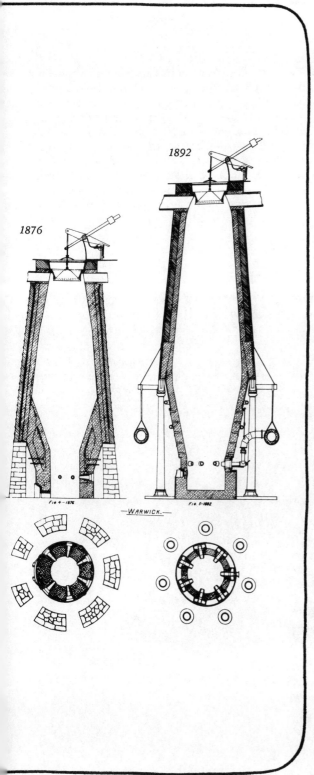

1892

1876

Fig 4 -1876

—WARWICK.—

Fig 5-1892

cerned with architectural aspects, at least to the extent of good workmanship.

Sometimes architectural differences reflected custom. The earliest ironmasters were from Scotland, England, Ireland, Wales, Germany, France, and elsewhere, and the furnaces they built here were most likely modeled after those they had built or worked in their country of origin. Other stylistic differences clearly had more to do with personal tastes and the conscious choice of a pleasing form over the less expensive utilitarian one which was all that was really called for. Treatises of the day noted the fact that it was the interior that was the principal consideration, and pointed to the "rude" furnaces in the western states—Ohio, Illinois, Tennessee, Kentucky, Missouri, Indiana, Michigan, Wisconsin, Minnesota—west of the Alleghenies, that is: furnaces of rough stones bound and held together by wooden logs that produced iron "as efficiently as the finest stack built of hewn stones or bricks." Many furnaces remain today masterpieces of the stonecutter's and mason's art, each piece cut, faced, and set so precisely. Indeed, furnaces of this era were less machinery than permanent architectural structures. They remained in blast, often, for fifty, seventy, eighty years, and longer, cared for by the original ironmaster, his sons, and his grandsons.

In its most usual form, the charcoal furnace of the early 1800s was square in plan, tapering from the base to the top, its four pillars joined by semicircular or triangular arches. But, as anyone who has visited several furnace sites even in the same county knows, there is nothing "usual" about many furnaces. Since to date the inventory of furnaces in Pennsylvania is the most complete, we might look there for some examples.

A Charcoal Furnace (c. 1851)

The outward form of furnaces of the mid-nineteenth century varied greatly, reflecting the builder's taste and regional style. But the general principles of construction had been established by c. 1851, and dimensions varied only slightly—according to the kind of charcoal and ore used in the furnace. The following dimensions are typical: height, 35 feet; width at base, 30 feet; width at top, 15 to 16 feet; trunnel-head (throat) opening, 20 inches to 4 feet. Charcoal and coal furnaces can be distinguished by the glaze on their hearth surfaces. Charcoal furnaces have a white glaze, which has been produced by the alkalies in wood ashes; coal furnaces have a black glaze, a result of the heating of iron and sulphur. Building stone and brick varied with a furnace's location, but sandstone, granite, and slate were the most common. Graywacke, a conglomerate, came into use after 1850.

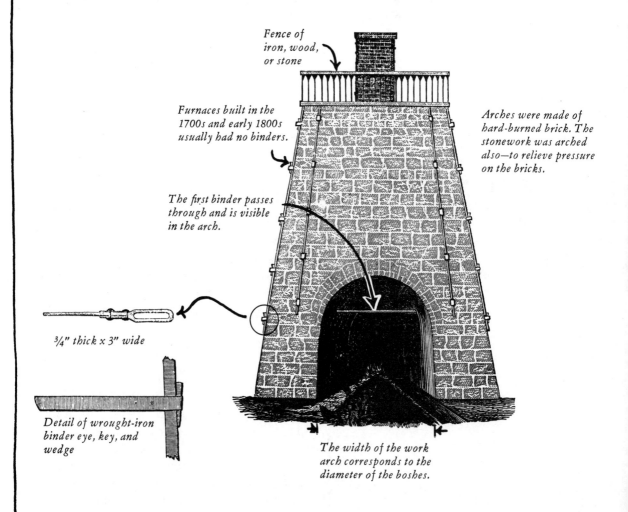

Fence of iron, wood, or stone

Furnaces built in the 1700s and early 1800s usually had no binders.

The first binder passes through and is visible in the arch.

Arches were made of hard-burned brick. The stonework was arched also—to relieve pressure on the bricks.

¾" thick x 3" wide

Detail of wrought-iron binder eye, key, and wedge

The width of the work arch corresponds to the diameter of the boshes.

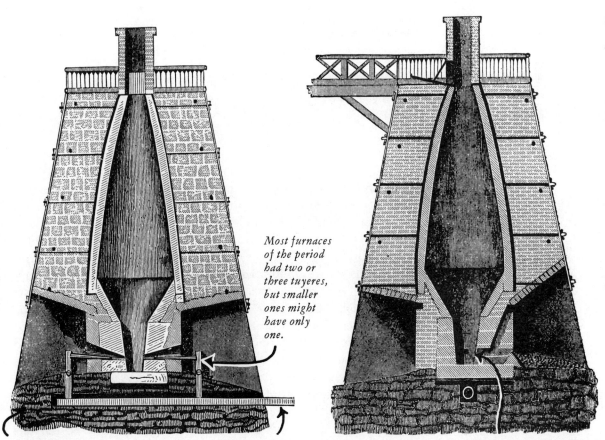

Most furnaces of the period had two or three tuyeres, but smaller ones might have only one.

The foundation stones were set without mortar—to allow moisture to pass through.

Sheet-iron or cast-iron pipes laid below the bottom stone conducted the blast from the blast machine to the tuyeres.

The hearth of charcoal furnaces was generally narrow and high.

SECTION THROUGH TUYERE ARCHES

SECTION THROUGH WORK ARCH

Instead of tapering, Wilroy furnace (Lawrence County) reduces in section in four setbacks or tiers, the smallest and uppermost forming the stack. A few, such as Canoe furnace (Blair County), were round; and Webster furnace (Venango County) is square at the base, but after the first twelve courses of stone it becomes neatly octagonal. The very little that remains of Forest furnace (Forest County) indicates that it was probably round at the back and square in front, the only such form found in Pennsylvania to date. Many of the furnaces of this region and in the South—Tannehill being an example there—were built with corbeled arches. These would be less expensive to build since there is no need to cut special stones for the arch, and there is no reason for centering the temporary wooden scaffolding that supports the arch until it is complete and self-support-

ing. In the corbeled arch each soffit (ceiling) stone projects inward about a quarter of its length beyond the stone below. Ross furnace (Westmoreland County) has two corbeled arches and two semicircular arches. But here, instead of the sloping sides of the arch beginning at the bottom course, the first five or six courses of stone are plumb one upon the other; then the triangular arch begins. Such an arrangement provides more shoulder and head room, but in this instance it also makes a more pleasing arrangement with the semicircular arches beginning the same number of courses above the ground. It is these kinds of little touches, so inconsequential to the furnaces' function but affording such pleasure to the eye, that to me reflect the ironmaster's and mason's mind. Without these well-turned and proportioned arches, the metal flowing from the hearth would be as fine and as

profitable as any, but as much as the structure was a smelting furnace it was also a monument to the ironmaster himself.

The first and most important consideration was the choice of location for a new furnace. Since there was no efficient means of shipping the great quantities of raw materials needed, it was essential that sources of ore and limestone and—most important—forests for charcoal be close at hand.

Furnaces consumed enormous amounts of charcoal, or "coal" as it was called then. A typical furnace built in the 1700s consumed about 800 bushels of charcoal every twenty-four hours. Getting this amount of charcoal required the charring of about twenty-five cords of wood, or an entire acre of timber—all of which produced perhaps 2 tons of iron. A large furnace might use five to six thousand cords during the nine or ten months it was in blast each year, the yield of about 250 acres of woodland. Among the interesting facts in Charles S. Boyer's *Early Forges and Furnaces in New Jersey* are the recollections of old-timers of the Pine Belt on managing woodlands for a blast furnace. They told him that 20,000 acres of pine forest, divided into sections of 1000 acres each, were required to keep one bog-ore furnace in operation. Each section provided enough charcoal for one season's blast, so that by the time the last 1000-acre section was cut, a twenty-year growth stood on the first section cut, and the cutting started anew. Engaging in an exemplary bit of reconstruction archaeology, Boyer inquired of the New Jersey State Forester if this were indeed possible. Yes, was the answer. Assuming that the charcoal burner, or collier, could

Blast Machines (c. 1800 until 1900)

BELLOWS

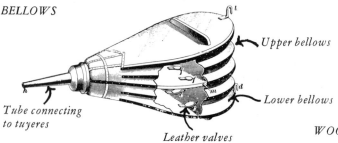

Upper bellows

Lower bellows

Tube connecting
to tuyeres

Leather valves

WOODEN BLAST MACHINE

The sides of the cylinder
were slippery with soap,
stone powder, and water.

Receiver

Hemp packing

Some machines were
built with square tubs.

Tubs of
ash or
dry pine,
4' x 4'

Sheet-iron pip[e]
carried the bla[st]
to the furnace
tuyeres.

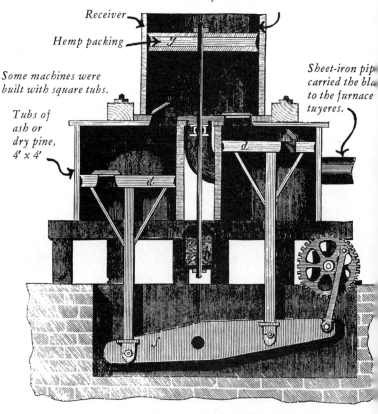

The packing for an iron-
cylinder blast machine
was made of hemp or
leather tube filled with
horsehair. Later, a
wrought-iron piston
"ring" was used.

Pine wood

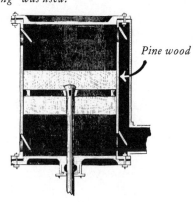

IRON CYLINDER

The wooden blast machine was driven by a waterwheel
or steam engine. It provided blast for a furnace or for
four or five forge fires. An even pressure was maintained
by a piston in the receiver, connected by an iron rod to a
box filled with iron and stones.

VERTICAL IRON-CYLINDER BLAST MACHINE

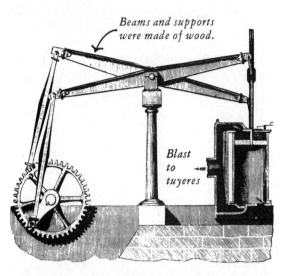

Beams and supports were made of wood.

Blast to tuyeres

The cylinders, pistons, pipes, valves, gears, and cranks of the vertical iron-cylinder blast machine were of iron.

FAN BLAST MACHINE (c. 1850)

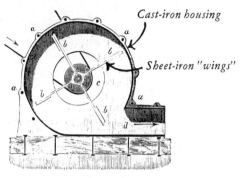

Cast-iron housing

Sheet-iron "wings"

The fan blast machine was used on anthracite furnaces, as well as on puddling and cupola furnaces. Its width was from 6 to 20 inches.

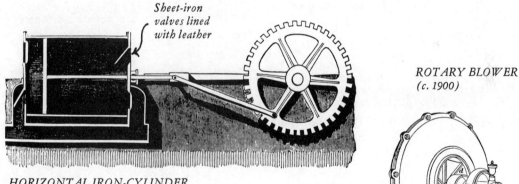

Sheet-iron valves lined with leather

ROTARY BLOWER (c. 1900)

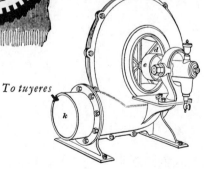

To tuyeres

HORIZONTAL IRON-CYLINDER BLAST MACHINE

The horizontal iron-cylinder blast machine was considered less desirable than the vertical because of the uneven distribution of its piston weight on the bottom of the cylinder and packing.

The rotary blower was a later version of the fan blast machine.

use cordwood ranging from 7 to 12 inches in diameter, the south Jersey pinelands could provide a cutting crop of charcoal wood every twenty years. Pine, of course, is less desirable than dense, fine-grained hardwoods like hickory—considered the best for charcoal. But along with white and black oak, ash, and chestnut, pine was used to fire American furnaces for over a century.

The land was covered with forests then. Wood was cheaper than coal and, besides, the forests needed to be cleared for pasturage and farmland anyway, making charcoal the favorite fuel of American ironmasters long after coal and coke were being used in England. As late as 1910, fifty-six charcoal furnaces were still in blast, about half of them in Michigan, Ohio, Alabama, and Texas, and others were being built. Most of these had had a long history, going back nearly a century. Here, for instance, are the histories of two furnaces still operating in the first decade of this century:

Dover Iron Company, Bear Spring, Stewart County [Tennessee]. Two stacks; one stack built in 1828, abandoned in 1834, rebuilt in 1854 and 1873, again abandoned about 1880, and again rebuilt in 1902–3; blown in February, 1903; partly destroyed by fire in August 1903; rebuilt in 1902–4; present size, 36½ × 9. Charcoal pits and kilns connected with the furnaces have an annual capacity of 1,200,000 bushels.

Bloom Furnace, The Clare Iron Company, Bloom Switch, Scioto County [Ohio]. One stack, 35 × 10, built in 1832 and rebuilt in 1846; burned December 7, 1887, and rebuilt in the spring of 1888; again rebuilt in 1901 [still in blast in 1904]. Charcoal pits with an annual capacity of 200,000 bushels are connected with the furnace.

A second but concomitant consideration in locating a furnace was the presence of a creek, river, or spring. From these the Crum Creek, Boiling Springs, Licking Creek, and French Creek furnaces and hundreds of other ironworks took their names as well as the waterpower to drive their blast machines. Ironmasters made the best use of whatever water they could find. S. G. Hermelin, who traveled around America in 1783 visiting mines and ironworks, observed that

At most of these blast furnaces there is no other water supply than from small brooks and springs, which is conveyed to a dam between the mountain heights, where the water goes to the blast furnace wheel, partly by [means of] a ditch and partly through a groove made of hollowed out tree trunks and also through wooden pipes. At most blast furnaces there are overshots for the wheels, which have a diameter of forty-four feet and can therefor be driven by a small amount of water.

Hermelin must have also watched the huge double bellows that provided blast for the single tuyere, or nozzle, of these early furnaces. They looked just like the traditional hand bellows that hung next to the hearth of every home a century and more ago, except that these were 25 feet long and several feet wide, made of wood and leather, and driven by immense waterwheels. Beginning at about the time of the American Revolution, however, the double-cylinder "blowing tub" was replacing the bellows. This machine consisted of two wooden cylinders placed side by side, inside of which were close-fitting pistons joined by connecting rods. As one piston moved down, drawing in air, the other

Carrick Furnace, and a cold-blast engine at Metal, Franklin County, Pennsylvania. The furnace was built in 1828 and blown out for the last time in 1884.

moved up, forcing air into the blast pipe. A later refinement was the addition of a third tub, or "dry receiver," in which floated a weighted piston. Air forced into this cylinder by the other two was kept at a reasonably constant pressure and made for a more constant and uniform blast at the tuyeres.

With the requisite timber and water-power at hand, the ironmaster could now choose the exact site for the furnace. Most often, the furnace would be situated next to a hill, the crest of which would be about the same height as the furnace. This made it possible for fillers to carry the raw materials in baskets or wheelbarrows directly from the bench to the top of the furnace and the opening, or trunnel head. A road or, in some instances, a tramway would be run from the base to the top of the hill, allowing for delivery of large loads of ore, limestone, and charcoal by cart or tramcar. Hills were not always exactly where you wanted them, of course, or

Blowing engine at the Carrick Furnace; it was built by Weimer Bros., Lebanon, Pennsylvania, in 1879. Steam was provided by the two under-fired boilers just behind the engine.

sometimes not available at all. In the flatlands of western New Jersey, it was necessary to build a long inclined ramp to the top of the stack, and upon which the fillers ran wheelbarrows. Otherwise, the practice of locating furnaces up against hills was widespread. After visiting over 170 furnaces in western Pennsylvania, Sharp and Thomas found only one exception to this practice, and an ingenious one at that. Lawrence furnace was not built in front of a cliff face but cut into it! Starting a few feet behind the edge of the cliff, a well was dug parallel and equal in depth to the face of the cliff, forming the stack, boshes, and hearth. Then another hole was dug down at the base of the cliff face, joining the hole dug from above. This became the work arch. The hole was then lined with firebrick, completing a furnace that was more an excavation than a structure. The furnace was simply fed from above as usual, except that the trunnel head was a hole in the ground. Two similar furnaces are known to have been built in Greenup County, Kentucky, and Lawrence County, Ohio, in the Hanging Rock region. Interesting, too, is that predating these, there were two furnaces similarly constructed in Scotland, which were in blast from 1782 until 1858, when they were apparently dismantled.

We've begun with the reconstruction of a charcoal furnace simply because during the eighteenth and nineteenth centuries, up to about 1870, this method of smelting iron predominated. A treatise on the manufacture of iron, published in 1851, noted that in that year there were but few coke blast furnaces in the United States, and none were in operation, not even the two largest coke ironworks

of the time, at Mount Savage in Maryland and the Great Western Iron Works in Pennsylvania. Even by 1850, considerable advances had been made, however, in the use of raw coal, and by mid-century there were more than sixty blast furnaces using anthracite coal in eastern Pennsylvania alone, and many others were in various stages of construction. But as we've already come to expect, the last quarter or so of the century would see all this changed.

The production of charcoal pig iron would increase still—516,000 gross tons in 1873, 538,000 in 1880, and 704,000 in 1890. But even at that, the iron produced in charcoal furnaces in 1890 amounted to little more than seven percent of the total iron production of the United States. Charcoal furnaces would continue to be built into the early 1900s, but coke and coal were now *the* fuels for America's ironworks and steelworks. In 1890 one ton of charcoal cost four times as much as a ton of coke from the Connellsville coke region of Pennsylvania. At the largest plant in this area, the Standard Coking Works, 690 beehive coke ovens, 12 feet in diameter by 7 feet high, were each charged with five tons of coal four times a week. The coke was then crushed and sorted according to the size of the pieces and shipped to the furnaces.

Coke furnaces, as they were first built in the 1850s, were similar in construction to charcoal furnaces. All of them were apparently built on the plan of the first successful coke furnace in the country, Lonaconing furnace in Allegany County, Maryland, which is 50 feet high, 50 feet square at the base, and 20 feet at the top, and measures 15 feet at the boshes. This furnace was noted for producing

A Coke Furnace (c. 1851)

Charcoal and coke furnaces were similar in construction, but coke furnaces were generally larger and required a higher pressure blast. Most coke furnaces of the mid-nineteenth century were built in the same style—based, apparently, on the Lonaconing furnace in Maryland. The furnace below was in operation at the Great Western Iron Works, Pennsylvania. Its dimensions are: height, 50 feet; width at base, 50 feet; width at top, 25 feet; diameter of boshes, 15 feet; hearth height (from base to boshes), 6 feet; hearth width at bottom, 36 inches; hearth width at top, 48 inches. The furnace had six tuyeres and hot blast.

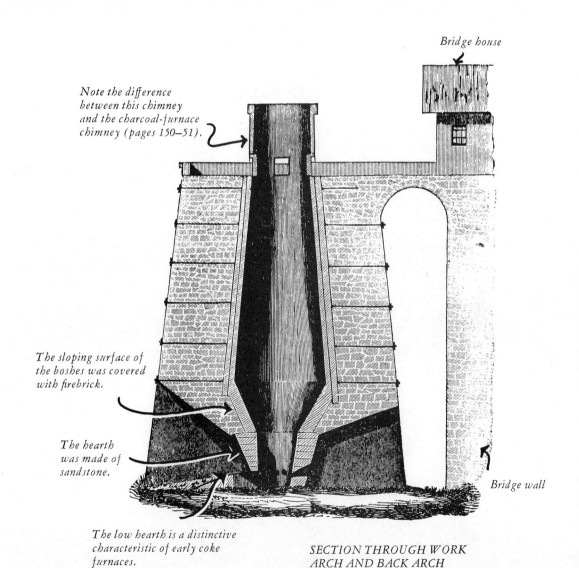

Bridge house

Note the difference between this chimney and the charcoal-furnace chimney (pages 150–51).

The sloping surface of the boshes was covered with firebrick.

The hearth was made of sandstone.

Bridge wall

The low hearth is a distinctive characteristic of early coke furnaces.

SECTION THROUGH WORK ARCH AND BACK ARCH

An Anthracite-Coal Furnace (c. 1851)

Outwardly, anthracite furnaces closely resembled charcoal furnaces, though they were commonly wider at the base, top, and boshes. They were not as tall as coke furnaces. But it was the interior of the anthracite furnace that distinguished it from the others: Two linings made up the in wall and there was a cylindrical space above the tapered boshes. The furnace illustrated here was built at Reading, Pennsylvania, and its dimensions are typical for the period: height, 37'6''; width at base, 30 feet; width at top, 25 feet; hearth height, 60 inches; hearth width at bottom, 60 inches square; hearth width at top, 72 inches square; diameter of boshes, 14 feet; slope of boshes, 67½ degrees; height of cylindrical space above boshes, 60 inches; diameter of trunnel head, 6 feet.

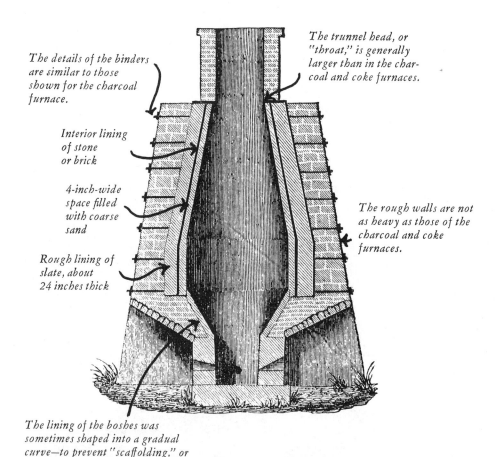

The details of the binders are similar to those shown for the charcoal furnace.

The trunnel head, or "throat," is generally larger than in the charcoal and coke furnaces.

Interior lining of stone or brick

4-inch-wide space filled with coarse sand

The rough walls are not as heavy as those of the charcoal and coke furnaces.

Rough lining of slate, about 24 inches thick

The lining of the boshes was sometimes shaped into a gradual curve—to prevent "scaffolding," or sticking and packing of the charge.

SECTION THROUGH WORK ARCH

good foundry pig iron whereas most coke furnaces of that day could produce only "white metal," iron especially suited to rolling. Apparently one of the problems in the changeover from charcoal to coke was the suitability of certain kinds of ores for the two smelting processes. It was quickly discovered that ores which had yielded high-quality metal in charcoal furnaces would not do so in a coke furnace.

The furnace shown in the illustration on page 159 was in operation at the Great Western Iron Works in 1851. This plant at Brady's Bend, Armstrong County, Pennsylvania—four furnaces and a rolling mill—was one of the first to roll T-rails, or railroad rails. Coke furnaces differed from charcoal furnaces in that they usually had six tuyeres, two in each of three tuyere arches, and a much larger hearth, this particular one being 6 feet high. The hearth is made of sandstone from the coal mines, but the upper part of the hearth is made of firebrick to the point where it joins the "in wall." The chimney of this furnace is built as an extension of the upper stack.

Stone coal, or anthracite, furnaces were quite similar, too, in construction to the charcoal furnace. "Stone coal," incidentally, was a useful term in the 1800s, distinguishing mined coal from charcoal, which was referred to as "coal" in those days. We'll have to look closely for the differences distinguishing coal and charcoal furnaces. Generally, coal furnaces were taller than charcoal furnaces but not as tall as those burning coke. The hearth of the coal furnace is immense when compared to charcoal furnaces of the same vintage. The furnace illustrated opposite, built at Reading, Pennsylvania, has a hearth 5 feet

square at the base, widening to 6 feet square at the top. The most noticeable difference, however, is to be found inside the furnace, where there is usually a cylindrical space above the boshes. Both the boshes and the hearth are made of coarse sandstone, but the sloping sides of the boshes are covered with a lining of firebrick. Above the boshes is an in wall that consists of two linings: an interior lining of firebrick, around which is a 4-inch space filled with coarse sand, and another wall of slate, about 2 feet thick. The construction details of the outer walls, such as the binders, are similar to those of charcoal furnaces. Sometimes these furnaces were built with steam boilers and heat exchangers at the trunnel head. The hot gases coming off the top of the furnace heated the blast and also generated steam, which was used to drive the blast engines. In the example on page 162, hot gases leave the furnace through six flues placed about 4 feet below the top of the furnace. They pass first under the steam boiler, then through the heat exchanger, and finally out the chimney. This particular arrangement is to be found on anthracite furnaces. It should be noted that the differences between coal and charcoal furnaces are not that crucial; many charcoal furnaces were later used for stone coal, apparently without modification. It seems that the second in wall had no other purpose than to serve in the event the innermost wall collapsed during a blast, making it possible to keep the furnace in blast until it was convenient to blow it out.

Though the furnace you've found may be hopelessly ruined and all evidence of the casting house long gone, there may still be some furnace products that can tell us even

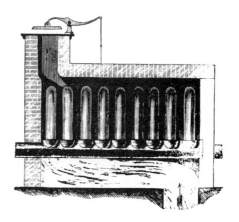

Detail of the Nassawango Iron Furnace hot-blast stove (see page 132). Air from the blast machine was forced through the iron pipes—heated by the furnace exhaust—and then to the tuyeres. The upper portion of the masonry housing for the pipes is missing, but the old drawing from Frederick Overman's *The Manufacture of Iron* (1851) provides one possible reconstruction.

more about its activities than the furnace itself. From one or two broken fragments of iron, or even the contents of the slag heap, we might be able to tell in what forms the iron was cast at the furnace, the type of metal taken from local ores, and whether the furnace's customers were foundries, forges, or rolling mills.

Our search begins on the casting floor. The casting house, or molding house as it was sometimes called, was usually nothing more than a roof of rough, hand-hewn planks supported by log posts, and served as a shelter for the casting floor and blast machinery. Some will be found with stone walls, a few courses or at least the foundation of which may yet be there. But in most instances we'll have to locate the floor by using a few simple hints. A large tamped area is almost certain to remain, and perhaps the post holes delineating the casting floor at the base of the furnace immediately in front of the work arch and hearth. The work arch can usually be identified by size, being larger than the tuyere arches, and in almost every instance is on the side of the furnace directly opposite the side facing the hill. In this arch may be found the hearth, possibly even the timpstone and damstone, but in the other three arches will be found a blank wall or a small hole through which the tuyere was inserted into the hearth.

While the product of every furnace was iron, the metal might take several forms on the casting floor. It might be cast into "pigs" and "sows," cast into various objects, or poured into molds that were "bedded in" the sand of the casting floor. Records of orders and receipts from the offices of many old furnaces indicate that both pig iron and use-ful articles were cast on the same floor. This was the case at Hopewell Village, Pennsylvania, where molten iron might become pigs or beautifully figured stove plates and Franklin fireplaces. On the other hand, the Andover Iron Works, one of the earliest in New Jersey, was known for its almost exclusive production of highest-quality pig iron. The old Hanover furnace in Burlington County, New Jersey, cast sadirons, fireplace backs, stoves, water pipes, and, for the duration of the War of 1812, 4-pound and 12-pound cannon balls. Actually, what was produced on the casting floor had much to do with the quality and type of iron that emerged from the hearth and the reason for building the ironworks in the first place. Some furnaces were built to make pig iron for the forge; others were built as part of an industry—a toolworks, a company specializing in cast-iron bridge parts or railroad wheels, an agricultural implement plant, a locomotive works—or for some other specific purpose. Different grades of iron each had rather specific applications.

The products and wastes of years and years of casting have become our historical clues. Splashed iron may be found on the lower courses of stone in the work arch or may remain from the last cast, tucked away in the corners of the hearthstones. Broken pigs are to be found scattered about the furnace and on the slag heaps, as are pieces of gate metal and broken or imperfect castings. At Bullion furnace, Venango County, Pennsylvania, there remains an irregularly shaped mass of iron that would probably weigh a ton or more. This might be a "breakout" resulting from some mishap, such as the damstone or tap-hole plug giving way unexpectedly. It

German *Stück Ofen*.

is possible, also, that some occurrence in the boshes or crucible forced the founder to hastily tap the hearth before adequate preparations could be made on the casting floor.

If you've found, instead, a large, regularly shaped mass of iron, this might be a "salamander"—which could mean that somewhere on the site there is or was a very special, and in America rare, type of furnace. The German *Stück Ofen* was much smaller than a charcoal furnace, 10 to 16 feet high and about as wide at the base. The blast entered through two tuyeres, usually, both on the same side, and the in wall might be either diamond- or egg-shaped.

But the most peculiar aspect of these furnaces was the way metal was taken from the hearth. In the work arch of the *Stück Ofen* will be found a large opening to the hearth but no familiar timpstone or damstone. After the furnace had been heated, but before smelting began, this opening was sealed with bricks, leaving a small opening through which

slag could be drawn off. After the smelting was complete, the furnace was blown out and, after some time, the bricks removed. Inside the furnace, then, was a large solid mass of iron called a *Stück Wulf*, or salamander. This was pried loose from the hearth with crowbars and lifted out with a pair of tongs suspended from a crane on chains. The salamander was immediately swung to an anvil under a tilt hammer and flattened into a 4-inch-thick slab, which was then cut into several blooms and hammered into iron bars. Meanwhile, the furnace would be charged again and the process repeated. It is uncertain whether many of these furnaces were built in America, but it is more than likely that immigrant German ironmasters and founders could have brought the *Stück Ofen* to America with them. One contemporary observer of an early-nineteenth-century furnace in New Jersey described the center core as resembling in shape "a large hen's egg standing on its largest end." This might well have been a German or Swedish furnace, the characteristic in wall being a smooth curve running from the trunnel head through the boshes to the hearth. This rounded in-wall form, incidentally, was used in Germany for reducing bog ores, and bog ores are found throughout New Jersey and in other states as well.

Slag, splashed iron, sows, pigs, salamanders, broken gate metal, and old cracked castings—what could we possibly learn from these? Well, if we're able to apply some of the ironmaster's rules of thumb and use our historical imagination, we can actually learn a great deal about a furnace's operations. Our approach will be empirical, just as was the ironmaster's.

In the absence of scientific laboratory

analysis, which would not come until much later, the early American ironmasters learned to identify types and quality of iron from its texture, the nature of a break, and, most telling, the iron's color. Terms such as "gray metal" or "white metal" would be too vague for a modern metallurgical engineer, but for ironmasters, founders, forgemen, and blacksmiths of the 1700s and 1800s they communicated precisely what each needed to know about the metal. Even the color of the slag taken during a charge and the color of the smoke and flame at the trunnel head were "read" as indicators of conditions within the furnace. An old guide to managing the charcoal furnace warns, "A heavy, dark top flame indicates that the furnace is cold, and that the burden is too heavy. A bright smoky flame, which throws off white fumes, indicates a too liquid cinder; that too much limestone is present; or that the burden is too light." The variables confronting the furnace manager seem overwhelming. The constituents of the ore—carbon, phosphorous, sulphur, various other metals and oxides—the qualities of the limestone flux, temperatures at various places in the furnace, the strength and temperature of the blast, the position of the tuyeres, and the proportions of raw materials added to the charge required decisions on the ironmaster's part hour after hour, day after day, throughout the months the furnace was in blast. For him the moment of truth came every twelve hours or so at the hearth, when the iron was let out.

At that moment color was the founder's clue. Now, many years later, color is our clue, too. While the old ironmasters and blacksmiths could discern subtle distinctions of quality in the color of pig iron, it will make

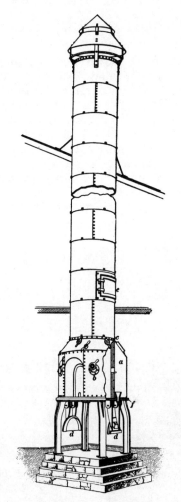

This, too, is an iron furnace—a cupola found in old foundries, where it was used to melt pig and scrap iron for casting; it was built around 1900.

our work more interesting just to be able to classify iron we've found at a furnace site as one of a few easily recognized types. The classification is based on the color and appearance, not of an exposed surface—which is most certainly oxidized—but of a fracture.

The Roast Oven and Cupola Blast Furnaces

These two structures are often found on the sites of old ironworks.

The roast oven shown here is of the "perpetual" type—meaning that ore could be added and removed continuously, rather than being roasted in charges. Such an oven was usually 12 to 18 feet high and held from fifty to one hundred tons of ore at one time. Note (a) the circular hearth, (b) the grate bars, which could be removed to let down roasted ores, (c) the side arches, which permitted access to (d) the draft holes, which admitted air when it was needed and permitted checking the progress of the roasting.

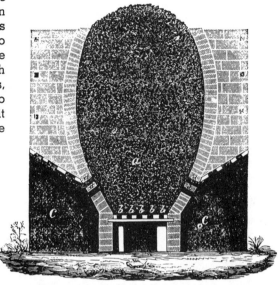

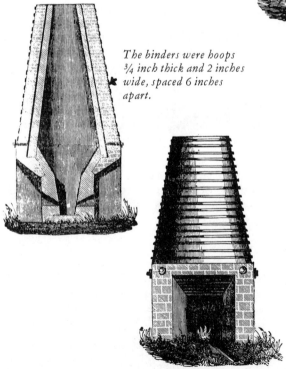

The binders were hoops ¾ inch thick and 2 inches wide, spaced 6 inches apart.

The cupola furnace was never widely used in the United States, as it was expensive to build, consumed more fuel than a square stack, and always broke its binders. The square bottom part of the cupola furnace on the left (Great Western Iron Works) is of stone; its top is of brick. The cupola furnace could be built entirely of brick or of stone. The name derives from its resemblance to the Great Western's foundry cupola. The height of a cupola furnace is from 15 to 20 feet; its width at base, 7 to 10 feet.

This is a destructive test, and since even fractures of a small area will reveal what we want to know, only obviously insignificant bits of small scrap should be used. The small hand lens in your archaeologist's tool kit is helpful, though it's unlikely that an ironworker of old needed one to classify iron as one of our broadly described varieties.

No. 1 pig iron is the darkest gray. It fractures easily with a dull, leaden sound and is so soft as to be dented easily with a hammer. Looking closely at the fracture, you'll see that it is coarsely grained and peppered throughout with little bits of black graphite or crystallized carbon. This iron has little tensile strength, but it was used to make the finest castings such as ornate stove plates and cast-iron housewares where great strength was not required. If No. 1 pig iron is remelted in a cupola or air furnace, the excess carbon will be separated out, and it becomes an excellent cast iron belonging to the next class.

No. 2 pig iron is much harder and stronger and shows a finer grain in the fracture. The color will be lighter, more uniform, without any noticeable bits of carbon or other impurities. The surface of a No. 2 iron pig or casting is smoother and is considered the best foundry metal for strong, smooth, high-quality castings. A slightly lower grade of No. 2 shows white crystals in the corners of the pig and in thin parts of a casting. When iron of this grade emerges from the hearth, it is more fluid than No. 1, it is a clearer red in color, and it remains molten longer.

No. 3 pig iron is still lighter in color, and the grain is finer and more regular. The surface of the fracture is smoother than in those of the lower numbers, and the iron is much harder. Because it is stronger and tougher than either No. 1 or No. 2, this grade of iron was preferred for large castings and structural ironwork requiring metal of high tensile strength. On the casting floor, No. 3 is not as fluid as No. 2, is freer from scum, and throws off sparks as it is poured from the foundry ladle or run into pig molds.

No. 4 pig iron is even stronger and is almost white in color. The silvery-white crystals of the fractured surface sparkle upon catching the sunlight. In a molten state this metal is whiter and appears hotter than the lower numbers and, like No. 3, throws off sparks when it is poured. It is used for only the heaviest foundry work and is considered unsuitable for small, light, or ornamental castings.

No. 4 forge is harder and even lighter in color than the last, approaching white. Even with a hand lens there are no graphite flakes discernible in the fracture. White iron is brittle, so brittle in fact that it may break with a sudden change in temperature; but it is hard enough to scratch glass. Iron of this type was referred to as "short," and, because it remains pasty in the molten state and will not flow freely, it is of no use for foundry work. No. 4 forge gets its name from its suitability for making malleable or wrought iron and would first be remelted in a puddling furnace before being hammered. A pig of white metal will ring like a bell when struck.

Mottled iron is actually white iron, scattered through which are spots of gray iron of varying sizes, visible on the surface of the fracture. Mottled iron was considered the best forge metal by many ironmasters, and while it was sometimes produced in the furnace, it was usually made by combining No. 2

Forges

Note: Early drawings such as these were somewhat idealized and are meant, here, as a general guide only.

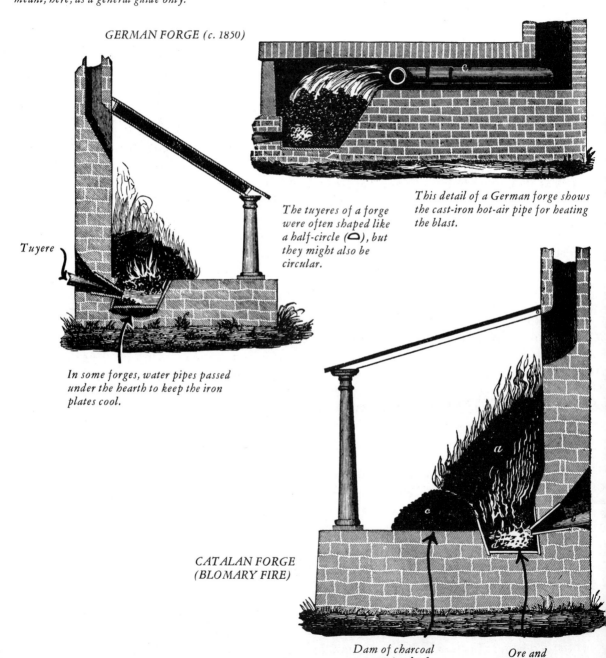

GERMAN FORGE (c. 1850)

Tuyere

The tuyeres of a forge were often shaped like a half-circle (⌒), but they might also be circular.

This detail of a German forge shows the cast-iron hot-air pipe for heating the blast.

In some forges, water pipes passed under the hearth to keep the iron plates cool.

CATALAN FORGE
(BLOMARY FIRE)

Dam of charcoal to contain the fire

Ore and charcoal

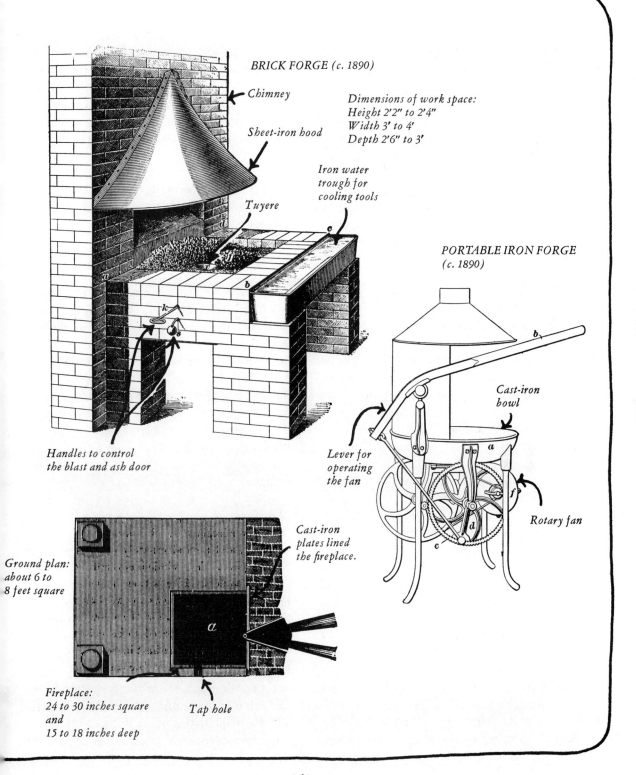

BRICK FORGE *(c. 1890)*

Chimney

Sheet-iron hood

Tuyere

Dimensions of work space:
Height 2'2" to 2'4"
Width 3' to 4'
Depth 2'6" to 3'

Iron water
trough for
cooling tools

PORTABLE IRON FORGE
(c. 1890)

Cast-iron
bowl

Lever for
operating
the fan

Rotary fan

Handles to control
the blast and ash door

Cast-iron
plates lined
the fireplace.

Ground plan:
about 6 to
8 feet square

Fireplace:
24 to 30 inches square
and
15 to 18 inches deep

Tap hole

and No. 3 pig iron before the cast.

As you may have already gathered from these descriptions, the pig iron that lay cooling on the casting floor was not usually a finished product. Still, many ironmasters prided themselves on furnaces that produced cast after cast of the highest-quality gray iron right at the hearth. Their pride was justified; ironmaking was an art then, and consistency at the hearth was as much a sign of well-trained managers, founders, keepers, molders, and colliers as it was of a well-built furnace and high-grade ores. While a variety of ironwares were cast from metal dipped right out of the hearth, iron castings to be subjected to heavier usage, such as those for bridges or steam locomotives, would have to be refined.

Under the archaeologist's hand lens the best No. 2 gray pig iron appears homogeneous. The metallurgist's microscope, however, would reveal minute flakes of carbon and short fibers which make even this iron unsuitable where high impact and tensile strengths are required. So to be useful for tools, agricultural implements, locomotive drive-wheel tires, steam-engine drive shafts, and bridge members, the carbon would have to be expelled and the internal structure worked into long, tough fibers that resisted being sheared, twisted, and pulled apart. This work might be done at the ironworks, but more likely the work of refining would be carried on in the foundries and forges which were the ironworks' customers.

At the forge the cast-iron pigs, scrap, and gate metal is remelted in the refining fire. This is the first step in converting the pigs into wrought iron. The process would be essentially the same at any forge. After kindling the fire, the finer's assistant would heap charcoal 12 to 18 inches high in the fireplace for gray metal, or up to 24 inches if white metal were to be worked. When the fire was just right, the finer would insert the ends of two or three pigs into the charcoal fire. The blast was now applied, and as the ends of the pigs in the fire softened, the rest was fed in and new pigs added until there were about 120 pounds of iron in the hearth. The iron was melted not to a fluid state again but just until it reached a pasty consistency. Using a long iron bar, the finer worked the pasty mass into a ball by continually raising and turning it until the iron was uniformly heated. When the finer felt the time was right, the bloom was lifted from the hearth with tongs, swung onto the anvil of a huge hammer, and beaten into a rectangular billet, 5 or 6 inches square and about 16 inches long. The carbon had been brought to the surface of the bloom in the refining fire, and now the hammering would remove this carbon, combined with the cinders, and would lengthen the fibers—producing a much stronger and different iron than that which had emerged from the blast furnace.

By the 1850s, an alternative for refining blast-furnace iron was becoming quite common in American ironworks: the reverbatory, or puddling, furnace. The reverbatory furnace differs from the forge fire in that the fuel—coal or coke—does not come in contact with the iron, but is burned, instead, in a fireplace or grate adjacent to but separate from the hearth. The hearth is heated partly by the flame heating the walls of the furnace, but most of the heat reaching the hearth is reflected off the roof of the furnace—hence the name "reverbatory." Although it eventually supplanted the finery furnace, the puddling furnace is itself an old form, apparently appearing first in Pittsburgh and throughout western Pennsylvania. Actually two forms of the furnace evolved: the single furnace, which is the older form; and a double furnace, which developed east of the Allegheny Mountains. The two furnaces look alike except that the double furnace has a larger, deeper fireplace. These old furnaces are cold now, but we can re-create their working from contemporary descriptions.

The iron floor of the hearth is covered with a layer of finely powdered cinders to a depth of 3 or 4 inches. A stone-coal fire is then kindled in the grate and left to burn for about five hours. The cinders eventually melt and are then smoothed up onto the iron plates forming the sides of the hearth so that the entire hearth is covered with a lining of fused cinder. The door on the side of the furnace is opened, allowing the lining to cool and harden, and then the broken pigs are thrown in. The door is closed and the fire brought up to working temperature. As the helper stirs the fire, getting it hotter and hotter, the puddler breaks up the now-pasty pieces of iron and mixes them with the molten cinders using a puddling hook. Since the tools are in the furnace much of the time, a trough filled with water is attached alongside the furnace; in this trough the puddling hooks and bars may be cooled. The puddler continues to work the iron and cinder mixture until the metal is, as he would say, "coming to nature." At this stage little round balls of molten iron about the size of peas appear in the cinder. They grow larger and larger as they adhere to one another. The furnace is at its highest heat, and the puddler must work quickly now to keep the mass of cinder and iron turning and uniformly heated. Then, with his bar or hook the puddler pushes the

smaller lumps together into several larger round balls, 12 to 15 inches in diameter and weighing about 70 to 80 pounds. The door is closed; a final and thorough heat is given the iron, and the helper now stands ready beside the furnace with an iron handcart. The door is opened, the puddler and his helper grasp one of the white-hot balls of iron with a stout pair of tongs, drag it onto the cart, and wheel it over to the hammer or squeezer.

The modern reader may not realize it, but the forge, before it was a refining furnace, was a small smelting furnace—the blacksmith making his own charcoal and gathering bits of ore from a nearby meadow or swamp. In America, over the years, a number of forges have evolved, all based on the same principle—a fireplace in which charcoal and ore were burned together, a bellows providing the blast—but varying somewhat in the details of construction. Most of the old forges are cold now, but many built around the time of the American Revolution were still in operation in the closing years of the nineteenth century, a few continuing to operate into the early 1900s. Among the oldest of these are the old Catalan forges tucked away in the remote hills of southern Appalachia, where they may still be today. Travelers to this region in the 1880s described charcoal forges, constructed and worked like those of a century earlier, still in operation. In northwestern North Carolina and adjacent counties of Tennessee, there were about forty or fifty forges of the old Catalan type, unchanged from and, maybe, going back to the Revolution. Some of these were known locally as "thundergust forges," because they could operate only when the meager mountain stream that powered the bellows and hammer was suddenly swelled by a rainstorm.

Puddling Furnaces

Single puddling furnaces were used at Pittsburgh and in general throughout the states west of the Allegheny Mountains. Few were built in the Eastern states, where the double furnace was most common. The construction of single and double puddling furnaces varied little—except that the double furnace had a deeper grate and two work doors. The grate of a typical bituminous single furnace would be 3 feet by 4 feet, and 10 to 12 inches deep.

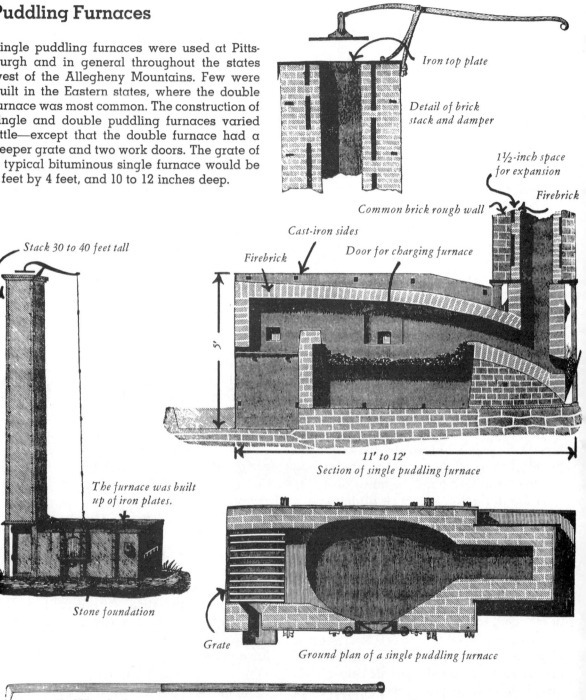

Iron top plate

Detail of brick stack and damper

1½-inch space for expansion

Firebrick

Common brick rough wall

Cast-iron sides

Firebrick

Door for charging furnace

Stack 30 to 40 feet tall

5'

11' to 12'

Section of single puddling furnace

The furnace was built up of iron plates.

Stone foundation

Grate

Ground plan of a single puddling furnace

Puddling hook

Puddling bar

Double furnace with iron water boshes

In double puddling furnaces with iron water boshes, water circulated through a space 1 inch wide between cast-iron plates 5 inches thick. Double furnaces with cast-iron hollow, or air, boshes for use with anthracite coal were common throughout New York State and New England. The grate of a typical anthracite double furnace would be 3 feet by 5 feet, and 20 to 24 inches deep.

Double furnace with cast-iron hollow boshes

The plates are held together by square wrought-iron bars or binders fastened with a key or screw and nut.

a   a   a   a   a

Deep grate

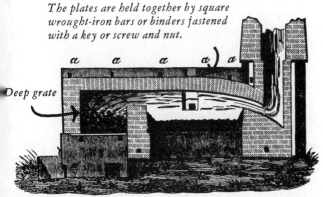

This is a double furnace for anthracite coal. In Pennsylvania, the boshes were made of soapstone.

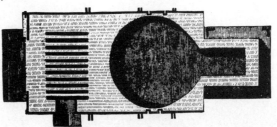

Horizontal section of anthracite double furnace

173

Forge Hammers and a Squeezer (c. 1851)

The weight of a hammer is a clue to its use. A 50- to 100-pound hammer was (and is) for drawing small iron bars and nail rods. A 300- to 400-pound hammer was (and is) for forging blooms of from 60 to 100 pounds in weight.

Cast gray-iron hammer

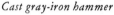

STEAM HAMMER

*TILT HAMMER
(GERMAN FORGE HAMMER)*

The tilt hammer's parts include: (a) the hammer itself, (b) the helve (of hickory or oak), (c) the anvil (of cast iron), (d) the iron stock, (e) a wooden log, 6 to 8 feet long, 4 inches in diameter, (f) foundation pilings, (g) the fulcrum, (h) cams, (i) a wrought-iron ring, which receives the impact of the cams, (k) a shaft (of wood), (l) a water-wheel, and (m) a cam wheel. This same hammer was also driven by belts or leather straps from a steam engine.

The kind of forge that developed in a particular locale was determined to some extent, as was the kind of blast furnace, by the origins of the early finers, forgemen, and blacksmiths who first settled there. But, like the choice of blast furnace, the kind of forge used had more to do with the kinds of ores and iron to be worked. In Pennsylvania, forges and the techniques for working were patterned after English forges and practices. The German forge is also to be found throughout Pennsylvania and in New York,

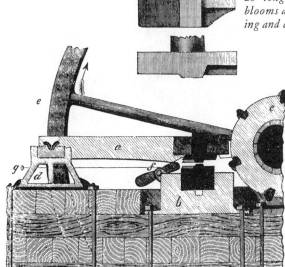

T-hammer, 16" wide x 20" long, for shingling blooms and for stretching and drawing

Timber foundation

T-HAMMER

The T-hammer is used for hammering slabs for boiler-plate and sheet iron. Its parts include: (a) the hammer itself, which weighs generally 4 to 5 tons, (b) the anvil stock, which weighs generally 5 to 8 tons, (c) the cam ring (of cast iron), (d) the fulcrum, (e) a flywheel, and (f–g) a handle which arrests the hammer, preventing it from striking the anvil or work.

NEW ENGLAND LEVER SQUEEZER

The foundation of the squeezer may be of stone, brick, or timber. Its parts include: (a) a bed plate, 6' long x 15" wide x 12" high, (b) a movable squeezer jaw, (c) a crank (steam- or waterwheel-driven), and (d) an anvil, 2' long x 14" wide x 4" high. The particular squeezer illustrated was made entirely of cast iron—its entire weight 4 to 5 tons—and was used to compress iron balls from the puddling furnace.

Flywheel, 3 to 4 feet in diameter

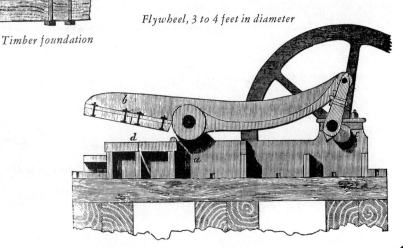

Vermont, New Jersey, and Missouri as well. German communities were here, to be sure, but a more relevant reason for using the German forge was its suitability for working the rich magnetic ores found in these areas. The Catalan forge was considered impractical for ores containing less than forty percent iron; it was considered best suited to the rich hydrate ores of North Carolina, Tennessee, and Alabama, or the red oxides of Arkansas. The Catalan forge was probably the earliest to be used in America and, though persisting

Rollers (c. 1851)

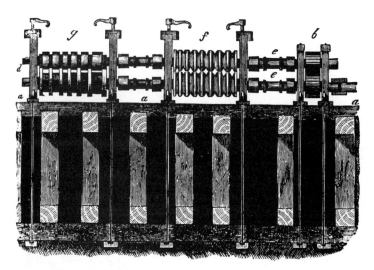

ROUGHING ROLLS

Shingled blooms went from the hammer or squeezer to the roughing rolls. The roughing rolls were made up of: (a) a timber foundation, below ground, (b) cogwheels, or gears, driven by steam engine, (c) cast-iron coupling rods, (d) flat rolls, and (e) roughing rolls.

DETAIL OF GROOVES IN ROUGHING ROLLS

The groove in the first set of rolls is 6 inches across. To reduce the bloom to a rod 1 inch in diameter, it passes through seven grooves that are progressively smaller: 6, 4 2/5, 3 1/5, 2 2/5, 1 4/5, and 1 inches. The rod may then be passed through flat rolls (d, at left) which form it into flat bar iron.

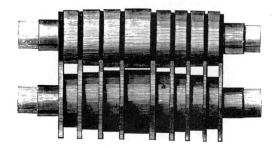

in its original form in the Appalachian backcountry, was largely replaced by the German forge by the mid-1800s.

This persistence of an earlier technique long after newer ones had taken hold is an interesting footnote to the history of iron-making in America and, for the historian and archaeologist, a significant one. Nothing, it seems, ever really became obsolete. Charcoal furnaces were still being built in the first decade of the 1900s, when by far the greatest number of furnaces were fired by coal and coke. When, in the 1890s, the iron industry boasted of a furnace that had made 502 gross tons of iron in a day (compared to a record 30 tons a day in 1850), Catalan forges were

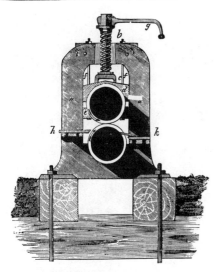

END VIEW OF A ROLL TRAIN

The parts of this roll train include: (a) its cast-iron housing—which would be 10" x 12" square for heavy bar or sheet iron, 8" x 10" for merchant bar, 6" x 8" for small bar, and 5" x 6" for wire, (b) the wrought-iron screw, (c) a safety cap (designed to break before any other part and thus prevent damage to the rolls), (d) a cap lined with brass or lead bearings, (e) a bottom bearing, (f) screws for regulating the height of the top roll, (g) a handle to adjust the height of the top roll, and (h–k) an apron to clean the rolls of iron scrap.

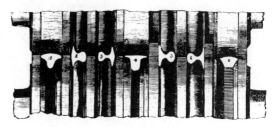

GROOVES FOR ROLLING RAILROAD RAILS

The square billet was first fed in at points 1, 2, and then 3. Its pass through point 4 pressed the top and bottom of the rail smooth. A pass through points 5 and 6 put finishing touches on the rail.

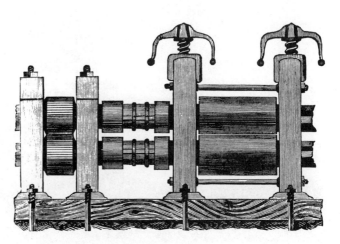

ROLLS FOR SHEET IRON

operating in Appalachia, and there was still a smithy in virtually every American town. Foundries still cast kettles and stoves, as they always had, and now there were iron locomotives; rails; water, sewage, and illuminating-gas pipes; bridges; architectural members; stationary steam engines for industry and portable steam engines for the farm; street railways; printing presses; fire engines; and machine tools. Even the blast furnaces themselves were now jacketed with sheet iron. For over a century, iron was a basic part of American life and, as steel, still is today.

Cable-tool drilling rig at Drumright, Oklahoma.

6. WHERE GUSHERS ROARED

Pithole, Pennsylvania. Though not one of the most euphonious names in the American landscape, Pithole was once one of the most important cities in the state, its post office ranking third only to Philadelphia and Pittsburgh. That was in 1865. In January of that year, a well was struck on the Thomas Holmden farm in a ravine on Pit Creek. Within weeks, on the same property, new derricks marked the Twin Wells, No. 54 well, Grant well, and Eureka well, each producing about eight hundred barrels of oil a day. Then, on the adjoining Rooker farm and nearby Hyner and Copeland farms, other wells were soon struck, all by the little group of entrepreneurs who called themselves the United States Oil Company. A city grew up around the wells in an incredibly short time; by September of that same year the population of Pithole reached an estimated sixteen thousand! But don't bother looking for it on the map; within two years the yield of all the wells had diminished drastically, the city's prosperity right along with it, and Pithole became all but deserted.

Pithole was a typical oil city. Similar stories could be told about similar towns all over America. At one time or another, from the early 1860s on, hundreds of boomtowns sprang up just like Pithole, towns with names like Sulphur City, Petroleum Centre, Oil Town, and Petrolia. Some are very much alive today; others disappeared when the oil

ran out. Oil towns, large and small, will have to be rediscovered. Along with them is certain to be found evidence of the petroleum industry of long ago: wood-frame derricks, oil rigs, powerhouses, lengths of cable and casing, tools, steam engines, refinery equipment, storage tanks, or, perhaps, along a deserted railroad siding, a loading rack and waiting string of crude-oil-blackened tank cars.

Like blast furnaces, many derricks will be found in backcountry habitats. So it was with the remnants of the West Oil Company, recently found standing in a secluded West Virginia woodland. This is West Virginia's historic Volcano district, a continuation of the Pennsylvania and eastern Ohio oil fields, the development of which began in the 1870s. About a mile and a half south of U.S. 50, near the town of Petroleum, stands a virtually complete drilling operation including derricks, a powerhouse, and the machine shop, all dating to the 1890s. In the powerhouse are still to be seen the wooden wheels and pulleys from which continuous "endless wire" cables once ran to several wells, driven by a single internal-combustion engine run on natural gas, a by-product of the well drilling. The wooden derricks stand naturally among the trees from whose antecedents the heavy timbers, planks, and wheel sections were hewn.

There'll be something for the amateur petroleum historian in almost every state.

179

Hundreds of thousands of wells have been struck over the years. The first were named in the same tradition as early blast furnaces. The Llewellyn well, the Eureka well, Spindle Top, and others took their names from the owner on whose property they arose, the drilling company, geographical region, or, perhaps, some topographical feature. As more and more wells sprang up on the same property, numbers were added to the owners' names to distinguish them—such as Butt's Well No. 1. But soon the derricks became so numerous that the name was dispensed with altogether, a new well becoming known simply as "No. 646," etc. Maps of a century ago showed "major" oil deposits in California, Colorado, Indiana, Kansas, Kentucky, Louisiana, Michigan, New Mexico, New York, Ohio, Oklahoma, Pennsylvania, Tennessee, Texas, West Virginia, and Wyoming. "Minor" fields had been located in Alabama, Arkansas, Alaska, the Dakotas, Illinois, Minnesota, Missouri, Montana, Nevada, Washington State, and Wisconsin. Much of this was due to the speculative energies of "wildcat" drillers, who, in the early days, were willing to try anywhere and everywhere. Later, petroleum production, just as iron and steel production, would be associated with a few regions.

The oil industry grew in America almost as fast as the city of Pithole. It all began in August 1859, when two drillers engaged by E. A. Drake and the Seneca Oil Company began to bore at Oil Creek about a mile from Titusville, Pennsylvania, the future site of Pithole. At first the effort seemed futile. Several attempts were made, but each time, before the drill could reach the rock where oil would be found, the shaft caved in and digging through the surface deposits would have to begin anew. Drake, hitting upon a new application of an old idea, drove an iron pipe down through the sand and clay to the rock, ensuring a clear shaft for the impact-type drill bits and establishing a practice used to this day. Work continued now, the bit monotonously rising and falling against the rock below, until suddenly, at a depth of about 69 feet, the drill dropped into a subterranean opening or fissure. The next day, oil under natural pressure appeared at the top of the well. The well produced only twenty-five barrels a day, diminishing to about fifteen later in the year. But news of Drake's success traveled fast, and the rush was on.

Seneca's parent company, the Pennsylvania Rock Oil Company, immediately secured all the available leases in the area, and within weeks new derricks appeared up and down the valley of Oil Creek and along the Allegheny River. Another well, almost within a stone's throw of the first, struck oil at 80 feet. Land values and population soared. Pennsylvania local histories record success after success during the years immediately following Drake's discovery—at Cherry Run, Pithole Creek, Benninghoff and Pioneer Run, the Woods and Stevenson farms, Dennis Run, and Triumph Hill. In June 1861, the first flowing well was struck, on the Funk farm, which at 460 feet yielded three hundred barrels a day. The Empire well, completed on the same farm in September, flowed at the rate of twenty-five hundred barrels a day and another, at the nearby Tarr farm, produced an unheard-of stream of three thousand barrels daily. On the 207 acres of the J. W. McClintock farm, which later became the site of Petroleum Centre, no less than one hundred and fifty wells were operating at the same time.

The history of petroleum use in America does not begin with Drake's well but, as we might expect, has precedents reaching back into the early 1800s and before. Rather than create a new industry, Drake's resourcefulness and the Pennsylvania Rock Oil Company's aggressiveness were actually responses to an already existing and growing need for oil. Mention of "oil springs" and "oil pits" appear in the writings of travelers in early America—in New York in 1632, at the now-famous Oil Creek in 1748, and at Santa Barbara, California, in 1792. Accounts of early settlers in Louisiana describe the gathering of a black pasty substance, which they used to lubricate wagon axles and protect iron tools from rust. But the earliest use of petroleum in America was medicinal, as a cure for rheumatism, coughs, sprains, burns, sores on horses, and other ailments. The main source of medicinal oil was in the vicinity of Lake

Oil rig, West Oil Company, Volcano, West Virginia; the rig was constructed around 1895.

Endless wire pumping operation at the West Oil Company north of Petroleum, West Virginia; it was built around 1895. One of the cables connecting the power-house (rear) to an oil rig remains.

Spring Valley oil field near Peru, Illinois, in 1901.

common fixture in every locomotive cab, the "tallow can" sat on its special shelf above the firebox doors, where its contents would be kept warm and liquid. Periodically, the engineer or fireman took the can down from its shelf and filled the "tallow cups" on each cylinder. (These "fixed" or animal oils, incidentally, are still used for lubrication in compounds with mineral oils.) The real impetus for an oil industry, for bringing up hundreds of thousands and eventually millions of barrels of petroleum out of the ground each year, was the growing demand for lamp oil.

In this day and age we need to stop for a moment and recall how homes and working places were lighted a century ago. In many American homes candles were still being used. But spermaceti, or whale-oil, lamps came into increasing use throughout the 1800s. So did petroleum from oil springs, filtered through charcoal to remove the impurities and objectionable odor caused by its sulphur content, but only where it was available locally. By the 1850s, however, the demand for lamp oil was greater than the supply provided through these simple means. The price for petroleum skimmed from marshes and pools reached forty or fifty cents for a small vial.

Promise of large quantities of inexpensive lamp oil came with the appearance in America of a new process, developed by English chemist James Young, by which oil was distilled from coal and shale. The rate at which these new refineries appeared was phenomenal, reflecting the American demand. Young received his patent in 1850 and, within the decade, over sixty plants were in operation around the country. There existed, in 1859, four refineries in Boston, five in

Seneca, New York, where a thin layer of yellowish-brown oil was skimmed off the top of marsh pools with a broad, flat board trimmed on one side to a knife edge. This foul-smelling oil with the consistency of tar was then heated, strained through flannel or woolen cloth, and sold under the name "Seneca Oil."

Lubricating cart axles and healing all manner of ailments, then, were important early uses of petroleum. But these needs could be met by simply collecting at oil springs and other natural sources on the ground, or by using animal and vegetable oils. Heavy mill machinery, waterwheels, and the like were usually lubricated with lard or tallow. As recently as the 1880s, tallow and, to a lesser extent, lard were still the most widely used lubricants for railroad locomotive and stationary steam-engine cylinders. A

New York, ten in western Pennsylvania, twenty-five in Ohio, eight in Virginia, and six in Kentucky. Portland, Maine; New Bedford, Massachusetts; Hartford, Connecticut; and St. Louis, Missouri, each had one or more plants. But these were all small-capacity plants. Besides this, whale oil was becoming expensive, for even then the great mammals were being hunted to near-extinction.

So the quest began. In the last year of the decade, forty patents were granted to Americans for petroleum lamps and burners (most using flat wicks). But how would America get the great quantities of oil needed for lighting its lamps and lubricating its machines? The answer came at Titusville.

The apparatus Drake used to penetrate deeply underground for oil had historical precedent, too. Long before the drilling rig and derrick were used to sink shafts down to oil deposits, they had been developed as part of the technology for boring water and brine wells. In fact, just about all the know-how needed to drill oil wells was already there when it was needed. The history of the oil derrick, tradition has it, begins in West Virginia, where, in 1808, the brothers Ruffner, drilling for brine, completed the first rock-bored well in America. The simple methods they devised were to become useful to an industry in a way they could not have possibly imagined. Their drill was a "spring pole" rig, known for centuries, but capable of reaching down 400 to 500 feet.

The Ruffners began by digging a well shaft down to the rock. Into this they low-

Wooden plank derrick in the area of Coalinga, California, about 1911.

ered a "gum"—a sycamore trunk hollowed out to about 4 or 5 inches inner diameter—which rested on the rock stratum about 13 feet below the surface. This was a prototype "casing," which then as now kept the soft surface strata from caving into the well. The next step was to make a spring pole from a sapling 40 or 50 feet long, set into the ground at an angle of about thirty degrees so that its upper end was directly over the well. To this end was attached a long iron drill with a

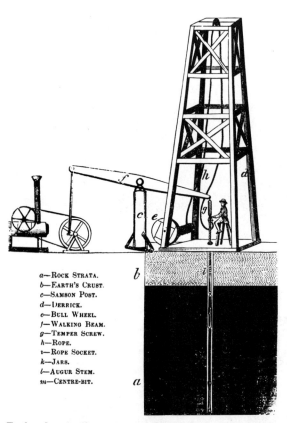

a—Rock Strata.
b—Earth's Crust.
c—Samson Post.
d—Derrick.
e—Bull Wheel.
f—Walking Beam.
g—Temper Screw.
h—Rope.
i—Rope Socket.
k—Jars.
l—Augur Stem.
m—Centre-bit.

Early sketch illustrating the operation of a cable-tool rig with the string of tools in position.

chisel-shaped bit about 2½ inches wide, which hung down into the opening of the gum. By pulling on the drill rod and then releasing it, they could hammer the bit into the rock over and over again, chipping it away bit by bit. As the well deepened beyond the reach of the drill, additional lengths of iron rod were welded on until they reached brine at 58 feet. To raise the concentrated brine from below without its being diluted by the water entering the well from the upper strata, another refinement was devised. Long tubes made of strips of wood bound together with a wrapping of twine were passed down into the well. The brine rose up through the tube into the gum, where it could be bailed out with buckets as in any ordinary water well. Later, the wooden tubes were replaced by tubes of tin soldered together; and these, in turn, by threaded-copper tubes, which could be screwed together.

The efficiency of drilling with a spring-pole rig increased greatly when, in 1831, William Morris introduced what he called "slips." Slips, or "jars" as they are now known, consist of two elongated and flattened chainlike links, each about 30 inches long, separating the heavy iron rod carrying the bit from the upper rod attached to the spring pole. The effect of the slips was to create slack in the line of tools. After the bit had struck hard into the rock, the links would slide together as the spring pole continued downward. Then, as the spring pole began its upstroke, the links connected with a sharp jar, loosening the bit from the rock. So, by the 1830s, all the basic elements of the drilling rig had come together. The wooden derrick would replace the spring pole as the steam engine would replace human power, but the process of impact drilling would remain essentially the same for the next century.

The Titusville derrick became the type of rig predominating in the petroleum industry. Although rigs varied somewhat in construction from one locale to another, all of them may be classified as one of two types, either as cable-tool or as rotary rigs. Cable-tool rigs, direct descendants of the spring pole, drilled wells by impact. A chisel-like tool, suspended from a hemp rope, was alternately raised and dropped, the falling force of the heavy string of tools driving the bit into the rock. In rotary drilling the bit revolves, penetrating the rock strata as a hand-drill bit penetrates a piece of wood. Looking at these two rigs (see pages 189 and 194) in detail will allow us to distinguish them and, with some accuracy, determine their vintage.

After a site had been selected, the first job was to erect the rig. The derrick was constructed of four strong uprights, or legs, which rested on heavy timber sills. These "mudsills" were usually sunk in trenches, but sometimes they were just set on the ground so that the whole derrick might be moved from place to place, the mudsills doubling in this case as sledge runners. In this case the foundation timbers would be locked together by keys or wedges, and so it would be with all the other wooden members of the derrick. No mortises or tenons or any permanent fasteners would be used, making it possible to take down the entire rig and set it up on a new site.

Early derricks ranged in height from 30 to 70 feet, the height being determined by the depth of the well or, more directly, by the length of the string of tools to be used. The derrick had to be tall enough to hoist the string of tools and length of casing clear of the wellhead. Here are the dimensions and weights of the various parts of the string, taken from a catalog of the Oil Well Supply Company (Bradford and Oil City, Pennsylvania) from around the turn of the century:

Rope-socket	3'	90 lbs.
Sinker-bar (4")	12'	400
Jars	6'	300
Auger-stem (4")	32'	1050
Bit	3'	140
	56'	1980

The deep wells of the Pennsylvania fields required tall derricks, 70 feet and higher, about 20 feet wide at the base, and 4 feet at the summit. Shallower wells, such as those found in Texas, the Gulf Coast states, and the Franklin and Mecca-Belden districts of Ohio (Lorain and Trumbull counties), usually called for derricks no higher than 30 feet and often less. Although wells in any one area would have to be sunk to various depths to reach oil in different strata, the maximum depths required varied generally from one oil field to another, accounting in part for regional differences in derrick heights and drilling-rig design. Here are a few figures compiled from drilling logs of the late 1800s for comparison:

Pennsylvania	300 to 3700 feet
Kentucky	650 to 1800
Indiana	900 to 1650
Kansas	800 to 1300
Texas	800 to 1100

Oil-Well Drilling Tools from the Pennsylvania Region (c. 1890)

A string of tools was formed with the rope socket uppermost. Attached to the rope socket were (left to right): the sinker bar, the jars, the auger stem, and a bit or reamer. The temper screw (far right) connected the string of tools to the walking beam, and the screw was then "let out" gradually as the drill penetrated the rock.

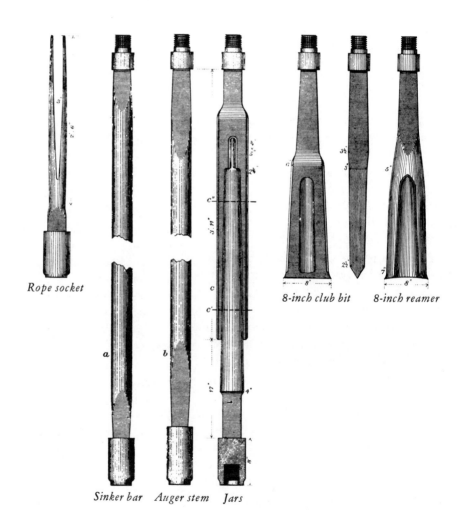

Rope socket

Sinker bar   *Auger stem*   *Jars*

8-inch club bit   *8-inch reamer*

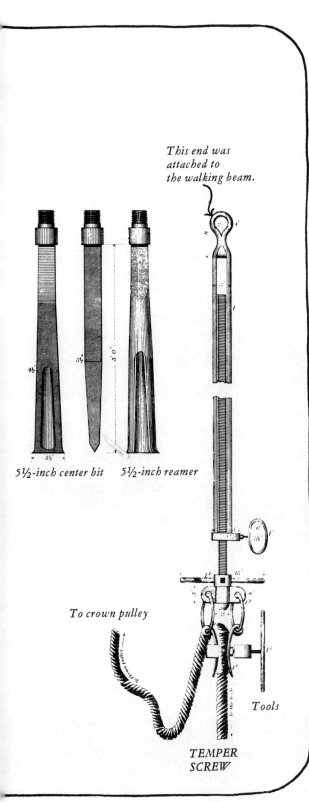

This end was attached to the walking beam.

5½-inch center bit   5½-inch reamer

To crown pulley

Tools

TEMPER
SCREW

The deepest well in the United States at this time was 6004 feet, in Connecticut; the second deepest, 5575 feet, was in Pennsylvania.

Steam engines provided the power for drilling and pumping. Near the new rig, then, would be mounted on a separate timber foundation a small steam engine of about twelve to fifteen horsepower. A drive belt or rope transmitted power from a pulley on the engine to the derrick's bank wheel, and steam for the engine would come from a stationary, locomotive-type boiler. In some instances each engine would have its own boiler, but a more common arrangement was a large, centrally located boiler providing steam to the engines of several wells. Still, the historian should be on the lookout for unusual arrangements like the endless-wire system at Petroleum, West Virginia (see page 181).

Rather than go further into the intricacies of constructing a rig—which can be understood more easily from the illustrations, anyway—we can better understand the relationship of all the mechanical parts we might find to the actual work of the rig if we visit a drilling operation and look over the shoulders of the crew as they set about drilling a new well.

Spindletop oil field, Jefferson County, Texas, in 1903. The plank road to the right was Boiler Avenue, providing access to the boilers and steam engines.

In the drilling crew of the 1800s were four men: two drillers and two tool dressers—a driller and a tool dresser working together in pairs. The workday was divided into two twelve-hour "tours." The drilling, once it was begun, went on continuously until the work was completed, one tour working from noon to midnight and the next from midnight to noon. Light was provided by a primitive iron lamp burning crude petroleum and re-sembling a teakettle with a spout on each side. Throughout the cold winter the crews would be warmed by a stove consisting of a sheet-iron cylinder in which natural gas from the well was burned.

The first step in drilling was to dig a shaft about 8 to 10 feet square down to the bed-rock, perhaps 10 or 15 feet below the surface. In the earliest petroleum wells, beginning about 1861, a wooden "conductor" of

6-inch timbers was carefully built in the shaft to keep mud and gravel from falling down into the well. The conductor, then, was a refinement of the Ruffners' gum. For the historian this detail is crucial, for at this and two subsequent junctures in drilling technology, there are changes in well linings which allow a reasonably accurate dating of old rigs. The uppermost part of the lining will usually be visible since it was the practice to extend the lining up through the derrick sills, floor sills, and derrick floor. The presence of a wooden conductor indicates that the well was struck sometime between 1861 and about 1868. Note in the illustration (p. 190) showing well cross sections from different periods that the wooden conductor was supplanted by drive pipes of iron in 1868. The interior diameter of the pipe and the thickness of the walls are further clues to the well's vintage. If the inside diameter of the drive pipe is about 6 inches and the walls about an inch thick, then the pipe is most likely cast iron (surface texture would be a clue here, too) and the well dates to the period between 1868 and 1878.

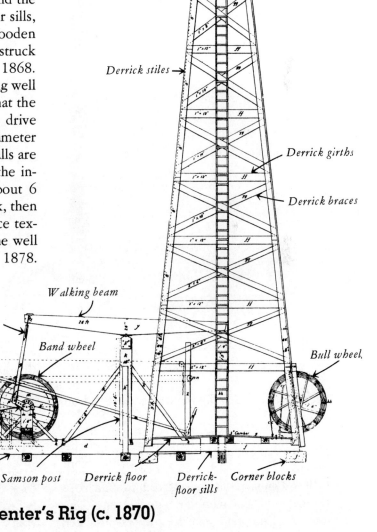

Carpenter's Rig (c. 1870)

189

Oil-Well Cross Sections (1861 to 1878)

These three cross sections show successive variations in well drilling and casing practice which provide a convenient means for dating wells. A wooden conductor of 6-inch-square timbers was used from about 1861 to 1868, when the cast-iron drive pipe and casing came into general use. In 1878, drillers began using wrought-iron pipes of a larger diameter and with a thinner wall. Inside diameter and wall thickness, then, are clues to the vintage of a well and to whether cast-iron or wrought-iron pipes were used.

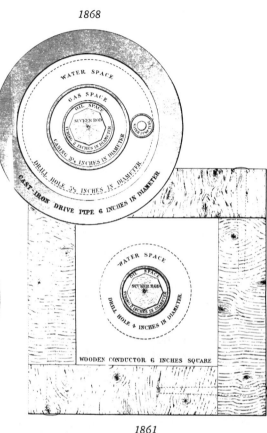

1868

1878

1861

If the inside diameter is about 8 inches and the walls of the pipe about $1/8$ to $1/4$ inch thick, then the pipe was rolled from wrought-iron sheets, and the well was drilled after about 1878.

With the conductor or drive pipe in place, preparations for drilling could then begin. Onto the derrick floor the drillers rolled a huge coil of untarred Manila rope some 2 inches in diameter. The free end coming out of the center of the coil was attached to the "bull rope," a rope running from around the bull-wheel shaft up over the crown pulley at the derrick's summit and down into the derrick. (See the illustration "Carpenter's Rig" on page 189.) The engine was started, the bull-wheel shaft revolved, and, with the men carefully guiding the cable, the entire coil was wound onto the shaft. To the free end of the rope now hanging down from the crown pulley was attached the string of tools, beginning with a rope socket—to which was attached the

California Cable-Tool Drilling Rig (c. 1900)

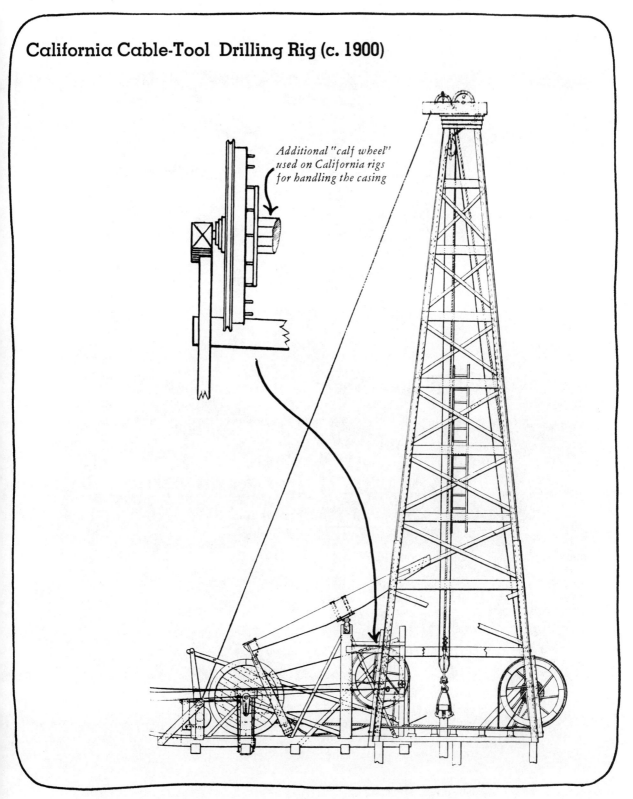

Additional "calf wheel" used on California rigs for handling the casing

View of cable-tool drilling rig at Drumright, Oklahoma, showing the band wheel, pitman, walking beam and samson post, and bull wheel (*inside the rig*).

sinker bar, jars, auger stem, and, last, the bit. The whole string was now suspended from the crown pulley, poised over the drive-pipe opening. Steadied by strong arms, the heavy string was lowered into the shaft until the rope socket was just level with the end of the walking beam projecting into the derrick. The string of tools was then attached to this end so that they were now suspended from the walking beam instead of from the top of the derrick, as before. The tools were run down to the bottom of the well. The driller reached for the chord which ran from a pulley near at hand out to the throttle valve of the engine. The single piston drove a small pulley connected by a belt to the band wheel, and as the band wheel turned, a crank or wrist pin imparted an up-and-down motion to the pitman arm and the walking beam. The string of tools was now moving up and down, up and down, chipping away at the rock below. A monotonous routine began. The driller, grasping a bar inserted into the temper screw, walked round and round, twisting the drilling cable so that the chisel-like tool would cut a round hole. Sensing the interval from the jar, the driller turned the temper screw, lowering the bit as it penetrated into the rock. When the temper screw had run out or the slowing progress warned the driller that the bit had dulled, the tools were then withdrawn. While the bit was being replaced, the string of tools once again suspended from the crown pulley was pulled aside so that a sand pump on its separate line could be run down into the well. This was done several times, whenever the tools were withdrawn, in order to keep the bottom of the hole free of sediment.

So it would go, day after day, morning tour and afternoon tour, interrupted only by the unwanted excitement of a break in the cable or string of tools requiring tedious "fishing" operations. Finally, if the site had been carefully selected and all went well, the driller, after eight or ten weeks, could enter into his well record: "January 30—struck oil-sand at 1664 feet."

Rotary drilling first appeared in the oil fields on the coastal plains of Texas, and did not come into general use until the late 1800s and early years of this century. Unfortunately for the historian, the transition occurred over such a long period of time that any meaningful dating of one or the other kinds of rig is impossible. Impact drilling with cable-tool rigs continued up into the 1930s. But rotary drilling predominates now mainly because of advances in bit design. When first introduced, rotary drilling was recognized as the most rapid and economical means of drilling in soft formations, but the early steel bits were useless where hard rock was encountered.

The derrick of the rotary-drilling rig is similar to that of the cable-tool rig just described. Two details distinguish the rotary-drilling rig and make for easy identification in the field: the revolving table that drives the drilling rods and bit, and the tools used in rotary drilling. Instead of a rope or wire cable, hollow drilling rods and bits are used so that a continuous stream of water circulates through the tools and back up to the top of the well. The purpose of this is to cool the bit, which becomes hot from the friction of working against the rock, and to carry rock chips and sediment up away from the bottom of the hole. Three bits were commonly used in the late 1800s and continuing into this

Rotary Drilling Rig (c. 1900)

Water was pumped into the drilling rods and bit at 40 to 100 pounds per square inch.

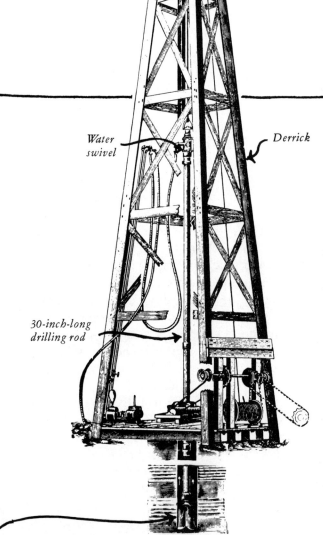

Water swivel

Derrick

30-inch-long drilling rod

Adamantine, or shot, drill for hard-rock drilling

Fishtail bit, used for soft strata

Early drilling rods were round in section. More recently, a special top section of drill pipe—square or octagonal in section—has been used. Drillers call this top section a "kelly."

century, each called by the kind of drilling to be done. Fishtail bits were used for soft strata, sand, and clay. When strata of dense, compact clay were encountered, the driller would change to a core-barrel bit. Hard-rock drilling required what was called an adamantine, or shot drill; this consisted of an extremely hard cylindrical bit that ground and abraded steel shot into the rock as it rotated.

Operating a rotary rig usually required four men—a driller, two derrick hands, and a fireman—or eight if there was to be a night tour. Their work begins much as does that of the cable-tool rig crew. From the hoisting drum at the base of the derrick, a rope or wire cable passes up over a pulley at the crown and down to the derrick floor. To this end is attached a block and fall, and then a

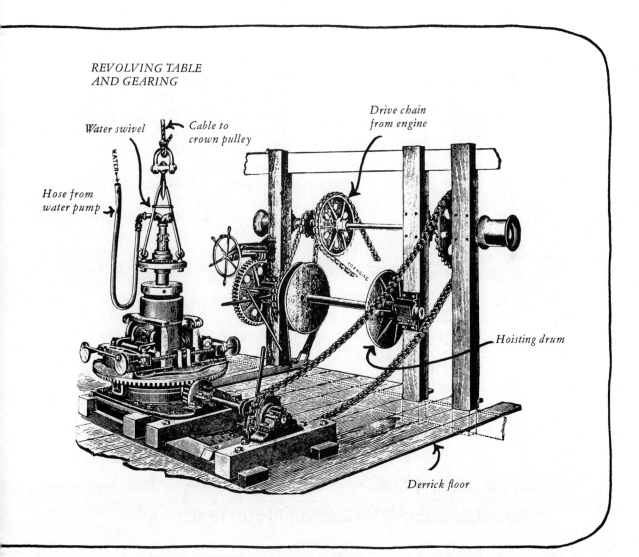

REVOLVING TABLE
AND GEARING

Water swivel

Cable to
crown pulley

Drive chain
from engine

Hose from
water pump

Hoisting drum

Derrick floor

"water swivel," which will carry water from a hose to the hollow drill rods. Then, to start the drilling, the first length of drill rod with a bit is attached to the water swivel. The water swivel, drilling rod, and bit, which are now suspended from the crown pulley, are lowered through the rotary turntable and clamped into place. The engine and pumps

are started, water begins to circulate through the drilling rod and bit, and the clamp is released, allowing the rod to slide down through the rotating table. As the upper end of the rod and water swivel approaches the table, the clamps are set, the water swivel is disconnected, another length of drilling rod is threaded to the first, the water swivel is connected once again, and the rotary-drilling process continues. Additional lengths of rod are added on as required, until the desired depth is reached. This procedure must, of course, be reversed when the bit dulls and is withdrawn. Most rotary-drilling rigs use a 13½-inch-diameter bit down to anywhere from 500 to 800 feet, which is the depth of the first string of 12-inch casing. The well may be finished with a 10½-inch bit and 9-inch-diameter casing, or the casing may reduce down to 6 or even 4 inches.

Throughout the United States, variations in the construction of historical drilling rigs are such that even the beginning petroleum historian has little trouble classifying a particular rig as one of the two principal types. This is not the case with the Canadian rig,

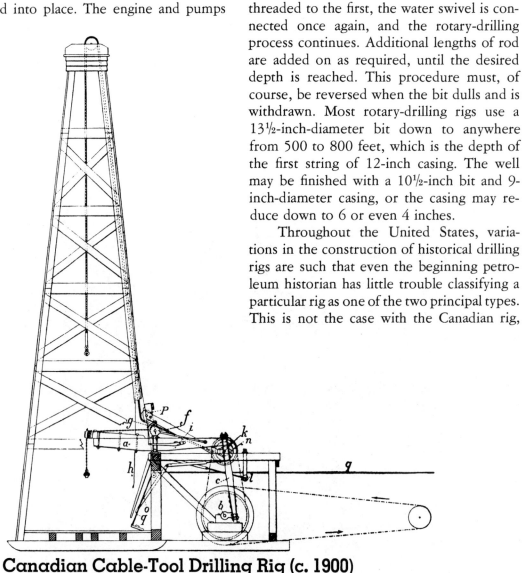

Canadian Cable-Tool Drilling Rig (c. 1900)

which differs in several fundamental ways reflecting the history of drilling in Canada. The earliest fields developed in Canada were in the area of Petrolia, Ontario, about fifty miles northeast of Detroit. Because the wells there tended to be shallower than most American wells—usually not more than 500 feet deep—and because of the tenacity of the clayey soils of the region, the construction of the drilling rigs used in the Petrolia fields was different from the later Pennsylvania, or "American," system. One difference apparent in the diagram (opposite) is the arrangement for transmitting motion from the engine to the string of drilling tools. Other differences would probably not be obvious in the field. Canadian drilling tools, for example, are lighter than those used on American cable-tool rigs. But most interesting are the slender, long-grained white ash boring rods barely 2 inches in diameter, which are used instead of Manila rope. The rods are usually about 37 feet long, joined one to the other by conical iron screw joints at each end.

The variations from the American system found in Canadian drilling rigs also reflect differences in drilling operations, though again the drilling operations are essentially the same. Canadian derricks of the 1800s were usually about 48 feet tall and 15 feet square at the base. The heavy timber foundation was not buried in trenches but, instead, was set on the ground so that wheels could be attached and the derrick moved from place to place. At the beginning of the drilling operation, no conductor or drive pipe was usually required; the clay of the region was too compact and heavy to fall in or allow any water to seep into the well. Instead, the drilling began with a clay auger 10 inches in

diameter attached to the threaded end of a clay-auger pipe some 30 feet long and 2½ inches in diameter. The auger rod was suspended from a pulley at the crown of the well, as in American practice, and then lowered by the winding drum until the auger point was in the ground. At this point, one end of a crossbeam was fastened to the clay-auger rod and the other to a yoke and horse, which screwed the auger into the ground as it walked around in a circle. Each time the auger became filled with clay, the crossbeam was removed, the auger hoisted up out of the ground, cleared, and the operation repeated. When gravel or sand was met, the auger was replaced with a "mudbit," which loosened the gravel so that it could then be lifted out with a bucket similar to the American sand pump. The mudbit was replaced when large stones were struck, this time with a corkscrew-shaped hook like a baker's dough hook. But once solid rock was met, the driller changed to bits similar to those used in Pennsylvania.

These different drilling techniques are reflected in the construction of the Canadian rigs. Finding an old rig, we might notice that the walking beam, pitman arm, and crank are quite short compared to their American counterparts. We might guess that such an arrangement would produce a shorter, faster stroke of the walking beam. The fact is that the pace of drilling in Canada was quicker. The bit struck at a rate of sixty blows a minute or more—a speed made possible by the shorter parts. Observers of early Canadian drilling operations have remarked that while each blow could be felt at the derrick floor, they could not be heard, the most noticeable sound being the inrush and outrush of air caused by the fast up-and-down movement of the bit and boring tools. Facilitating this fast movement, also, was the chain used in place of rope to suspend the boring rods from the walking beam. The chain passed through the cast-iron cap of the walking beam, a ratchet wheel, and a pawl on its way to the drum of a small winch. By raising the pawl the driller would release the chain, allowing it to unwind from the drum and lower the tools into the rock.

The boilers and steam engines of Canadian rigs differed little from those in the Pennsylvania fields except that they seldom if ever burned natural gas and were not fitted with reversing gear.

Regardless of the drilling process used, when the drilling was complete and the presence of oil duly noted in the well record, the next and last step was to bring the oil up. For this work a pump valve, or "sucker," was attached to the lower end of a length of tubing and lowered down into a pipe, or "working barrel," in the well. On the sucker are a series of three or four leather cups

Pumping rig and storage tank, Volcano, West Virginia; they were built around 1895.

Pumping Oil (c. 1890)

The illustration shows the arrangement used for separating gas and oil from a pumped well. The oil was pumped into a gas tank inside the derrick; here it was separated from the gas and pumped into the oil tank at the same time water accumulating in the well was pumped out—into the tank at the left. In flowing wells that did not need pumping, the pump rods would not be necessary, the walking beam would be dismantled or deactivated and the oil allowed to flow directly into the separator. Collected gas was used to light the drilling rig, to provide heat for the drillers in cold weather, and sometimes to fire boilers for steam engines.

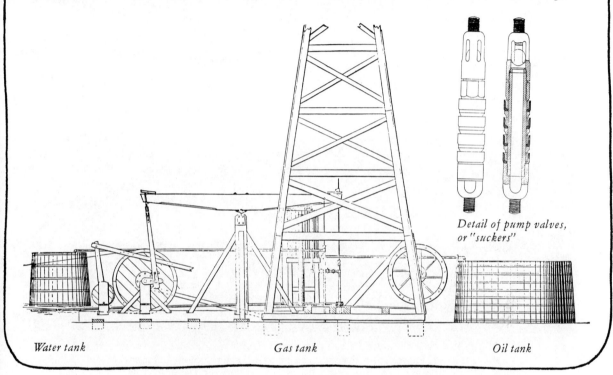

Detail of pump valves, or "suckers"

Water tank   Gas tank   Oil tank

which are forced against the inside of the working barrel. The sucker moves up and down inside the working barrel, lifting the oil up to the surface much as a water pump or any other simple pump does. The sucker is down in the well, connected by a string of "sucker rods" to the walking beam at the base of the derrick. On earlier wells the sucker rods were usually of white ash or hickory, circular or octagonal in section, about 25 feet long by 1½ inches in diameter. The sections of sucker rod were joined at each end by male and female threaded-iron ferrules. It is also likely that you will find an iron pump rod in use, suggesting a later well. When the oil reached the surface it was piped to a storage tank. Tanks were often centrally located to receive the oil from several pumping wells.

199

Detail showing the bull wheel and pump with the upper section of the sucker rod and cable still attached to the walking beam. The equipment belonged to the West Oil Company, Volcano, West Virginia, and was built around 1895.

That's how it was at hundreds of oil fields around America. Up until the 1870s, the crude petroleum was usually refined in the vicinity of the well, making it likely that we'll also find storage facilities and small refineries on or near historical oil fields. But then it became more economical to ship crude by tank barge, railway tank car, pipeline, and tank road wagons to the large refineries growing up at Cleveland, Pittsburgh, Buffalo, Boston, New York, Philadelphia, and Baltimore.

Much of the oil in those days was transported in iron-hooped oak barrels holding about 42 American gallons, coated on the inside with glue to prevent leaking. At Oil Creek, teamsters carted in barrels by the thousands, to be filled and loaded on boats bound for the refineries. The scene must have been hectic indeed. The empty boats

Storage tank, or "pool," Okmulgee County, Oklahoma, around 1916.

were towed up the shallow creek by horses that waded in the stream. After being loaded, the boats sat too low in the water to make the trip back down to Oil City. Here they waited for days and weeks for a sudden storm and freshet or the completion of a temporary dam downstream. When the freshet arrived, a fleet of boats left at once, carrying as many as forty thousand barrels. At one time there were over one thousand boats and thirty steamers, with crews totaling more than four thousand men engaged in the traffic on Oil Creek alone. It had all begun at Titusville, not twenty years before.

King-post truss, Dos Rios, California.

7. ADVENTURE WITH A GREEN BRIDGE
Helping Children to See the Past

Imagine an activity for children that involves roaming the outdoors, exploring new places, following "treasure" maps, solving history puzzles, working together with small groups of friends and parents, being able to ask all the questions a heart could desire, drawing pictures, taking photographs, learning—an activity that works in the country as well as on city streets. It costs little more than the price of some drawing materials, a couple of topographical or city street maps, and, perhaps, some film. The activity is aboveground archaeology.

A lot of nice things can come from such a project. Children become acquainted with historical structures and places in their own community. Young amateur historians, who have explored their neighborhoods on bikes and on foot, often spot treasures overlooked by grown-ups in their inventories. Through aboveground archaeology they experience history in an active sense, doing the work of historians. But, most important, such activities make history what it once was for children—a natural way to get a sense of place and roots.

The history of how things are made and how work is done may be closest to the interests of children. Many of us rediscover history as adults, often in the search for self. We may be surprised, even embarrassed at first, to discover that this new interest in history as an adult is the reawakening of a childhood pleasure. Railroads, steam engines, clothing and its styles, dolls, tools and machinery, fire engines, furniture, airplanes, ships, lift bridges, flour mills, subways, farm machinery, old buildings, automobiles are recalled to mind not as artifacts but as wondrous objects that fascinated us when we were young.

There is nothing really difficult about getting kids involved in industrial archaeology. Many teachers are introducing children to the past—introducing children to themselves, really—through family and community history. The historian's techniques taught in these classes—listening to tape-recorded oral histories, collecting photographs and postcards, visiting libraries and museums, searching the back files at newspaper offices, going on "history walks," collecting in attics and basements—are also the techniques of industrial archaeology.

More often than not, the subject does not await formal introduction. Kids are aware of artifacts adults had forgotten long ago—bridges, for instance. A few weeks ago a local paper published a picture of a nineteenth-century king-post truss bridge that had begun to slip away from its ancient masonry abutments. How many winter snows and spring freshets the little bridge had endured, few in our town could remember. But the children knew the little span well. Their delight was in passing over it on the school bus every day,

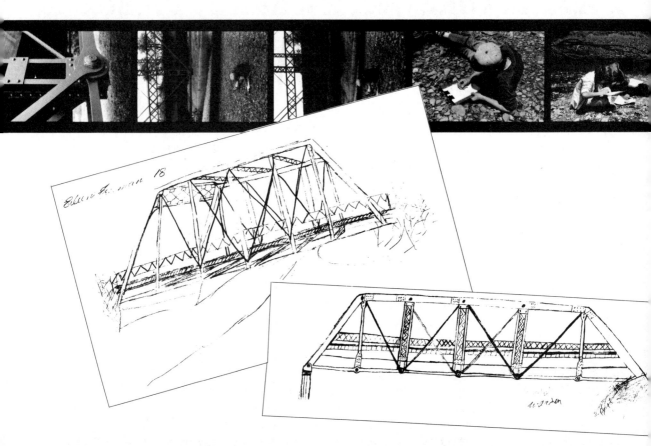

and some had become quite attached to it. At least they were curious. The story of the old king post's predicament got us to talking and wondering about other bridges we had all seen, but especially this one. What held it up anyway? How old was it and how did it get there? We started making little sketches to explain the purpose of the simple truss of timbers and rusted iron rods. The discussion turned to other bridges hidden in the mountains along unpaved county and private roads. The children's discoveries included an iron railroad bridge dating to the 1880s (something we learned when one of the kids called the County Engineer's office), now carrying a rutted dirt road high over a creek. And there were other bridges that had been found.

I began sketching some truss forms on the board. Interests and energies were up, and there was no escaping it. Plans were made over county road maps and topo maps. Parents with station wagons and pickup trucks were called, and off we went in search of history. The result was our own inventory of the several pin-connected iron through trusses scattered in the hills around us and on the valley floor.

In my experiences, learning to see means *sketching*. For most children (and, I

suspect, for most adults), recording a structure is not a separate task but is integral to the whole process of seeing and understanding it. Drawing requires us to observe with more care than we are used to. Even the simplest sketch helps us fix distinguishing details in our mind. This is certainly true of kids and bridges. A bridge is line, really nothing more. The relative "weights" of the web members translate directly into different line widths on the paper. Here the forces of tension and compression are almost visible.

There is to be nothing elaborate about our "recordings." Such informal, freehand sketches are lively and more expressive. With

children, recording begins, then, with simple and inexpensive materials. Masonite sheets (¼ inch or ⅜ inch thick) are cut up into 18″ × 24″ drawing boards to which are attached two large board clips. Each young historian gets a board and lots of paper (such as newsprint). I collect and bring along pencils, charcoal sticks, erasers, some little pencil sharpeners, sandpaper pads for sharpening leads, and the cake of black wax left over from the day we made rubbings at the cemetery. Later we will add to this collection a few plastic triangles and a T-square.

Our first work was a bridge many of the children knew already, an iron Pratt-type

By Marjo

through truss with a new coat of glossy green paint. That made it even more attractive to the children and, as I would soon realize, it had some practical value, too. The rust and blotches of primer found on many old bridges act as camouflage, obscuring details. But a newly painted surface catches the light, bringing out rivets, built-up members, builder's plates, pin connections, and decorative ironwork in sharp relief. Of course, this does not mean that old, rusty things are to be avoided. But for a first experience, particularly with elementary schoolchildren, the extra clarity of form and detail is helpful.

At first, we were at a loss to describe what we saw. Soon we began using a new vocabulary to describe "posts," "diagonals," and other members. Some of the children were content with recording the bridge in its scene. Others quickly accepted the suggestion to take a closer look. Down through their pads of paper the children worked, recording the details (including the wildflowers and a little nest tucked into the latticing). Other things happened, too. The bridge was touched, too, so that "iron" and "rivet" and "oak planking" became real. The builder's plate on the end post became a fine rubbing. The children delighted in rivet patterns, latticing and lacing, the rough masonry abutments, and in just being outside together.

On our return, there was a lot to talk about. We had drawings to put up—not someone else's but our own.

From our experience with the green bridge have come a desire to share our discoveries, and many questions: How do rivets work? Why are some bridges higher (deeper) than others? How are iron and steel made? Why do bridges have different shapes? It's time for the children to meet Ithiel Town and to look at all kinds of bridges in the books we've collected from the library. It is time also for scissors, scraps of cardboard, paper fasteners, and the little experiment in truss design on pages 59–60.

These experiences in seeing and recording forms and textures, in being close to industrial artifacts, will reinforce other activities we will be doing throughout the year. There's to be a field trip to record nearby railroad structures, and a visit to a local flour mill with machinery and a steam engine dating to the early 1900s. And there will also be a museum visit. A museum trip is for us a "collecting" and recording session, not a tour. When we go to a museum, the pencils and drawing boards go, too, just as they would when we are headed for the field. Here we can "discover" and record farm implements, tractors, winepresses, the marvelous toy steam engine on the floor of an 1890s sitting

By Jenny Moss

room, a collection of wooden carpenter's planes, and logging equipment. Again, the emphasis is on seeing the details that help us to understand the workings of a drilling rig or a foot-treadle-powered lathe. The experience is a more lasting one because a historical object has been studied carefully, drawn and redrawn until it is almost as familiar to us as it was to the builder and operator—and then has been "brought home" to keep.

How much of all this is remembered? Parents tell me that when the family returns to the museum later, the children return to their "discoveries" and confidently explain what they are and how they fit into their past. Neither is traveling by car the same, anymore; bridges along the highway are now events on a long drive, and to parents must now be explained the difference between a "Pratt" or a "Warren." I think an awareness of historic structures in the community leads to a deeper attachment to that community. I know that there is genuine disappointment when the neighborhood's last treasure has been recorded. Before that happens, though, the teacher—now hooked on aboveground archaeology—has already explored other places in which to visit the past.

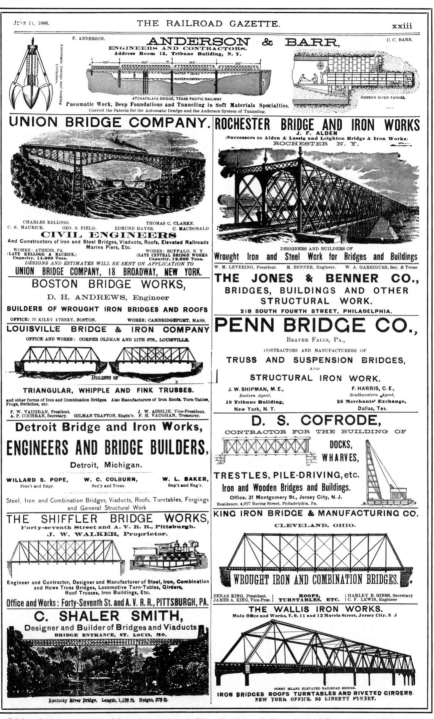

Old advertisements like these from *The Railroad Gazette* of June 11, 1886, are rich sources of illustrations and information on early American industry.

LIBRARY ARCHAEOLOGY
A Bibliography

The literature of early American industry is extensive and includes many works that provide the general background for perceptive, sensitive fieldwork and the beginnings of a historical imagination. Carl W. Condit's *American Building* (Chicago: University of Chicago Press, 1968) has, among others, fascinating chapters on buildings, bridges, train sheds, and roof trusses which create a historical backdrop to salient engineering developments. The structures and sites illustrated through measured drawings and photographs in Theodore Anton Sande's *Industrial Archaeology: A New Look at the American Heritage* (Brattleboro, Vt.: The Stephen Greene Press, 1976) and in the *Historic American Engineering Record Catalog* (Washington, D.C.: U.S. Government Printing Office, 1976) by Donald E. Sackheim awaken us to the unlimited possibilities for industrial archaeology from lighthouses to brewhouses. Simple techniques for recording structures, artifacts, and early manufacturing processes with camera and tape recorder are described in David Weitzman, *Underfoot: An Everyday Guide to Exploring the American Past* (New York: Charles Scribner's Sons, 1976), which also offers in "Meetings with the Miller" a model for preserving skills no longer practiced.

The identification and dating of structures and equipment requires close attention to detail and an eye for distinguishing features. For this, early catalogs, advertisements, trade journals, and, especially, textbooks for students and working engineers and builders are most helpful. Treatises and textbooks from the 1800s and early 1900s, offering a kind of inadvertent history, still repose in larger public and university libraries. Therein can be found the engineering drawings and engravings that help us to determine "new" and "old" practices in, say, bridge-connection details, or furnace construction, or locomotive-cylinder design. The books included in this group are, for the most part, contemporary primary sources containing illustrations and descriptions of sufficient detail to help us identify and date the artifacts we discover. Some include anecdotal accounts of the setting up and operation of early machinery, which allows us once again to put back into "working order" an abandoned, rusted machine.

These general suggestions will get you started and, then, to continue on your own, begin with Brooke Hindle's *Technology in Early America: Needs and Opportunities for Study* (Chapel Hill: University of North Carolina Press, 1966), which consists of bibliographical essays on books and periodicals on early American technology, many of them from the 1800s, and to which has been added a very useful directory of artifact collections in museums all over the country. Hindle's book is helpful in a number of ways. Many of the books he lists have bibliographies of their own, and the periodicals chosen are often filled with drawings and photographs not found elsewhere. The headings and subheadings of Hindle's table of contents serve as a checklist for searching the subject index of your library's card catalog.

New finds are coming to light every day, and new books and articles on industrial archaeology as well. To keep up with these there's a lively, illustration-filled newsletter published by the Society for Industrial Archeology. Membership in the society also brings announcements of conferences and field trips around the country and news of preservation groups. For information on membership and the newsletter write the Society for Industrial Archeology, National Museum of History and Technology, Smithsonian Institution, Washington, D.C. 20560.

Mirrors of Rust

The number of books available on railroads is, in itself, a statement of their importance and of our fascination with the steam locomotive. Early developments in locomotive design—materials used in locomotive construction, types and wheel arrangements predominating in various periods, boilers, running gears, and decorative treatment—are illustrated in John H. White, Jr., *American Locomotives: An Engineering History 1830 to 1880* (Baltimore: Johns Hopkins Press, 1968). White has also prepared an annotated edition of Angus Sinclair's *Development of the Locomotive Engine* (Cambridge: The M.I.T. Press, 1970), originally published in 1907. Here is a lot of information that will help in the identification and dating of locomotives; the editor's "Afterword" summarizes devel-

opments up to 1950. The evolution of basic elements such as fireboxes, cylinders, engine and trailing trucks, side and main rods, and tender trucks of locomotives built from 1860 to 1950 is described in Alfred W. Bruce, *The Steam Locomotive in America* (New York: W. W. Norton, 1952).

For an even closer look, there are the thousands of drawings depicting locomotive engineering in its every aspect, to be found in serial industry publications such as *Locomotive Dictionary* and *Modern Locomotives* (both New York: Railroad Age Gazette, various dates from 1897) and *Locomotive Cyclopedia* (New York: Association of American Railroads, 1934). Drawings of railroad cars can be found in the various editions of *Car Builders' Dictionary and Cyclopedia* (New York: Simmons-Boardman, 1880). The *Railway Signal Dictionary* (New York: Railroad Age Gazette, 1908) identifies the array of structures encountered in track walking, such as crossing signals, interlockings, battery wells, relay boxes, and block signals.

W. M. Camp's *Notes on Track* (Chicago: published by the author, 1903) is unique as a contemporary account of track construction and maintenance practices in the late 1800s. Full of drawings of early switch components, snowsheds, tunnels, bumping posts, ties, mileposts, and specialized track-laying and maintenance tools still to be found in the corners and cobwebs of old section houses, this book is especially useful in identifying the odds and ends of old work trains, including all manner of track-laying machines, ballast cars and spreaders, tie-plating machines, weed-burning cars, derricks, inspection cars, snowplows, ditching cars, and crew boarding cars.

(Note: Many of these books are being reprinted for railroad-model builders.)

First advertisement for the Janney coupler to appear in Poor's *Manual of Railroads*, 1884. The Janney came into use in the 1880s, replacing the link-and-pin coupler that had caused the death and injury of thousands of brakemen every year. It was during the 1880s, also, that states began to pass laws *requiring* automatic couplers like the Janney.

Bridges of Timber and Iron

America's bridge builders were practical men and, when they wrote, it was in the working language of the carpenter-builder and in the tradition of Ithiel Town. Squire Whipple's *An Elementary Treatise on Bridge Building* (original edition, 1847; New York, 1873) is a pioneering work that influenced bridge-construction techniques well into this century. The particulars of early wooden and iron railroad-bridge construction, photographs of typical bridges of the period, and a splendid collection of foldout patent drawings (some of which have been used in this chapter) are to be found in Theodore Cooper, *American Railroad Bridges* (New York: Engineering News Publishing Company, [1889?]). Elementary-school mathematics will get you through solutions to stress and proportioning problems for a number of truss forms, worked out in Alfred P. Boller's *Practical Treatise on the Construction of Iron Highway Bridges for the Use of Town Committees* (New York: John Wiley and Sons, 1890), but most people will be content with his general sections describing the distinguishing details of web members and connections. J. A. L. Waddell's *The Designing of Ordinary Iron Highway Bridges* (New York: John Wiley and Sons, 1884) seems, at first glance, too technical, until you discover toward the back a very useful "Glossary of Bridge Terms" and several foldout working drawings of iron highway bridges. And there's an exemplary model for individual and group bridge-recording projects—historical introduction, inventory form, recording sheet, bridge photography—in the five volumes of *Metal Truss Bridges in Virginia: 1865–1932* (Charlottesville: Virginia Highway & Transportation Research Council, 1975–76) by Dan Grove Deibler.

Roof Trusses

These less glamorous descendants of the bridge truss are usually overlooked by historians, but in Carl Condit's chapter "The Iron Railroad Train Shed" (in *American Building* [Chicago: University of Chicago Press, 1968]), they attain a social significance as indicators of the fierce competition among the railroads and of American tastes growing more extravagant in the years after the Civil War. Numerous plans and drawings of connecting hardware, framing joints, and splices for roof trusses (and railroad trestles) of timber and iron will be found in Henry S. Jacoby, *Structural Details or Elements of Design in Heavy Framing* (New York: John Wiley and Sons, 1909). These can be compared with the later iron-and-steel roof trusses illustrated in George A. Hool and W. S. Kinne, *Steel and Timber Structures* (New York: McGraw-Hill Book Company, 1942). Photographs and drawings of unusual roof truss forms are included in the *Historic American Engineering Record Catalog 1976* (Washington, D.C.: U.S. Government Printing Office).

The Ironmaster's Gift

For most of us, some introduction to ironmaking and refining is needed, because the processes are not as generally known and because it is not easy to infer from what remains at most sites how a furnace worked.

W. David Lewis's little booklet *Iron and Steel in America* (Greenville, Del.: The Hagley Museum, 1976) explains the basic manufacturing processes and places ironmaking

and steelmaking in a historical context. My principal contemporary source for this chapter is Frederick Overman, *The Manufacture of Iron in All Its Various Branches* (Philadelphia: Henry C. Baird, 1851), which describes in considerable detail each step from the extraction of ore to the several refining and manufacturing processes. Here, too, are hundreds of engravings of tools, furnaces, forges, blast machines, and rolling mills of over a century ago. Information for dating historical furnaces from the 1700s can be found in Arthur Cecil Bining, *Pennsylvania Iron Manufacture in the Eighteenth Century* (Harrisburg: Pennsylvania Historical Commission, 1938), which appends a list of names, locations, and builders of Pennsylvania ironworks. James M. Swank's *The Manufacture of Iron in All Ages and Particularly in the United States from Colonial Times to 1891* (Philadelphia: The American Iron and Steel Association, 1892) gives the history and specifics of ironmaking in each state and explains some of the European antecedents of American manufacturing processes but, unfortunately, lacks any useful index.

Life on an iron plantation and working a furnace is re-created in Joseph E. Walker's exceptional study, *Hopewell Village* (Philadelphia: University of Pennsylvania Press, 1966), with such clarity that it brings life back to a quiet, deserted site. Finding ironworks or early sites in your state is a real possibility if you can find one of the early directories published, some annually, throughout the late 1800s. In one of these, the *Directory of Iron and Steel Works of the United States* (Philadelphia: American Iron and Steel Association), can be found the addresses or (in backwoods areas) the locations of ironworks, descriptions of the furnaces in use, histories of furnace operation, and listings of forges and foundries. Once you've done the work of locating those old sites, you might publish your own guide, like Myron B. Sharp's and William H. Thomas's *A Guide to the Old Stone Blast Furnaces in Western Pennsylvania* (Pittsburgh: The Historical Society of Western Pennsylvania, 1966), perhaps to form the beginning of a network for amateur historians.

Where Gushers Roared

Much of what is available on the petroleum industry is too technical for the generalist; it is concerned mostly with specific chemical processes. An exception is Boverton Redwood, *Petroleum* (London: Charles Griffin & Company, 1906). The maps of oil fields in America, engravings of tools, oil rigs, drilling operations and refinery equipment, early drilling records, and a survey of drilling operations in each state alone make this a rich source of information for the industrial archaeologist. But then the author includes, too, anecdotal accounts of erecting and operating a rig using well drillers' terms of the 1880s, including the use of various tools. Volume 2 of this work (1923) includes an interesting chapter on oil lamps and burners imported into the United States from Europe, and other lamps, such as the Rochester lamp, manufactured here later.

ACKNOWLEDGMENTS

Despite the lone name on the cover, *Traces of the Past* is a collaboration by interested friends whose enthusiasm added joy to the writing. It all began with a suggestion from Laurie Graham at Scribners, who then helped me turn an idea into a book and whose love of history shows on every page. Once into the work, I knew I'd need help from others with more experience, busy people often engrossed in projects of their own. But their responses to my timid requests were overwhelming. Robert M. Vogel welcomed me to the Smithsonian, made me comfortable in the office with the huge roll-top desk and boxes of drawings and photographs piled to the ceiling, kept up with the progress of the book over the years, and gave the manuscript a thoughtful, incisive reading. Robert also introduced me to other of his colleagues at the National Museum of History & Technology, among them John H. White, Jr., who answered my questions, shared his knowledge of American railroads, and got me into a vast picture collection. Eric N. DeLony led me through the treasures of the *Historic American Engineering Record* files, suggested useful approaches to early American technology, and offered an architect/historian's view of new directions in industrial archaeology. To Eric's staff, especially Isabel T. Hill, go my thanks for helping with the selection of photographs and for shortening the distance between California and Washington, D.C. Lots of ideas came as well from photographer Bill Barrett, Christopher Duckworth of the Ohio Historical Society, Jeff Dean at the State Historical Society of Wisconsin, Myron B. Sharp, Richard Drew of the American Petroleum Institute, and Robert M. Frame of the Minnesota Historical Society.

ILLUSTRATION CREDITS

Pages 2, 4, 5, 6, photos by Wm. Edmund Barrett; pages 8, 25, from W. M. Camp, Notes on Track (Chicago: published by author, 1904); page 9, Railway Signal Association, Railway Signal Dictionary (New York: 1912); page 13, found in Wendell P. Hammon's Archives & Artifacts store, Sacramento, Calif.; pages 16–17, adapted from George L. Fowler, Forney's Catechism of the Locomotive (New York: Railway Age Gazette, 1911); page 19, reproduced from Alfred W. Bruce, The Steam Locomotive in America, by permission of W. W. Norton & Company, Inc. Copyright 1952 by W. W. Norton & Company, Inc. Copyright renewed 1980; pages 4, 21, drawings by Richard Wilson; pages 22–23, drawings courtesy Railway & Locomotive Historical Society; pages 26–30, from Baldwin Locomotive Works, Record of Recent Construction (Philadelphia: Burnham, Williams & Co., 1902); pages 33, 37, 38, photos by Wm. Edmund Barrett; page 42, from Charles S. Boyer, Early Forges & Furnaces in New Jersey (Philadelphia: University of Pennsylvania Press, 1931); page 43, U.S. Geological Survey; pages 46–47, Poor's Manual of the Railroads of the United States (New York: H. V. & H. W. Poor); pages 48, 49, Historic American Engineering Record (HAER), National Park Service, Wm. Edmund Barrett; page 52, drawing and photo, Historic American Engineering Record, National Park Service; pages 54–55, HAER, T. Alan Comp, Donald C. Jackson, and Arnold David Jones; page 56, HAER, Wm. Edmund Barrett; page 57, HAER; page 62, from Theodore Cooper, American Railroad Bridges (New York: Engineering News Publishing Co., n.d.); page 64, courtesy, Society for Industrial Archeology, Smithsonian Institution; page 65, National Museum of History and Technology, Smithsonian Institution; page 67, courtesy, Historic Preservation Division, State Historical Society of Wisconsin; page 68, courtesy, Historic Preservation Division, State Historical Society of Wisconsin; page 69, HAER, Jack E. Boucher; page 71, National Museum of History and Technology, Smithsonian Institution; page 72, from J. A. L. Waddell, The Designing of Ordinary Highway Bridges (New York: John Wiley, 1884); page 74, National Museum of History and Technology, Smithsonian Institution; page 76, from J. A. L. Waddell, cited above; page 77, courtesy, Historic Preservation Division, State Historical Society of Wisconsin; page 78, National Museum of History and Technology, Smithsonian Institution; page 79, HAER; page 80, HAER, Michael Masny, delineator; page 81, National Museum of History and Technology, Smithsonian Institution; page 88, Oregon Department of Highways; page 89, National Museum of History and Technology, Smithsonian Institution; pages 90–109, from Theodore Cooper, American Railroad Bridges (New York: Engineering News Publishing Co., n.d.); page 101, HAER, Wm. Edmund Barrett; page 110, National Museum of History and Technology, Smithsonian Institution; pages 112–13, from J. A. L. Waddell, cited above; pages 114–15, from Hale Sutherland and Harry Lake Bowman, Structural Design (New York: John Wiley, 1938); Thomas Clark Shedd, Structural Design in Steel (New York: John Wiley, 1934); pages 116–17, George A. Hool and W. S. Kinne, Movable and Long Span Steel Bridges (New York: McGraw-Hill, 1943); pages 118–19, Historic Preservation Division, State Historical Society of Wisconsin; pages 120–21, HAER, Wm. Edmund Barrett and Jack E. Boucher; page 122, HAER, Jack E. Boucher; pages 123, 124, 130, George A. Hool and W. S. Kinne, Steel and Timber Structures (New York: McGraw-Hill, 1942); page 125, National Museum of History and Technology, Smithsonian Institution and HAER; page 126, HAER, Jeffery Jenkins, delineator; page 127, HAER, Jack E. Boucher; page 131, HAER, Robert McNair, David Bouse, and Toni Ristau, delineators; photo by Jack E. Boucher; page 132, courtesy, Society for Industrial Archeology, Smithsonian Institution; pages 135–37, from Myron B. Sharp and William H. Thomas, A Guide to the Old Stone Blast Furnaces in Western Pennsylvania (Pittsburgh: The Historical Society of Western Pennsylvania, 1966); page 138, drawings from Arthur Cecil Bining, Pennsylvania Iron Manufacture in the Eighteenth Century (Harrisburg: Pennsylvania Historical Commission, 1938); pages 141, 144–45, 150–51, 154–55, 159–60, 162, 164, 166, 168–69, 172–77, drawings from Frederick Overman, The Manufacture of Iron (Philadelphia: Henry C. Baird, 1851); pages 148–49, courtesy, Eleutherian Mills Historical Library; pages 142–43, courtesy, the Ohio Historical Society; pages 152–53, drawings by Doug McCanne; pages 157, 162, National Museum of History and Technology, Smithsonian Institution; page 165, from Shop and Foundry Practice (Scranton, Pa.: International Textbook Co., 1901); page 178, courtesy, American Petroleum Institute; page 181, HAER, Wm. Edmund Barrett; pages 182–84, American Petroleum Institute; pages 186–87, 189–91, 194–95, and 196, drawings from Boverton Redwood, Petroleum (London: Charles Griffin & Company, 1906); pages 188, 192, American Petroleum Institute; pages 198, 200, HAER, Wm. Edmund Barrett; page 199, from Boverton Redwood, cited above; page 201, American Petroleum Institute; page 202, photo by Sheena Schroeder; page 204, drawings by Eileen Freeman and Mike Warden; page 205, drawing by Kevin Harlan; page 206, drawing by Marjo Wilson; page 208, drawing by Jennifer Moss; page 209, drawings by Scott Hixon; page 210, advertisement from The Railroad Gazette (June 11, 1886); page 213, Poor's Manual of the Railroads of the United States (New York: H. V. & H. W. Poor); page 215, from Boverton Redwood, cited above.

INDEX

Entries in **boldface** indicate illustrations.